ESCAPE FROM TEHRAN

By Assad Aram

to Sarah

Freedom
Assad W. Aram
march 9 - 2014

ISBN: 1492347620
ISBN 13: 9781492347620

ABOUT THE AUTHOR

Dr. Assad Aram graduated from the School of Dentistry at the University of Tehran. He earned a master's degree in hospital administration at the University of Minnesota. In 1964, he returned to Iran with his American wife, Helen.

Dr. Aram was the principal architect of the modern medical health care system in Iran, including the country's emergency medical network. He was CEO of Iran's National Health Insurance Organization and later became Vice Minister of Health and Welfare. Prior to the Iranian revolution, the Shah had Dr. Aram arrested with other top government officials. Most of those officials faced the firing squad. The author was one of the few who miraculously escaped.

*This book is dedicated
to my lifetime partner and devoted wife, Helen,
and our brave, resilient children—Lisa, Cathy, and Cyrus—who,
at a very young age, experienced grave fear and uncertainty.
It is also dedicated to my seven grandchildren,
who are the "noor of my life."*

*To the brave Iranian leaders and technocrats
who were imprisoned with me.
Our long hours of discussion, behind bars,
were a major source of information for this book.
Most of these leaders were executed without trial.
Their last wish was to publish the truth.*

Some names have been changed to protect the individual.

ACKNOWLEDGMENTS

I would like to thank Susan Wels for her professional, constructive editing and dedication. I thank her for helping me bring *Escape from Tehran* to life, and I'm deeply grateful for her enthusiasm and patience. I would also like to express gratitude to Susanne Pari for her expert editorial evaluation and recommendations. Finally, I would like to thank my family for their encouragement and support. Lisa Monetta spent countless hours coordinating various aspects of the book, for which I am very grateful.

TABLE OF CONTENTS

CHAPTER 1

POLITICAL SHOWDOWN BY
THE NEW GOVERNMENT

On September 5, 1978, without cause or warning, in a matter of hours, I lost my family, my profession, and my identity, and I was certain my future had been stolen, too. This is the story of a descent into hell—my own and my country's—and a reconstruction of historical events, many previously unknown, that plunged Iran into a dark age of political and religious terror.

That day, a Tuesday, began routinely enough. In the morning, I had greeted distinguished physicians from the United States, welcoming them to Tehran in my role as vice chancellor of Iran's Imperial University and Medical Center. When I returned to my office, I received a call from my daughter Cathy. Her voice shaken, she told me two SAVAK agents were at home asking for you. I tried to calm her and said it is a misunderstanding and told her to have them come to my office. Shortly after, two men walked in and introduced themselves as agents of SAVAK—the country's brutal security service—and told me that they had a warrant issued by the Martial Law Commander. They then ordered me to accompany them, escorted me outside, pushed me into an unmarked car, blindfolded me, and drove me to a destination they would not disclose.

I told myself not to panic, to be calm, that I had nothing to fear. For months, riots and violence had been tearing the nation apart, and the Shah was fighting for his political life. But I knew that I had served him and Iran honorably and honestly as the university's vice chancellor and undersecretary of Iran's Ministry of Health and Welfare and the Director of National Health Insurance Plan.. By any standards—man-made, God-given, or decreed by the Shah—of what could I possibly be guilty? By whose law was I going to be judged?

After half an hour, the car came to a halt. I sensed we hadn't driven very far and were still within city limits. Firm hands hauled me out of the vehicle and rushed me up a set of steps. After a pause, I heard a door swing open and was led through a bewildering set of turns until, finally, hands suddenly released me, and I staggered blindly, trying not to fall over.

My blindfold was ripped off. The first image I saw was a surly officer, sitting at a polished desk and gazing up at me. I realized that I was in prison. The officer asked me to spell my name and surname, then nodded curtly to the guards. They grabbed me, dragged me across the hall like a piece of meat, emptied my pockets, and took their contents—a watch, a wallet, and a fountain pen. Then they took my clothes and watched me, with blank expressions, as I put on a prison uniform. Without a word, they then blindfolded me again and pulled me along a stairwell. After two hundred feet, we stopped abruptly. I heard a deafening clang, and they pushed me into a cell. The guards then tore the blindfold from my face, and I watched as a metal door slammed shut.

I was in a tiny cell, just three feet wide and eight feet long. Its only contents were two ragged blankets. I spread one on the floor and covered myself with the other. A single, weak electric light swayed from the ceiling. There was a small, dark window, but it was too high up to see anything outside. No light came into the cell, even though it was a sunny day.

For the first three days I spent in that hole, I ate nothing at all. I had no appetite. Through the hinged window in the door, guards passed me food on an aluminum plate that had been bent into the shape a bowl. They also gave me a cup of water that was so filthy that I couldn't tell if the water had soiled the cup or the reverse. But I managed to swallow the water and scratched a line on the wall each time the guards brought food—two lines a day.

From time to time, I heard terrible voices screaming or pleading for mercy. Inmates were being tortured, and I strained to hear their words, but it was impossible to understand them. I later learned that the cries were prerecorded and played on loudspeakers to intimidate new inmates; it worked very well. Inner voices, though, were torturing me even more.

Why was I here? Why me? What had I ever done? I had never really believed that, in my country, human beings could be imprisoned in such a place. The dungeon I was in, I later learned, was the notorious prison run by SAVAK's anti-sabotage security force. Known as "The Committee," its members were empowered to adopt any decision—legal or extrajudicial—to deal with those detained as security risks. Almost invariably, detainees would die under torture, disappear, become turncoats who worked for SAVAK, or survive with broken bodies and souls.

Isolated from the world, in this brutal place, I was at SAVAK's mercy. The possibilities terrified me. I knew that the agency's chief, Parviz Sabeti, was a callous, unfeeling creature who ran the security agency as his personal fiefdom. He took pleasure, a colleague had told me, from watching the torture of prisoners. Sabeti, whose nickname was "Mr. Security," had been named Adjutant to the Shah, but even the Shah avoided contact with him and refused to give him an audience. I knew that my situation was grave and that Sabeti would never hesitate to do anything that he wanted to or believed necessary.

Outside the prison's round, four-story walls, protesters were rioting and chanting "Death to the Shah," and security forces were battling violent mobs incited by Ayatollah Khomeini. Inside my barren cell, however, surviving on filthy water and bread, I had no idea what was happening or even what time it was when I woke up or fell asleep. I only knew that twice a day the guards opened a small window in the door to pass me food and water and check that I was still alive. Once a day, they asked me if I needed to go to the toilet. If I needed to do so at any other time, there was nothing that I could do to attract their attention.

After one week, when I had scratched fourteen lines on the cold stone, the door of my cell opened again with a wrenching screech, and I saw the shadow of a huge man. I was quickly blindfolded again and shoved out of my cell into the hall. I tried to ask the guard where we were going, but after so many days in silent, solitary confinement, I had no voice. He pushed me forward with sharp, animal barks, and I stumbled down the corridor for several minutes. When we came to a halt, he removed my blindfold. The light dazzled me, and it was a moment before I realized that I was back where I had started, at the desk of the prison's duty officer.

This time, my tired eyes recognized a familiar person next to him—Dr. Shoja Sheikh, a renowned orthopedic surgeon and Iran's former Minister of Social Welfare and Health and Welfare. I had served as Dr. Sheikh's second-in-command at both ministries. One month before, however, Iran's new Prime Minister, Jamshid Amuzegar, had removed us from our positions.

I had started my new job the next day, as vice chancellor of the Imperial Medical Center. Dr. Sheikh had returned to his private practice at Tehran's Pars Hospital. Now, I was shocked to see him here, with wild hair and a long, unkempt beard, in dirty, crumpled prison pajamas. Dr. Sheikh looked as awful as I felt, and I saw a tear rolling down his unshaved cheek.

The duty officer allowed us to talk for fifteen minutes, but Dr. Sheik and I had no answers to questions that consumed us. What were they going to do to us? What accusations would they try to pin on us? Would our families be safe? Would we ever see them again? The duty officer gave us no answers—saying only that, one way or another, our fates would eventually be revealed.

Days later, I was again blindfolded and led, stumbling, into a large communal cell that held scores of men. Dr. Sheikh was there with Reza Neghabat, Iran's former Undersecretary of Health and Welfare. I was glad to see them, to have company in misery, but my new, larger quarters were hardly an improvement. Instead of the silent, brooding isolation of solitary confinement, I now had to deal with the noise and stink of a vast crowded pen. The three of us struggled to stake out a corner as our own space. In some ways, it was harder to hold onto our humanity in such a place. Once a week, we were all herded into a dirty pit, euphemistically called the "shower room," and forced to stand in muck while water trickled onto us from pipes that had been perforated with hand-drilled holes. We were treated like cattle, deprived of even the most rudimentary means of personal hygiene, and had no hope for any semblance of due process or justice.

Soon, other former cabinet members and officials appeared in the cell, including reformers who had worked to bring progress and development to Iran. Mansour Rouhani—the former Minister of Agriculture and a well-known businessman—joined us. So did Fereidoun Mahdavi, former Minister of Commerce, and Daryoush Homayon, former Minister of Information.

Rouhani had also been Minister of Water and Power. In fact, he had spent the last thirty years of his life holding the ten highest positions in Iran's government, half of them at the cabinet level. Rouhani was an extraordinary problem solver and manager, and the Shah called him the bulldozer of government. A major contributor to the modernization of Iran, he had helped create the country's agro-industrial plan and establish a modern electrical grid throughout the country. He also had a great deal of information about the secret activities of wheelers and dealers in the regime and explained to me how a parallel government in the Shah's Ministry of Court operated through despotism and corruption.

Fereidoun Mahdavi had come from one of Iran's most prominent families and had spent most of his youth in Europe. He was greatly influenced by European culture and had adopted the discipline of the Germans, the zest for political debate of French intellectuals, and the gentlemanly manners of the English. Above all else, however, he was a patriotic, courageous, and bold Iranian. Mahdavi had been a follower of National Front leader and former Prime Minister Muhammed Mossadeq, who had supported democracy and the nationalization of oil resources. After Mossadeq was deposed in a 1953 coupe d'état, Mahdavi was arrested and spent a year in jail. Then, in 1971, Prime Minister Amir Abbas Hoveyda appointed him Minister of Commerce. An energetic, honest official, Mahdavi was determined to fight corruption. That struggle made him a target of SAVAK and eventually led to his second arrest. In 1977, when street demonstrations and chaos were growing more widespread and organized, Americans had pressured the Shah to seek the cooperation of the National Front. Hoveyda, who was then Minister of Court, remembered that Mahdavi had maintained his contacts with members of the group and sought his help. Mahdavi met with National Front members in Iran and France and successfully devised a plan for cooperating with the Shah's government. The Shah would remain as constitutional monarch, retaining his power as the Commander-in-Chief of the Armed Forces. Several National Front members would join the cabinet, however, and Iran would hold a free national election. Mahdavi believed that he had negotiated an agreement that could save Iran's government and flew from Paris to Tehran, expecting to have an audience with the Shah. Instead, SAVAK agents met him at Tehran's Mehrabad Airport and escorted him directly to prison, where he joined us.

Daryoush Homayon, a distinguished journalist, was a close friend of Ardeshir Zahedi, his brother-in-law and Iran's ambassador to the U.S. In 1968, Homayon had convinced Prime Minister Hoveyda that a free, independent newspaper was vital to Iran's political life. Soon, his daily newspaper, *Ayandegan*, began publication. Homayon was its part owner and editor in chief, and its writers including reformists and political dissenters. *Ayandegan* boldly defended freedom and democracy and, despite warnings from SAVAK, soon developed the largest circulation in the country. Homayon was later appointed Minister of Information, with access to classified information.

Hewas arrested by SAVAK in September, 1978, along with other Hoveyda cabinet members.

While Homayon was in prison with us, he met frequently with Ardeshir Zahedi, who traveled regularly between Iran and Washington, D.C. Whenever Zahedi came to Tehran, he would send for Homayon, who would leave jail and visit with him for up to ten hours. When he returned to our prison group, he would give us all the news. Most of it gave us no cause for hope.

Colonel Rasoul, a union leader and former police officer, also joined us in prison. It was Rasoul who was able to tell us that we were in the Anti-Sabotage Committee's detention center. Since our guards and wardens were Rasoul's former subordinates, our situation began to improve a little. The food got a bit better and, most importantly, Rasoul had newspapers smuggled in. From the papers, we were able to see that SAVAK was distorting the facts and portraying us as corrupt officials. As revolution swept the country, Sabeti and his ilk had imprisoned us, like gift-wrapped sacrificial lambs, to take the blame for the excesses and failures of the Shah's regime. Some commentators, in fact, were demanding our summary trial and execution. We also learned that, of all the top officials who had been arrested, only Dr. Sheikh, Neghabat, and I had been subjected to vicious, dehumanizing solitary confinement. We assumed that Sabeti had ordered our "special treatment" as payback for an old grudge, since Dr. Sheikh and I had written a scathing official report on SAVAK's use of torture. All of us, however, recognized the somber truth, too terrible to say out loud—that no matter who won, the Shah or Khomeini, we were doomed. The Shah had put us in prison, but Khomeini's blood-thirsty lieutenants had no love for us. We had no choice but to wait and see which side would destroy us.

As my imprisonment continued, I could hardly sleep more than two or three hours a day. My appetite was gone, and I was sinking quickly into despair. In those dark days, Mahdavi came to my rescue. He told me that no matter what allegations we were charged with, we were in reality political prisoners. "They are abusing our rights," he said, "and you and I have to fight for our freedom and liberty. This is a great objective target. Remember Ghandi and Lumobo. You have to stay healthy and strong by eating the food and exercising daily, and you must strengthen your mind by reading and discussing our situation." His words inspired me and pulled me out of my depression.

Mahdavi began organizing discussions to keep our minds clear and sharp while we were in jail. A few members of our prison group were often angry, kept to themselves, and did not participate in these sessions, but Mahdavi, Rouhani, Dr. Sheik, and I took part from the beginning. Later, Homayon joined us. For two hours each evening, we would try to make sense of what was happening by pooling our collective knowledge. These discussions became the highlight of our day, and we all eagerly looked forward to them.

We would begin by discussing the rumors and news that we gleaned from the Iran's newspapers, radio and television broadcasts and family visitations. We would then compare them with reports in the *New York Times* and *Le Monde*, which Mahdavi managed to receive regularly. After that, our discussions would open up broadly, and we would compare the current situation with past events. Members of our group were well-educated, and each had ten to twenty years of experience in high government positions. Some were even able to maintain their contacts with current leading officials, and a few had daily communications with revolutionaries.

As new inmates arrived, they joined our sessions and added new information. The newcomers included Dr. Iraj Vahidi, Minister of Water and Electricity; Manouchehr Azmoun, Minister of Labor; Reza Sadaghiani, Minister of Agriculture; Dr. Manouchehr Taslimi, Minister of Commerce; General Jafar Sadri, Head of National Police; Reza Kianpour, Minister of Justice; and Senator Reza Nikpay. Eventually, our group also included Houshang Nahavandi, Minister of Housing and Development, and Majid Majidi, Director of Plan Organization, as well as two others who asked not to be named. So many long-time government officials were sharing the same space that we could check and compare untold details of past events and political conflicts against each other's individual memories.

For six months, around the clock, I lived with this group, many of the most important people in Iranian politics. We had nothing to do but talk with each other, and we had insight on all sides of every issue. In some ways, inside our prison, we were more knowledgeable about what was going on in Iran than anyone outside, in the middle of the chaos. Now, as we waited together for an unknown, frightening fate, we had nothing to do but try to make sense of it all.

It was clear to me that the information we were sharing was profoundly significant and important to Iran's history. Even if none of us left prison alive, I felt determined to ensure that a record of our discussions would somehow

7

survived. So I wrote shorthand summaries of these conversations and hid them inside the waistband of my trousers. Every time my wife, Helen, visited me, she brought a laundry bag filled with clean clothes and took home my soiled clothing for washing. In this way, I passed her the record of our discussions, which she smuggled out of prison and preserved. Those notes formed the basis of my recollections and reconstruction of the history of Iran's revolution.

CHAPTER 2

MAZANDARAN

I was born on the shores of the Caspian Sea, where the high peaks of the Alborz Mountains cleave the green expanse of Mazandaran from the arid central plateau of Iran. When I was a child, it was the most beautiful place in the world. As I look back toward the Mazandaran, across the distance of memory, it occurs to me that this arduous mountain terrain gave the region and its inhabitants their identity. For centuries, hiding in its rugged ravines and jagged passes, our people resisted the Arab invasions that streamed down from the north and west. Even after the rest of the ancient kingdom of Iran had been overrun, the Mazandarani people maintained a thousand-year struggle. We clung to our culture and religion with such dogged determination that Arabic never found its way into the Mazandarani dialect. We have always taken pride in what made us different, from the rice we ate instead of bread to the freedom and beauty of Mazandarani women.

My family lived in Sari, a small, lush city on the southern coast of the Caspian Sea. The surrounding natural springs and citrus orchards made it a favorite spot for the Mazandarani on weekends, and tourists prowled the old ruined fortresses along the seashore—the last memory of ancient Arab assaults. By the beginning of the twentieth century, however, the Arabs were no longer Iran's main enemies. Britain and Czarist Russia had been playing a great game for control in Asia. After Iran signed constitutional reforms into law in 1907, they divided the country into two spheres of influence. The Czar's "Persian Cossacks Brigade" commanded the northern part of Iran, and Britain's "South Persia Rifle Forces" patrolled the south. Under the gun barrels of these great powers, a central Iranian government—under the incompetent Ahmad Shah Qajar—kept the peace but accomplished little. The countryside slumbered in feudal fiefdoms under the thumb of sheiks and tribal chiefs. Ahmad Shah himself lived most of his time in Europe, and rumor had it that he threatened not to return to Iran unless the British agreed to raise his salary. Such were our leaders in those days.

Then, in 1917, the Bolsheviks overthrew the Czar and established the Soviet Union. The revolution shook the capitalist world at its foundations. Repercussions were felt strongly in Iran's north and south, which seemed to be on the brink of civil war. Initially, the Soviet Union offered Iran friendship, promising to restore its territorial integrity by declaring the Anglo-Russian agreement of 1907 null and void. But the British considered this a serious threat to their interests and extended their sphere of interest into the north. The young Soviet Union reacted harshly—seizing Anzali, a city on the Caspian Sea, and establishing it as the center of Iran's Communist Party.

Anzali was a wake-up call for the British. They surveyed the deep socioeconomic and political turmoil fueled by decades of anarchy and corrupt government and realized that a chaotic Iran would be fertile ground for the spread of communism. The solution, the British concluded, would be a strong, central government led by someone they could rely on to keep the peace for them. They selected a veteran politician named Seyyed Zia. He was glad to be a British stooge; he had actually been living without earshot of Ten Downing Street when he was chosen. But even the British realized that Zia would never be able to maintain power on his own. They also needed a man who, in their view, could build Iran's army into a modern force for national stability. So they picked Reza Khan, a Mazandarani who had been a commander in the Persian Cossacks brigade before the Russian Revolution. Despite his time with the Russian forces, Reza Khan had always been a true patriot, and he jumped at the chance to rebuild Iran's military. The country had not had an army of its own for years. Free of any attachment to the past and without entrenched interests fighting him, Reza Khan could create a modern force from the ground up that would be loyal only to Iran and answered to him.

As he built up Iran's army, his star rose while Zia's dimmed, and it was not long before Zia was the executive in name only. Reza Shah filled the military and then Parliament with men who were loyal only to him and shared his patriotism and desire to expel the British. His methods were not democratic; like Kemal Ataturk of Turkey (whom he admired), he believed that dictatorial methods were the only means of freeing his country. When the British, for example, tried to separate Khuzestan, an oil-rich state in the south, from Iran by installing a tribal chief named Sheikh Khazal as its leader, Reza Khan put the Sheikh under lifetime house arrest and kept the country whole.

He also engineered the termination of the Qajar dynasty. In 1925, his supporters in Parliament, by an overwhelming vote, declared him Reza Shah Pahlavi, the new Shah of Persia. That move ended a century of rule by a dynasty that had drawn a salary in British pounds. Shortly after, he forced the British to withdraw their forces from Iranian soil.

As Reza Shah strove to build Iran into a modern nation, he often turned his attention to the Mazandaran. He routed a new railway network through the province. Soon after, industrial factories and workshops began popping up like mushrooms after the rain. Jointly owned Russian and Iranian companies began trawling the Caspian Sea for caviar. Although most of the harvest went north to Russia, many rubles flowed south in exchange. Most of all, the Shah's land reforms revolutionized agriculture in the Mazandaran, and as it flourished, the picturesque sight of women working in rice paddies, wearing colorful *shaliteh*, drew thousands of tourists. Hotels were constructed to house them—modern buildings and comfortable seashore villas—and parks and resorts of the region were soon filled with visitors from all over Iran and the world. At the same time, the Shah centralized Iran's government in Tehran, the capital city. Until his ascent to power, Tehran had largely been isolated from the world. Now, it was the center of the new independent, modernizing nation.

CHAPTER 3

COMING OF AGE

My grandfather, Haji Ali, made his living by farming and trading. When he died, at the end of the nineteenth century, my uncle, Mirza Mahmud, became head of the family and took charge of my father, Ahmad, and their sister, Ama. Mahmud was a capable manager and shrewd businessman, and he expanded the family business. Before long, his trading office in Sari expanded into an import and export business between Iran and Russia, and he eventually set up an office in St. Petersburg. He spent half his time in that beautiful city and bought a house there. Later, my father joined him and studied pharmaceutical sciences at the Czar's schools.

In those days, before the revolution, Russia was a welcoming place for Iranian businessmen. When the Bolsheviks took charge, however, Mirza Mahmud lost most of his wealth. When I was a child, my uncle was a frail and bitter old man who took refuge in my father's home after the Bolsheviks ruined him. There were sacks of worthless Czarist bank notes in our attic, gathering dust in huge sacks. As kids we used them to play games like Monopoly and tossed handfuls of them into the fireplace to add zest to the flames. None of the adults stopped us.

My father was a happy and humorous person, and he commanded respect; everyone in our family, including my mother, called him *Aga*, or "Sir." In his youth, he had been a reformer and freedom fighter, and the example he set was always important to me. In 1908, he had joined the constitutional movement's struggle against Iran's dictatorial government; in those circles he had been known as "Mirza Ahmad the pharmacist." Living clandestinely for years, only a step or two ahead of security agents, he published an underground paper that poked fun at Iran's dictators. The newspaper—called *doogh*, a drink made with yogurt or sour milk—gained a wide underground following in northern Iran. Later, when Reza Khan became commander in chief of the armed forces, he rewarded my father's patriotism by designating our family's pharmacy business as the only official pharmacy in the state.

My mother's family fared less well under Reza Shah. Her father had been a landlord who lived lavishly and died young. Reza Shah's land reforms stripped her family of its only source of income. A mutual friend introduced my father to my mother's brother Habib, who hoped that my father would train him as a pharmacist. Habib, in turn, introduced my father to my mother, who was then only fourteen. Though she was thirty years younger than my father, they would marry years later and have five children.

I was born on December 18, 1928, two years after Reza Shah ascended to the throne. In those days, over 60 percent of the country was illiterate, but my mother made sure that I walked a mile to school every day, along streets that were lined with intoxicatingly fragrant citrus trees. Our family was happy, on the whole, and we had a comfortable life. But when I was still a child, my father began to drink. As years went by, he became more dependent on alcohol and lost his interest in his work. By then, my uncle Habib was fully capable of running the pharmacy on his own. As my father grew ill and stayed home more and more, my uncle took full control of the family business.

Eventually, after wasting away for a long period of time, my father died. We were still well off and had no reason to doubt that we would have a secure future. But after my father's death, Habib seized control of the family and my father's estate. He soon let us know that the good life we enjoyed would be disappearing, because my father's wealth, he claimed, was much less than we had always believed.

My mother had been raised in a family tradition in which male supremacy was unquestionable and unchallenged. Younger sisters lived under the absolute control of their fathers or older brothers, and my mother's obedience to her husband transferred to her brother once she was a widow. Though she had children and independence, she would never have dreamed of sitting down in the presence of her brother unless he had given her permission to do so. And even though my mother had inherited valuable property from her father and should have been entitled to rent and income from his estate, Habib managed her share of it as he saw fit. It would have been unthinkable to ask him what happened to her inheritance.

As we adjusted to my father's death, we became acquainted with austerity and privation. My mother had to work on a farm to supplement our meager income. It hurt me to see her in the fields, but what else was she suppose to do? In those days, there were no other options for women; the only jobs available were degrading or demanded hard labor. But my mother was able to endure hardship and humiliation; she hid her troubles from her children and never allowed her agony to affect us.

My uncle was always kind to me and treated me like one of his own children. I used to spend a great deal of time in his house. Even when I was in school, I had responsibilities in his household, such as doing the daily shopping. Eventually, I began working in the evenings as an errand boy in the family pharmacy. Afterwards, I would take supper with my uncle's family and would only return to my mother's house after collecting some food which my grandmother—a woman well known for her kindness, generosity, and trusting nature—carefully measured out for me.

I enjoyed working hard. When I was twelve, I began doing jobs as a technician in the family pharmacy. Though I didn't receive wages, I took great pride in being useful to the business. I loved my uncle as if he was my own father and never hesitated to put in an honest day's work for him. But I noticed that the pharmacy my father had built hardly benefited my mother at all. Under my uncle's management, the family business was going strong, but he imposed great financial hardships on his own sister; each day, she would rise with the sun and take her two year old son Darius to work without complaint.

One day, with tears in my eyes, I begged my mother to demand her rightful share of the pharmacy income from her brother, even though I knew she would never do it. "Son, my dearest one," she answered me with a pained smile, "I prefer to do as much as I can. I don't wish to ask my brother for anything."

Life, I was learning, could be ugly and hard, and in 1941, when I was in elementary school, the shadow of World War II touched our community. In the 1930s, Hitler's Germany had been looking for a foothold in the Persian Gulf region and gave Iran economic and technical assistance, at the request of the Shah. He believed that Iran had much to learn from Europe. By the end of the decade, with war on the horizon, hundreds of German experts were

14

at work modernizing Iran's economy, helping to create a new Iran and establish security and unity within the nation. The Shah progressively introduced more liberal European laws and regulations into Iranian society and sent as many Iranians abroad as he could to acquire modern knowledge and help build up the country.

At the same time, Iran's ties with Britain were under stress. For years, Iran had been receiving markedly reduced royalties from Anglo-Persian Oil, while the coffers of British oil companies grew ever fatter. So in 1939, Reza Shah canceled Britain's oil concession. Matters quickly came to a head. The British were enraged at being deprived of the profits of Iranian oil and brought the matter to international arbitration, without success. The League of Nations forced the British oil companies to agree on a new contract with Iran that provided for increased royalties.

Two years later, however, Winston Churchill found a way to punish Reza Shah for his rebelliousness and alliance with Nazi Germany. In 1941, Great Britain and the Soviet Union jointly invaded Iran and reoccupied it, exactly as they had after the Two Power's Agreement of 1907. The U.S.S.R. bit off the north while the British occupied the south and used the pretext of Iran's relations with Germany to remove Reza Shah from the throne. The monarch was arrested, forced to abdicate, and lived out the rest of his life as an exile on South Africa's Morris Island.

Reza Shah's inexperienced twenty-three-year-old son, Mohammad Reza, was named the new monarch. A self-indulgent playboy, he had no interest in political challenges and held little real power. To run the country, the British—who had years of experience manipulating Middle Eastern governments—established an "Executive Committee" that could be counted on to secure British interests. Made up of a few experienced, pro-British Iranian politicians, the Executive Committee handpicked top members of the cabinet. The young Shah rubber-stamped its orders and took credit for all its decisions.

Today, I look back bitterly on our army's disgraceful defeat and the ouster of the Shah. Iran was humiliated under the occupation of two foreign powers. But some of the most vivid memories of my youth, during World War II, were of watching films that the Soviet army showed us in the town square, since the northern town of Sari had no movie theater. I especially remember watching Lenin giving a speech in Farsi. I was amazed to see this man, whose name we had heard, speaking in Farsi about the bravery of Russian soldiers who were fighting the Germans. I had never imagined that a person like Lenin could speak our language, and it stuck in my mind. Of course, the propaganda film was dubbed, but I didn't understand that.

Sometimes, as kids, we would sprinkle pepper dust on roses and, with inviting smiles, offer the flowers to Russian soldiers on duty. When the soldiers sneezed, we would laugh and run, having done our duty against the occupiers. I also remember the day that I met an American soldier. He offered me chocolate, chewing gum, and a pen and showed me a photograph of his own son that he kept in his wallet. He seemed different to me, and I was touched.

Time marched on, and I watched the world change as I was growing up. Life was often a struggle. In the 1940s, malaria, a debilitating disease we barely understood, was still widespread in the Mazandaran. Everyone got the enervating, sweat-racked, shivering fever at predictable intervals. It was only eradicated after World War II with the help of Truman's Point Four technical assistance program. In Tehran, typhus—carried to Iran by Polish refugees—and other epidemics also made life miserable. Still, despite hardships, there was always something that brought smiles to our faces. Spring's budding flowers were followed by the heat of summer, then autumn with its falling leaves and the crisp cold of winter. In the long, freezing winter nights, I loved crawling under the *korsi*—a table with brazier underneath and a quilt wrapped around it to keep in the warmth—to eat oranges and tangerines with my siblings. I still carry those moments of pleasure with me.

Once, when I was on the verge of manhood, I went with a group of boys and girls my age to Farahabad, where the Tejan River flows into the Caspian Sea. As we were walking, someone suggested that we cross the river. There was no obvious place to do it, and the river was wide and deep, but we spotted an abandoned boat on the other bank and thought we could use it. To get hold of it, though, someone had, to swim across the roaring river, which seemed to be at least a hundred meters wide.

With the boldness of youth, I declared that I was the best swimmer and prepared to jump in. The river's width and rough waters filled me with confidence; I was a good swimmer, and all I could see was an opportunity to show off. I dove in and, though the water was choppy, managed to swim two-thirds of the way before my strength suddenly began to fail and I could make no more progress towards the other side. The harder I tried, the more exhausted I was. Glancing back, I realized how far I had come from my friends on the bank and that I lacked enough strength to swim back to them.

In desperation, I relaxed my aching muscles and tried to float on the surface, but the current kept pulling me under. I tried to put my feet on the riverbed to rest, but as soon as they touched the muddy floor, I started to panic. The river was carrying me toward the sea. I could hear my friends shouting, calling me to return to their side of the river, so in desperation I tried to swim back. All of a sudden, I felt I could do it. I had been swimming against the current! Now, every stroke was easier, and my confidence grew. When I finally reached the shore, I realized what many youths understand too late—how close I had come to death and how lucky I was to make my escape.

As I grew up, I looked forward to the time when I would be able to help the family. My sister had found a job while she was in high school, and when she completed her studies, she took a job as a primary school teacher. Her salary—and the decision to rent out part of our house—allowed my mother to give up her arduous work outside the home. But although I was making great progress at the pharmacy and had gained a lot of experience attending to prescriptions, giving injections, and dispensing all kinds of first-aid, I was still not receiving regular pay. Only occasionally would I be able to bring a tip from a satisfied customer home to my mother. Still, seeing what a difference my sister's wages made in our lives, I started to think about a career in medicine as a path that could give me possibilities and hope. I had never been able to devote much time to my studies at school, but I had always managed to rank first or second in my class. I began to think that my work at the pharmacy could help me launch a career.

Sometimes, too, my job at the pharmacy gave me things to see. In those years, people in need of medical care had nowhere to go but their local pharmacies. Most pharmacy technicians provided injections and other types of services that patients normally receive in hospital outpatient wards. Since most assistant pharmacists were young men, however, female patients were reluctant to take off enough clothing to receive their shots. In our pharmacy, those women would ask to be treated by me, because I was only thirteen and had an innocent, boyish. I was happy to be chosen. Despite the inhibitions of my traditional upbringing, my eyes were opening wider and wider.

One day, my uncle sent me to a woman's house to give her an injection for gonorrhea. In the 1940s, antibiotics like penicillin had just come into general use. Compared to previous treatments, it could have miraculous effects on infectious diseases. To treat gonorrhea patients, the drug had to be injected into the thighs every four hours, and I was sent to an address in a remote part of town to administer the medicine personally. When I arrived, a tough-looking man met me at the door and took me to meet an old woman of about sixty, who, after grilling me about my work experience, took me into another room. When I entered, I saw a beautiful young woman lying on a bed, wearing heavy makeup and only a tantalizing see-through nightgown. She was clutching the sheet, her face twisted in fear. "You're not going to hurt me, are you?" she pleaded. Dumbfounded, I didn't know what to say. I could only shake my head and assure her that I would not. I gave her the first shot, and the old woman led me out of the room to a bed in the courtyard garden that was piled with sheets, pillows, and blankets. I was to stay there between injections, which I would administer to the young woman at four-hour intervals.

Sleeping in the open night air was a normal practice in the country at that time, so I had no difficulty bedding down outside in the large courtyard. There was a pool in the middle and a number of rooms strung together in a one-story structure surrounding the garden. The doors of the rooms opened onto the courtyard through a low staircase. The smell of citrus trees made it a pleasant place, and I was happy to stay there, reading my schoolbooks and daydreaming.

I lay down on my bed after a light supper, but had trouble going to sleep. There was a lot of coming and going in the place, and it suddenly occurred to me that, though many adults lived there, I had not seen any children. A large number of residents, in fact, seemed to be scantily clad women wearing heavy makeup, like the lady I was treating. I also noticed how many visiting young men were being led to rooms where they would stay for short or long periods. I was young and shy, but it didn't take me long to realize, with a shudder, that I was in a house of prostitution. Boys my age picked up information here and there, and we would sometimes hear the most horrible stories about dangerous, prostitutes in such places who caused diseases.

My first thought was to run away, but I was more curious than scared. My patient was afflicted with several diseases, I told myself, and what kind of doctor would abandon a patient out of fear? In the end, my sense of adventure got the better of me, and I suddenly realized what a wonderful opportunity this was to see what went in this forbidden place.

I lay on my bed for hours pretending to sleep, but I kept one eye open and observed everything. Men arrived one by one, and sounds of laughter and merrymaking were heard everywhere. Half-naked women appeared at their doors, holding hands with the visiting men, and I strained to hear the strange, passionate sounds emanating from their rooms.

After I stayed in that house for forty-eight hours, the woman running the place handed me an envelope. I opened it outside and found that it contained thirty-two *tomans* in bank notes—more money than I had ever had in my life. I could hardly contain my joy. It must, I imagined, be enough money to sleep with as many as six prostitutes! I was no longer afraid of these ladies, who looked friendly, beautiful, and looked. Even though I was a young boy and would never have dared to have sex with one, I knew that I had a great story to tell my friends.

CHAPTER 4

POLITICS OF INDEPENDENCE

As I entered the final years of my secondary education, I began to look out at the country I was inheriting. I didn't like what I could see. Iran in the 1950s was falling into an economic quagmire; in the public sector, corruption and nepotism were becoming a way of life. The Shah's government was weak and subservient to foreign powers, and the bureaucracy was on the verge of collapse. Even worse, economic stagnation was causing instability and political unrest. Widespread poverty, unemployment, and the lack of adequate infrastructure and public services created fertile ground for demagogues and politicians who promised to put an end to the chaos. A general feeling of indignation and shame at being under foreign occupation only fanned nationalist flames higher and brighter.

Britain and the Soviet Union, of course, had no intention of letting things get out of hand. They moved quickly to set up client political organizations to maintain their control. But the Soviets had a definite advantage in this competition. The communist Tudeh Party, the first organized political party in Iran, had been founded years before, in 1941, with the active support of the U.S.S.R.'s. Championing the cause of workers, laborers, and underdogs worldwide, communism was an attractive ideology for Iran's intelligentsia and young people and especially appealing to students like me.

Tudeh means people, and the party was built on the twin pillars of intellectuals and workers. Its ranks were filled with experienced cadres, communist leaders who had already mastered the art of partisan political activism in revolutionary activity in Europe and the Soviet Union. These people formed the party's organizational backbone, and they could call on the overt support of Red Army units whenever they needed it. The Tudeh Party's official newspaper, a propagandist mouthpiece publication called *Mardom* ("The People" in Farsi) was staffed with experienced leftist journalists and was quite successful for a political party paper. The articles I read in *Mardom* strongly influenced my thinking.

I began to attend some Tudeh Party cell meetings and found myself drawn toward communist thought and ideology. Seeing Lenin speaking Farsi when I was younger had impressed me, of course, but this attraction was based on the idealism of youth and the wisdom of a little experience. When I read *Mardom* articles decrying the ways the rich exploited the poor, I thought of my uncle enjoying the fruits of the pharmacy my father had built while my mother slaved in the fields. When Tudeh's leaders declared that all people should live equally, I listened with rapt attention. Who could deny the attractiveness of such a vision?

In a sense, the communists were the only game in town. Britain's political proxies could not fool anyone into thinking they cared about anything but furthering British interests in the country. The various nationalist groups were somewhere in the middle, between Tudeh's revolutionaries and pro-British, pro-establishment politicians, and they lacked financial resources and organizational skills. Tudeh, the majority party in northern Iran, was rapidly gaining power throughout the country.

By the time I was a senior in high school, however, a third foreign nation was beginning to have an influence in Iran. The U.S. government was beginning to recognize Iran's strategic importance, especially given its shared thousand-mile border with the Soviet Union. Iran, for its part, was happy to have a new ally that could, perhaps, counter the influence of Britain and the U.S.S.R. In 1942, the United States dispatched thirty thousand troops to Iran at Britain's request. In those days, we didn't know anything about the United States, but the arrival of American soldiers gave us a chance to see and compare them with the devils we already knew. The Russians always seemed to be hard up and kept to themselves, preoccupied with their own affairs. But the Red Army, an instrument of the Soviet government, was a constant source of public anger, since Moscow often used it to interfere in Iran's domestic affairs. As for the British, we saw first-hand that most of the lower-rank troops were natives of India and other colonies and how those soldiers were commonly mistreated by their English officers. We also knew that Britain wanted to colonize Iran, and such conduct made a poor impression on Iranians. The American soldiers, on the other hand, were well paid and seemed outgoing and generous. And since the United States had no colonial history in Iran, U.S. troops became comparatively quite popular.

American businessmen also started appearing in Iran. In 1943, the U.S. government had asked Arthur Millispaugh to lead an advisory mission providing technical assistance to the Iranian government to help modernize the country's tax system and upgrade America's diplomatic presence in Iran from a legation to the embassy level. Hard on the heels of these developments, two major U.S. oil companies began negotiating with Iranian authorities to operate in Iran. The Soviet and British governments vehemently opposed these moves; in their minds, Iran belonged to their joint sphere of influence. They viewed these companies as encroaching on their national interests, and they got their way. American companies withdrew from the talks and apologized, and The Soviet Union and Great Britain separately warned Iran that it could not award oil concessions to other countries. In response to these warnings, the Iranian Parliament approved a bill submitted by Dr. Mohammad Mossadegh, a rising nationalist politician, forbidding the Iranian government to offer new oil concession rights to any foreign entity while Iran was still occupied by foreign armies, including the British and Soviets.

On January 1, 1946, American and British forces left Iran, complying with the agreement between Iran and Allied governments that occupation forces would withdraw from Iranian territory within six months after the end of hostilities. The Soviets, however, refused to leave. They began interfering in Iran's internal affairs, forming an armed militia group to separate the province of Azerbaijan, which bordered the Soviet Union, and establish a puppet communist government in that northern region. The strategy succeeded and led to the formation of the Azerbaijan Democratic Republic, led by Jaafar Pishevari, a well-known Iranian communist. The Soviets then sponsored another separatist movement in western Iran, which they called "Democratic Kurdistan," and the nation seemed threatened by complete territorial disintegration.

In response, the United States and Britain filed an official complaint with the United Nations Security Council, charging the Soviet Union with failing to meet its obligations to withdraw its forces from Iran and meddling in Iran's internal affairs. Diplomat Averell Harriman personally gave Stalin a strong ultimatum from President Truman, telling him to evacuate Iranian territory at once and warning him that the U.S.S.R.'s continued occupation of Iran was becoming an obstacle to world peace. In fact, Truman let it be known that if the Soviets would not leave Iran voluntarily, he would "nuke them out."

On March 24, 1946, the U.S.S.R. announced that it would evacuate Iranian territory within a month. As soon as the Red Army left, the Iranian Army, supported by the people of Azerbaijan, liberated the province from the hold of Pishevari, who fled to Moscow. The separatist rule of Soviet puppets in Kurdistan also crumbled when the Iranian army arrived, restoring the country's territorial integrity. The United States, meanwhile, was beginning to spend hundreds of millions of dollars to train and equip the Iranian armed forces.

As Iran began to look forward to a future free of colonial control, I was thinking hard about my future plans in life and determined to enroll at a university medical school. There were no institutes of higher education in Sari, however, and only the universities of Tehran, Shiraz, and Tabriz offered courses in medical sciences. So I began to prepare myself mentally for enrolling at Tehran University. Preparing myself financially, however, was another matter. I asked my uncle for help and was stunned by his reaction. He immediately and vehemently opposed my educational plans and told me that my future would be at the pharmacy.

"This business helped your father make a living," he insisted. "Today, I am earning my livelihood at this pharmacy, and tomorrow it will provide a living for you. After your father's death, I became the owner of this establishment, and after I go, you too, in turn, will come into possession of the family inheritance."

I was cynical about this promise, given everything I knew about my uncle, but he tried to sweeten the pot.

"You have already shown a good deal of talent and interest in this profession," he added. "Now you will acquire more experience and knowledge through on the job training. You will also develop better communication skills. All these advantages, I am sure, will enable you to obtain the required certificate as a licensed pharmacist."

He tried to convince me that it was my duty to keep alive the tradition of sons following their fathers' footsteps—that it was my responsibility as well as an honor to perpetuate the family's name and profession. By now, however, I realized that his only real concern was his own self-interest. It was to my uncle's advantage to hold on to a hardworking, honest, undemanding employee. I also knew that it was impossible to get a pharmacy license without studying at a pharmaceutical school in one of the big universities.

Without hesitating, I rejected his offer. "I have already made up my mind to continue my studies in Tehran," I declared.

My uncle then told me how impossible it was to get accepted by Tehran University, since many applicants were competing for a small number of slots. I would have to take a difficult and highly competitive university entrance examination, and he insinuated that my chances of success would be very slim. Finally, he let me know that, even if I managed to win a place at the university, I would have to support myself. "How do you propose to pay for the very high expenses of living and studying in Tehran?" he asked. "How will you do it?"

But I was unwavering. My mind was made up. I vehemently believed that hard work and determination would lead to success and that my life would be better without him.

I still remember the day when I packed my few books and modest belongings in an old suitcase and prepared to leave my birthplace for Tehran. After I kissed my mother, sister, and brothers good-bye, I passed under the Holy Qoran to prepare for the journey, as custom dictates. As I left the house, my mother performed a final ritual, pouring a saucer of water over my footsteps behind me as I departed.

Later, on board the train heading for Tehran, I examined my life savings, carefully pulling the banknotes out of a small bag my mother had hung around my neck. I counted them carefully. I had 150 tomans in all (about $60 at the time)—a sizable enough sum to give me some measure of confidence. In eight hours, I realized with hope and happiness, I would step onto the platform at Tehran's train terminal and begin an exciting new, independent phase of my life. But I was anxious, too. I would have less than three days to prepare for the university's entrance examinations. Time was short, and with no time to learn the city's layout, how to get to and from the university, or even where I would stay—and how I would pay for lodgings—I was wondering how I could possibly get everything done in time.

Fortunately, when I arrived in Tehran, my mother's youngest sister, Aunt Sedigheh, was on the platform to meet me like a guardian angel. She, her husband, and their ten-year son received me with open arms and insisted that I stay with them. My fears erased, I gratefully agreed and started buckling down and focusing on my entrance examinations.

After days of frenzied preparation, I took the test and was rewarded with a place at Tehran University's School of Dentistry. I was slightly disappointed, since my intent had been to study medicine, but I knew that path would still be open. If I began my studies at the dental school, I would be able to enroll in the medical school the following year without having to retake the entrance exams.

As the first weeks went by, I found that the difficulties of student life were not as great as I had feared, and I found little to complain about in my new environment. I was not happy to impose on my aunt's family, although they never complained, but my aunt's great motherly love and her husband's immense generosity made me feel almost as comfortable as if I were at home. And, to my surprise, by the end of my first year at the School of Dentistry, I found that I was beginning to warm to the idea of becoming a dentist. If I continued on in the Faculty of Dentistry, I could graduate two years sooner than if I transferred to medicine, so I decided to continue my studies there. The sooner I completed my degree, the sooner I would be able to make my own way in the world.

In the meantime, I began to look around for some way to earn money on the side. I had always been good at puzzles, so I began submitting crossword puzzles to the daily newspapers. After a few had been accepted, I was given a steady job preparing the daily crossword for the *Etelaat* newspaper. Since I was now writing for the paper, I started to read it regularly for the first time. The university was becoming the hub of political activity in Tehran, so politics were unavoidable anyway. Demonstrations were becoming almost daily occurrences, and clashes between students and police were increasingly common as things heated up.

In those days, the Tudeh Party was very active, and a great many intelligent and dedicated young men and women belonged to it. Under its umbrella, students quickly became experienced operatives. Since I had been introduced to leftist ideas in high school, I naturally gravitated toward Tudeh activists. The egalitarian philosophy of the communists matched my own ideals and aspirations, and I supported their campaigns against injustice and vocal defense of the rights of underprivileged classes.

As I got more involved, I began writing articles for left-leaning papers. I even wrote a novel, which I called *The Cry of the Crowd*. In it, my aim was to write a story, dealing with police corruption, that would have more effect and influence than mere journalism. The novel was distributed and even sold well for a modest undertaking. One day, however, several police officers visited me and made clear that if I didn't suppress the book, they would save me the trouble, suppress it themselves, and throw me in jail. It was an easy choice. I had the novel suppressed, and the police left me alone. But my part-time writing was now earning me enough money to meet expenses, and I was able to send small but regular sums of money home to my mother and sister. I think they were as pleased about my success as they were about the money.

CHAPTER 5

THE PATRIOTIC FRONT

Iranian politics, however, were heating up, and I soon began to question my allegiance to Tudeh. In February 1949, the Shah narrowly escaped an assassination attempt. The would-be assassin was killed on the spot, and the authorities declared he had been a member of the Tudeh Party. Soon after, they outlawed Tudeh, declaring the party an illegal entity, and the Shah's security forces launched an intense anticommunist campaign against the organization. Tudeh's operations were restricted on all fronts, the party went underground, and many of its leaders fled to the U.S.S.R. Although communism didn't entirely lose its appeal in Iran, its organizational unity was fractured.

Iran's fight against Tudeh drew the attention of the U.S. government, which, quite rightly, saw the party as an organ of the Soviet Union. The United States decided to throw its weight behind the Shah, and the presence of Americans in Iran became more visible. Max Thornburg, the State Department's adviser on oil matters, arrived in 1947 with an economic and financial team that helped create the foundations of a state economic planning and development apparatus. The country produced its first seven-year economic plan, and American grants and low-interest loans—as well as direct military assistance and advice—kept the economy off the brink of bankruptcy and helped modernize the Iranian Army.

Iran's government welcomed U.S. support. By 1950, however, nationalistic feelings were on the rise, especially after the suppression of Tudeh. Nationalists were becoming a force in Iranian politics at the same moment that Iran's oil resources were becoming the hottest topic in political debates. What brought things to a head was the announcement by oil industry experts that Iran's national share of income from its oil resources was a tiny fraction of the total, even though its vast deposits were being exploited and exported. American advisers were also pointing to the country's large oil reserves and asking why a nation so rich in natural wealth should receive generous development assistance from the U.S. that was intended for poor countries. The British, in fact, held an exclusive concession for Iran's oil at half the market price and were drawing massive royalties from oil sales. When the Iranian public found out that the income tax that British Petroleum paid to the British treasury was a great deal higher than the royalties it paid to Iran, nationalist passions reached a boiling point.

At the height of anti-British sentiments, a pragmatic Iranian politician named Dr. Mohammad Mossadegh gained wide popularity by waving the flag of national pride. Backed by the Iran Party and other nationalist groups, Mossadegh led a broad-based coalition, known as the National Front, which quickly became the country's strongest political force in the country. Until then, the Tudeh Party, even though it was underground, was still the country's preeminent political force. Now it found itself playing second fiddle.

Although the nationalists wanted Iran to control all of its oil resources— ousting the British Petroleum Company (BP) in the south and the Soviets in the north—Tudeh wanted to preserve Soviet oil concessions. The party advocated instead nationalizing only the oil industry in the south, where Soviet oil interests would not be affected. In the end, Tudeh's refusal to join the campaign for full nationalization alienated many of its most able supporters. A group of intellectuals, led by political theorist Khalil Maleki, left Tudeh in protest and established a new party that joined Iran's National Front. Officially named the "Iran Labor Party," it was popularly referred to as the "Third Force," an alternative to the communists who were looking north and the capitalists who were looking west.

More and more, I found myself agreeing with the nationalists. Iran was clearly being colonized. Why should the British and Soviets reap all the benefits from oil resources under Iranian soil? It reminded me of how my uncle had been wringing every last drop of value from our family's business. I looked hard to find convincing reasons why the Tudeh Party was opposing oil nationalization. I found none that satisfied me.

Like a religious convert, I began to see things clearly. I threw aside the Tudeh Party's doctrines and suddenly realized I could think through social and political problems on my own, without adhering rigidly to party guidelines. I could even think and speak freely about Stalin, referring to him as the despot that I knew he was instead of the kindly "Father of the Masses" I had been trained to call him.

More importantly, I could now join others in speaking freely against Soviet interference in Iran's affairs. Support for Dr. Mossadegh and the patriotic front was spreading far and wide. As the Shah and Houses of Parliament began yielding to their demands, the power of British and Soviet surrogates began to wane. The Americans seemed to be happy with the changes. U.S. Ambassador Henry Grady stated that he hated Britain's colonial policies, and General Dwight D. Eisenhower, then Supreme Commander of NATO, wrote Dr. Mossadegh to express support.

In 1951, Mossadegh was voted in as the new Prime Minister. On April 30 that year, he submitted a bill to the Majlis to nationalize the country's oil industry. Britain's oil interests were subsequently seized by the state in the name of Iran and its people. The British demanded that the U.N. Security Council restrain Iran from the confiscations, but the council officially condoned Iran's right to control its oil industry. Britain, however, was not about to accept this state of affairs and resorted to an old colonial tactic: gunboat diplomacy. British warships placed Iran under an economic blockade and announced that any country purchasing Iranian oil would have its cargo confiscated on the high seas. As a result, Iran's oil exports abruptly collapsed.

U.S. Secretary of State Dean Acheson attempted to mediate between Iran and Britain but did not succeed. In a surprise move, all the clerics and politicians in the British camp were mobilized to oppose Iran's nationalist government. Even Ayatollah Kashani, Dr. Mossadegh's most important clerical ally—who had as much influence in the National Front as Mossadegh himself—did an about-face and suddenly opposed his former comrade-in-arms. Soon, several other heavyweight politicians abandoned Mossadegh and began supporting the opposition. Even these high-profile defections, however, could not dent public support for Mossadegh's government, which only increased as it became more embattled. So Britain's machinations went into overdrive. The British intelligence service circulated a report claiming that Mossadegh's government would soon be overthrown by a military coup and replaced by a communist regime, led by the Tudeh Party.

This was baseless propaganda, and in Iran, only fools would have believed it. The British, however, were trying to exploit American fears about communism's global spread. They alleged that unless Mossadegh was replaced by a pro-Western government, Iran would fall into the orbit of the Soviet Union. The Tudeh Party was, in fact, in no position to seize power, but Americans did not seem to realize it. Although the U.S. had been supporting Mossadegh, it now withdrew its support for Iran's oil policy and conspired with Britain to bring down the nationalist government. In a coup d'état on August 19, 1953, Britain's cronies, the Rashidian brothers, teamed with Kermit Roosevelt of the CIA to organize riots in the streets of Tehran, sack Mossadegh's house, and force the Prime Minister to flee. By noon, the coup leaders had captured the Tehran Radio Station and announced the formation of a new pro-American cabinet. The next day, Dr. Mossadegh and his closest aides were arrested and imprisoned. The Shah, who had left the country for a week in Italy, returned to Iran, and a new government took power that resolved the dispute over Iran's oil industry in favor of Britain and the United States.

The overthrow of Mossadegh's cabinet opened the door for U.S. oil companies to enter Iran. A consortium of Western oil companies signed a new agreement to exploit Iran's oilfields, and American companies seized a sizable share, at BP's expense. Britain's influence in Iran began to weaken, and the British would never forgive America for their loss of power.

CHAPTER 6

BANDAR GAZ

Ironically, in the turbulent days of the early fifties, I lived in more comfort than I had ever known. During the last years of my study at the School of Dentistry, I always seemed to find well-paying jobs to fill my evenings and holidays, at newspapers and dental and other medical clinics. Going to dental school was a way for me to get into the medical field. After one year, I could have transferred to medical school. I decided, however, to complete dentistry studies and specialize in oral surgery. Then, after I passed my final exams and graduated, I was called up for National Military Service. Within days, I was dispatched to basic training.

I was commissioned as a second lieutenant and assigned to the Seventh Tabriz Regiment, in the northern city of that name. During my service, I worked until four in the afternoon examining soldiers who needed dental care. In the evenings, I worked with an older dentist in his private practice. In those days, I was young and full of boundless energy. Since he was almost ready to retire, I managed his clinic, which became very busy and successful. My patient load expanded rapidly, and I began to rub shoulders with the well-to-do class of Tabriz society. Life was good; I had a substantial income and could see even better prospects on the horizon. For the first time in my life, I was not struggling with financial handicaps, and I became familiar with a lifestyle that had been alien to me.

Once a month, I served as one of two duty officers at the Tabriz army hospital, in charge of security and emergency calls for a twenty-four hour period. I often learned a great deal from the doctors I worked with. One of my counterparts was an old-timer, a kind, sociable man named Captain

Mahmoodi. On night duty, when there was nothing to do between calls, we played backgammon and talked.

Mahmoodi had originally joined the army as a noncommissioned officer, but his hard work and courage had earned him a commission and eventually promotion to the rank of captain. He told me stories about his long army career—in action against Russian troops at the Khoda-Afarin border point and many skirmishes with Turkish and Kurdish rebels. Once, over a game of backgammon, he told me a story that I've never forgotten—about his encounter with a gang of eight insurgents on the summit of a mountain near Tabriz. The insurgents, he recalled, refused to recognize any government presence, and their vicious raids had terrorized the local community. When Captain Mahmoodi's unit was dispatched to engage them, the troops easily spotted the insurgents, pursued them over difficult terrain, smoked them out quickly, and arrested all eight of the rebels. That very day, the insurgents were tried and sentenced to execution.

The soldiers of one platoon, Mahmoodi told me, were ordered to form a firing squad, but the conscripts were new and inexperienced; even with five bullets each, they didn't finish the job. The sergeant sent a solider to fetch more bullets, while the prisoners moaned in agony. "I was close by," Mahmoodi remembered, shaking his head in amazement, "and it was a horrible sight. Finally, the sergeant got fed up and started shouting at the prisoners. 'Be patient! Keep quiet! I've sent someone for more bullets, so, please! Have some respect!'"

My patience, too, was being tested. When I had completed my eighteen months of national service, the owner of the dental practice suggested that I remain in Tabriz and settle in that city permanently. It was an attractive prospect, since my income was high for the area, and in Tabriz I was learning the intricacies of a dental practice. I had also developed deep affection for the town and the people of Azerbaijan. But the discipline and sense of duty I had learned enabled me to tolerate hardship. Despite my profitable practice and many friends in Tabriz, my heart was in Tehran. I felt my studies were only half-finished, and I had dreams that could only come true if I returned to the capital.

In those days, graduates of Tehran University's medical schools weren't allowed to set up practice in the city until they had completed military service, as well as a year of public service in their profession in a provincial town. So, before I could return to Tehran, I moved to Bandar Gaz, a small town on the Caspian Sea. At one time, it had been a bustling seaport famous for its caviar, and there were still old buildings that bore witness to its past prosperity. The U.S.S.R. still kept their caviar station in Bandar Gaz, but the port had returned to swampland, and the people of Bandar Gaz were making their living once more as simple farmers.

I chose to do my mandatory service in Bandar Gaz for a number of reasons. One was its closeness to Sari, 50 kilometers away. Another was that I would be serving a deprived community like the one I grew up in, with meager access to even basic medical services. Dental care facilities were non-existent. When I arrived in Bandar Gaz, the only qualified medical person in the city of forty thousand was one physician, assisted by a midwife and a single pharmacy. Bandar Gaz had a thirty-bed hospital, headed by its sole physician, and its staff —two first aid-technicians and four nurses—had no additional doctors.

I was the first dentist who had ever been posted in Bandar Gaz. My services were in such demand that a crowd of anxious sufferers had gathered around my residence, waiting for treatment, when I arrived. I set up a small, well-equipped dental clinic and took on as many patients as I could handle. I was happy to be welcomed, and patients were eager to show to me their appreciation. They came from far and wide, often bringing me locally made gifts, and they thanked me with heartfelt words for choosing their town. If I had not come, they told me, they would have had to travel long distances, incurring expenses and wasting valuable time, to get dental treatment.

When I first arrived, the chief assistant to the town's doctor was especially glad to see me and asked me if I could treat patients at the hospital when the doctor was out of town. I reminded him that I wasn't qualified to act in the physician's stead, but what else could I say? I had had a bit of experience sorting out medical emergencies, thanks to my work at the army hospital in Tabriz and the family pharmacy. I wasn't really qualified, but the doctor's aide was correct that my presence there would be better than leaving hospital patients unattended. So I agreed to handle first-aid calls and minor emergency cases whenever the doctor was away. For cases beyond my ability, I would contact hospitals in the nearby towns of Gorgan or Sari for specific instructions. I could also arrange for more serious cases to travel by car to the nearest town, since there were no ambulances. Thanks to our improvisations, the town doctor's occasional absences did not mean that poor patients were deprived of care.

Most of the time, when the physician was gone, my days were routine. One day, however, on Ashura, the anniversary of the martyrdom of Shia Imam Hussein, disaster struck. Ashura—the most important religious holiday for Shia Muslims, the majority of the Iranian population—remembers the Imam, who was martyred some fifteen centuries ago. On that day each year, people honor him by organizing processions of black-clad mourners— young and middle-aged men who sing rhythmically and beat their chests in tune with the drummers and the thunder of the marchers' footsteps. On that hot, fateful day, residents of a nearby village sacrificed a cow and placed its carcass in a cart. They then marched through the hamlets for several hours, with the sun beating down on them, while they pushed the sacrificial cart in front of the procession. When they arrived at the town's mosque, they butchered the cow, cooked it, and served it to the mourners.

Under the hot sun, the meat had gone bad, and the food they served up was spoiled and rancid. By five p.m. the first wave of mourners began arriving at the hospital, and within hours, it was crowded with patients. We had to accommodate some of them on the floor and outside in the hospital courtyard. I hardly knew what to do. I contacted doctors in the next town for advice, but they could only give me basic instructions over the telephone. I had too little information, but with the help of the town's two medical aides, four nurses, the pharmacist, the midwife, and scores of local volunteers, we managed to treat more than a hundred patients.

There were no fatalities, thank goodness, but the incident left a deep impression on me. Who was accountable for this sorry state of affairs? How could scores of suffering patients have no recourse but a single health center that was clearly incapable of handling the load? I knew that the people of Iran, even given their limited resources, would gladly support better medical services, but there was no planning or organization to make such services available. The country's population, moreover, was fast outstripping its number of qualified physicians. Our medical system was broken, but what was the solution? As a result of my experience in Bandar Gaz, I decided to expand my professional focus from oral surgery to medical administration, so I could improve access to quality medical care throughout Iran.

When my mandatory service in Bandar Gaz came to an end, I made my way back to Tehran and quickly found a position in a government clinic that was part of the Social Insurance Organization (SIO). The position was highly sought-after, and I gained it with help from an influential friend. Others, I quickly learned, had also used favoritism to get their job. I was assigned to assist two dentists who were, despite good reputations, incredibly arrogant and irresponsible. Sometimes they would only work an hour or two a day before leaving the clinic; they almost never completed their six-hour quota of work. When other workers protested, the management was so reluctant to reprimand them that they decided to hire me to handle the patient load.

Government health jobs were very desirable in those days. We joked that the Social Insurance Organization was an "insured" source of income, since government employees were never fired, no matter how much they might deserve termination. But most physicians and dentists earned the major share of their income in private practice, so I too began working to set up a dental practice in a bustling corner of downtown Tehran. In keeping with tradition, I had my official job in the mornings with the SIO and attended to my private patients in the afternoons. Unlike my colleagues, however, I carefully performed my duties at the government's dental clinic, putting in my full six-hour shift and doing everything I could to make patients happy. As a result, in a short time, the clinic's patient load went from around eight a day to more than thirty. Everyone was happy. The two old-timers were satisfied that the clinic was thriving without more effort from them. I was pleased with the situation, too. Working at the government clinic gave me valuable experience that I could eventually use in my own practice. Because standards of dental hygiene were poor and treatment was inadequate, patients often developed infections, deformities, and other complications. Many required surgery and treatments for gum diseases and problems in their upper and lower jaws. I was ready to take on these challenges, and my surgical work was very successful. Satisfied patients were a good source of advertising, and they helped my private dental practice prosper. My income was enough for me to live in a comfortable house in the capital's prime district, and I began to enjoy a stylish, cosmopolitan life.

Iranians tend to have regular gatherings—called *dowreh* in Farsi—of particular friends. *Dowrehs* can be held on a weekly, fortnightly, or monthly basis. Everyone takes turns playing host and inviting some of their own friends, and in time, some of those guests may be accepted as regular members. *Dowrehs* are still the center of Iranian social life. They give members the opportunity to meet people, engage in business, indulge in political horse trading, spy on others, discuss poetry or music, gamble, pick up lovers, or search for a spouse; after the revolution, *dowreh* participants organized Quran readings. Back in the 1950s, my attendance at *dowrehs* and my sociable nature contributed to my success in business.

There were limits, however, to the growth of my practice. I was interested in oral surgery but had no training in it and had to study foreign textbooks to learn modern techniques. This was not unusual, because the Iranian health care system was in a sorry state. A high-ranking official in the Iranian Ministry of Health once showed me a summary of a report finding that Iranian health care suffered from a shortage of doctors, trained personnel, and hospital beds, as well as poor management, inadequate leadership, and a lack of coordination among the various medical care sectors. With better organization and dynamic management, the report concluded, it would be possible to increase the provision of medical services fourfold.

The author of the report was Dr. George Hamilton from the University of Minnesota, an academic who had come to Tehran at the invitation of the U.S. Advisory Group. I thought a great deal about Dr. Hamilton's observations. He had suggested practical, attainable solutions for sorting out some of the system's deficiencies—but to make these changes, Iranians needed to obtain necessary training. Since Iran's medical education system could not provide it, countries like the United States would have to supply the required education and technical assistance. The U.S. Advisory Mission in Iran, Dr. Hamilton suggested, could initiate health management courses under the joint auspices of the Ministry of Health and Tehran University.

I was sure that the country would act on Hamilton's proposal, so I asked my friend at the Ministry of Health to let me know when and if the training program was organized. In the meantime, I intensified my efforts to master the English language and began to think seriously about going abroad to study the latest oral surgery techniques. American universities were pioneers in the field, and I became determined to find a way to travel to the United States.

When Tehran University inaugurated the Medical Care Services Management course, I was among the first thirty students to enroll. An American professor, Sheldon Miller, was in charge of the program, and the subjects were interesting and instructive. When Miller explained hospital management techniques, however, I found it difficult to visualize the spaces or surroundings he described. When he talked about hospital rooms and wards, he was referring to equipment and facilities that I had never heard of or seen; he could easily have been talking about hospitals in outer space.

After the program ended, I contacted Mr. Miller and told him that, as my grades and exam results indicated, I had learned everything in the course quite well. "But the truth is," I added, "that if you put me in charge of running a hospital today, I wouldn't know where to begin."

Professor Miller was sincere and tried to address my concerns. The course, he explained, taught from the same academic texts that gave American students an overview of the subject, but students in the U.S. were also required to go through hospital residency. "Frankly," he acknowledged, "there is not a single hospital in Iran where you could get that kind of training." And he was right.

Since I was still enthusiastic, Miller encouraged me to enroll at an American university and offered to help. It was exactly what I was hoping to do. All the newest technology seemed to come from the United States, especially in medicine, and it would be the best place in the world for me to advance my skills. He suggested that the University of Minnesota would be a good choice for studying medical care management; it was a top-flight university, and Dr. George Hamilton, the most respected specialist in the field, was on its faculty.

Still, I wasn't sure whether I wanted to study oral surgery or medical care management. For dental surgery, I decided on Georgetown University; for medical care management, the University of Minnesota was the clear choice. So I applied to both, and the decision was made for me. With Georgetown's acceptance letter in hand, I prepared to travel to the United States.

CHAPTER 7

WASHINGTON, D.C.: GEORGETOWN UNIVERSITY

When I first arrived in Washington in the summer of 1959, I thought I knew a lot more about the United States and Americans than I really did. But within weeks, I was in a state of shock; everything was very different than I had expected. My English was not nearly sufficient, and because of the poor exchange rate between Iranian and U.S. currencies, it was also much more expensive than I had anticipated. I found it was a struggle to just take care of the basics.

Initially, I tried to stick to fast foods. Hamburgers did not exist in Iran, so for the first two days I could only muster the words "apple pie coffee." The third day, I got adventurous and tried to order chicken, but I somehow managed to say "kitchen" instead. When the waitress sarcastically asked if I wanted "a whole kitchen?" I paused in confusion. Unable to articulate a cohesive thought, again I ordered "apple pie coffee." The next day, after a friend explained that hamburgers were good food, like Persian kebabs, I tried to order a hamburger. The waitress understood but asked promptly whether I wanted onions, ketchup, what kind of bread, and whether I wanted fries "to go with that." I was stumped. "Apple pie coffee, please," I said again.

Eventually, I found a list of university-recommended rentals, and I ended up taking a room from the elderly widow of an American army colonel. She was a kindly woman, well informed about American politics, and I learned much from her stories about the eventful life she had lived with her husband. Sometimes we would simply watch American television together, and her friendly welcome not only helped me strengthen my English, but also helped me assimilate in this strange new place.

With no car, I needed to travel around the city by bus and learn Washington's complex transportation system. This was no simple task. One day, I had to take the Zone 5 bus to Massachusetts Avenue and the Iranian Embassy. After I waited for twenty minutes, the bus still hadn't shown up. So I asked a passerby for assistance. He asked a shopkeeper near the station "where the damn Zone Five bus" was, and the shopkeeper pointed to where I was standing. The man then suggested I clarify the zone number with the bus driver. When the bus finally showed up, I asked the driver, "Is this the damn Zone Five bus?" The driver laughed and cheerfully shouted, "This *is* the damn Zone Five Bus, *I am* the damn driver, and *you are* the damn passenger!"

At the university, I spent most of my free time with two Iranian students, Ali Ershadi and Sadeq Qotbzadeh. We didn't see eye to eye about politics but developed the kind of friendship that grows when fellow expatriates are far from their home country. Ali Ershadi came from a middle-class family in northern Iran, and after graduating from Tehran University's Economics Department with honors, he had received a scholarship to study for his Ph.D. in the United States. Politically, his affiliation was with the Iranian socialist group, and he detested religious fanaticism. Sadeq Qotbzadeh, on the other hand, came from a family in the merchant-class, known as *bazaari*. The *bazaaris* are an old fashioned religious group who continue to trade in the centuries-old market in southern Tehran, once considered the pulse of the Iranian economy. Qotbzadeh was only an average student, but he was steadfast in his friendship and his devotion to his homeland. Though he was not a practicing Muslim, his family background placed him within the religious wing of the National Front.

Though far from home, our discussions always stayed close to the latest news and rumors of events in Iran. I had grown out of my attachment to communism, and I found myself increasingly committed to the kinds of free-market economics practiced in the United States. Neither of my comrades, however, shared this line of thinking. Our long hours of debate invariably left us exhausted, without any sort of consensus or conclusion. We were young, of course, and it's the nature of young people to hold strong convictions.

In March of that year, the Iranian ambassador invited a group of Iranian students—along with various important dignitaries, congressmen, businessmen, well-to-do Iranians, and the media—to a reception at the Statler Hotel. Across Asia, wherever Farsi is spoken and Persian culture observed, *Now Ruz* is a time when we all come together and celebrate. In the United States, it was doubly important, a time when we could gather and meet each other.

The new ambassador was Ardeshir Zahedi, the son of the general who had led the coup that ousted Mossadegh and returned the Shah to power. Zahedi was married to the Shah's eldest daughter, Princess Shahnaz, whose mother was the Shah's first wife, Princess Fawziyyeh of Egypt. But there was more to Zahedi than his family connections, as we came to find out. As he prepared to host his first *Now Ruz* reception, he decided to directly confront Iranian students opposed to the regime.

In those days, of course, dissidents in Iran were unable to engage in active opposition; the Shah's regime stifled all political activities, especially among students at Tehran University, who formed the nucleus of opposition to the Shah's rule. As a result, only students abroad were able to engage in political activities against the regime. There were not many dissident Iranian students in the United States, since most were in the U.S. on the government's dime. A few of them, however, were loud enough to attract media attention, and the general public had begun taking notice.

It was easy to guess, therefore, that the ambassador's grand reception might turn into a golden opportunity for these students to take a stand against the regime. After dinner was served, an Iranian student, specifically handpicked by the embassy, was ushered to the podium to give a speech. But as he was preparing to utter his first words, another student dashed over and grabbed the microphone. Before anyone could stop him, he began shouting, "You do not represent the students! Today, on the anniversary of the oil nationalization, the rights of the people of Iran have been usurped! We salute Dr. Mossadegh, the great leader of the Iranian nation!"

The embassy officials rushed toward the student with the microphone. As they dislodged him from the podium, I suddenly saw my friend Sadeq Qotbzadeh coming to his aid with other students. In the ensuing melee, a giant coffee container landed on the table where Zahedi and his wife, Shahnaz, were seated.

It didn't take long for police squads to arrive; they appeared so quickly that the embassy must have foreseen some sort of scuffle and warned them in advance. They arrested Qotbzadeh and eight of his fellow activists. Although some of the guests left, the rest of the New Year's ceremony continued at the hotel as scheduled.

That night, at Zahedi's request, Qotbzadeh and the other students were released from custody. My friend was not in the least deterred by his detention. On the contrary, he began cutting most of his classes and spent the bulk of his time in political activity against the regime. Because Qotbzadeh's was in the United States on a student visa, his absence from the university eventually gave the embassy a reason to revoke his passport, but Iranian officials could not force him to leave the country. He had an American girlfriend whose uncle was an influential senator, and it seemed that the distinguished statesman was able to keep Qotbzadeh from being deported.

In the meantime, he was engaging in the kind of anti-regime activities that bordered on outright sabotage. He soon gave up his studies altogether and associated with suspect characters. As his activities intensified, American intelligence operatives began taking notice. At that point, Qotbzadeh's connections were no longer helpful, and he was first deported from the United States. Years later, he would reemerge as a key revolutionary leader in Iran, one of Khomeini's "godsons." Many people, in fact, believe that there would have been no Iranian revolution without Qotbzadeh.

To improve my English, I occasionally attended a special lecture class for foreign students. When I had a question, I would often strike up a conversation with the young female professor, who was an excellent teacher. One day, she came to me with a problem. She told me that most of her students seemed to enjoy her teaching methods, but one young man in her class, who had only recently arrived from Iran, appeared to have serious problems. Whenever she tried to engage him in conversation, he would pin his eyes to his feet and refuse to look her in the eye. "Either he dislikes something about me," she said, "or he doesn't like my class. He's wasting his time and money if he stays, but I can't do anything with him. Perhaps you could speak with him?"

His name was Abdullah, and he was delighted to talk to me. "My father is a well known bazaar merchant in Tehran," he said, immediately adding, "We are a very religious family." I had already surmised that. With his short beard, white shirt, and unshaven face, he clearly came from the religious *bazaari*. Abdullah, however, confided in me, gravely, that he suspected his father's faith.

"I think he only pretends to be religious," he continued, describing in detail the trappings of modern living that his father adopted. Not only did he often go to Europe, Abdullah added, he actually *enjoyed* it! He praised his grandfather's piety, however, and hoped to emulate him. His father had insisted on sending him to school in the United States, while his grandfather wanted him to study theology in Najaf, the center of Shia theological studies in Iraq. Abdullah's sympathies were with his grandfather, but his father saw religion as a sign of backwardness. "He says that our religious traditions are blocking our march toward progress and development," Abdullah told me. "He says that we must learn modern ways of life and business, so he sent me to the U.S. to learn these new methods and take them back to Tehran."

The amazing part of Abdullah's story was how he had arrived in Washington, D.C. His father had told him that, in accordance with his grand-father's wishes, he was going to Najaf, Iraq to study theology. So Abdullah went to the airport and boarded a plane he believed was headed for that seat of Islamic learning. He was surprised that the other passengers didn't look like pilgrims, but he put aside his misgivings, even though the flight was longer than he expected. When the plane landed in Washington, however, the game was up. "In the arrival lobby," Abdullah said, "a man was waiting for me who took me to an apartment in Georgetown and gave me money. The next day, he brought me to this English class, and here I am."

Abdullah was a shy young man, and he was deadly serious. I suspected that he was not as unhappy to be in America as he maintained, but the impossibility of pleasing his grandfather caused him great anxiety. He went to his classes, but laboriously observed the strictest Islamic rules—offering up prayers five times a day and eating only *halal* meat, which is prepared according to special instructions, like kosher foods. In order to eat properly, Abdullah even bought live chickens and slaughtered them in his bathtub, carefully following Islamic precepts. Once, his house cleaner spotted bloodstains in the bathroom and called the police—a misunderstanding that was only cleared up after a long ordeal. Abdullah scrupulously abstained from looking at women who were not properly covered, and our young teacher's enthusiasm was a source of great difficulty for him. How could he learn English from someone he could neither look at nor address directly?

I didn't have any solutions for Abdullah, but it helped him to talk over his troubles with someone who could understand them. I gave him some advice on how to make his way without compromising his beliefs and explained his situation to the English teacher, who promised to keep his circumstances in mind. The problem must have been resolved, since Abdullah persevered. From time to time, he would visit me, and, though we always talked about the difficulties of being Iranian in the United States, he gradually seemed to be adapting to his new environment.

I, however, was beginning to feel restless at Georgetown. For some time, I had been debating whether to continue my specialization in dental and oral surgery or pursue studies in medical administration. I finally decided that the latter choice would open up wider vistas. After all, I thought, who wanted to be limited to the inside of the human mouth? So even though I was excelling in my training at Georgetown, I began to explore other opportunities. In Tehran, Mr. Miller had mentioned the highly regarded health care management program at the University of Minnesota, where Professor George Hamilton was on the faculty. Hamilton had been part of the U.S. advisory group, and his books and essays were used as textbook examples in many American universities. I knew that Minnesota was where I needed to go.

Each year, Professor Hamilton chose twenty students from a large pool of applicants. I was overjoyed to receive his letter of acceptance. I was even more elated to find out that Ali Ershadi had also enrolled at the University of Minnesota to continue his studies in economics. So Ali and I made our way to the Midwest.

CHAPTER 8

UNIVERSITY OF MINNESOTA

On the banks of the great Mississippi River, the University of Minnesota's stately buildings had a look of grandeur. Our neighborhood, known as "Dinky Town," however, was far from grand. In Dinky Town, Ali and I shared a house with five fellow students, a number of whom came from other countries. We also quickly discovered that eleven co-eds lived in the house next door. Since we were all young, there was constant traffic between the two houses, prompting other students to refer to the houses jointly as "Seven-Eleven." I wonder what Abdullah would have thought.

The course of study I enrolled in was a two-year program—a year of classes followed by a year of residency. I was accustomed to studying the human body, but the contents of the course—everything from economics to statistics and accounting—were quite different from what I had imagined I would be learning in medical school. I was expanding my horizons in countless ways at once; even Professor Hamilton's manner of teaching was new to me. Instead of dry lectures, he used the Socratic method. He turned each day's subject matter into a play, with the classroom as his stage and his students as players. We acted the lessons in the textbook, improvising around current events and suggesting decisions we would make. At the end of each lesson, Dr. Hamilton would evaluate and gently guide our performances, steering us toward the best data that we had available.

At night, back at the Seven-Eleven, Ali and I would compare notes on our separate courses, reflecting on how much we had wasted our time and energy grappling with the inadequacies of education in Iran. There were few people who could share that conversation, since there could not have been more than thirty Iranians in the entire city. Apparently, Iranians were not drawn to the icy climate of Minnesota, although I never minded it.

One of the few Iranians I knew was a physician who had started calling himself "Moe" when he realized how difficult it was for patients to pronounce his name. He was an OB-GYN resident at St. Mary's Hospital, and we found that our temperaments matched well. In late December 1962, as everyone was preparing to celebrate Christmas and New Years, he insisted that I join him at a New Years Eve party. It would be my first chance to meet his girlfriend, he said—adding, with a grin that was audible across the phone line, that he had set up a blind date for me. Moe didn't give me any details, and as I set down the phone, I could only imagine what was in store.

As we drove to pick up the two girls, Moe was full of anticipation. A moment later, I realized why. Joan, who got into the backseat next to me, was a brunette with lots of charisma. But Helen, the slim, beautiful blond who sat in the front seat with Moe, took my breath away, and I found it difficult to cóncentrate as we drove. Joan was jovial and likeable, but I wasn't able to give her my full attention; I was following Helen's every move out of the corner of my eyes. She was quiet and serene. Though I was usually talkative on such occasions, I matched her silence as we drove, and I caught Moe staring quizzically at me through the rear-view mirror.

It was bitterly cold. The restaurant Moe had chosen was a beautiful lakeside spot, nestled in snow and lavishly decorated for Christmas, with lights that reflected brilliantly off the water. It was the sort of scene I had only imagined or had seen in movies. As we hurried from the car into the warmth of the inn, I found myself reflecting on the difference between the New Years that I had lived through in the past and the one that I was now about to celebrate. In Iran, *Now Ruz* signaled the beginning of spring, the rebirth of life and warmth, as green shoots and blossoms emerged from the receding winter. Here, in the middle of America, on a frigid night, I wondered what kind of new life was about to sprout.

As we sat down for dinner, Helen became lively and talkative, but I wasn't myself; I had little to say to Joan while Moe chatted with Helen. Between courses, Moe caught my eye and asked in Persian, under his breath, "What cat has your tongue?" Only with effort and a few drinks did my frozen countenance start to thaw. I danced with Joan and managed to hold up my end of the conversation. She was a nurse and full of admiration for Moe. Then, when I danced with Helen, the band was playing a tango, and I had to be careful to maintain decorum. Helen made that more difficult because she was not inhibited. Then, in a sweet tone, she told me that she was delighted to discover that I was her blind date.

I was too surprised to know what to say and stammered, "*You* were supposed to be my date?"

"Whose date did you think I was?" she said, laughing.

By now, I was recovering from my shock. Helen had barely finished her sentence when I pulled her close and began making up for lost time. Later, as we were all finishing coffee and dessert, Moe caught my arm and said, laughing, in Persian, "I wish I had made you drink your whisky sooner!" At the stroke of midnight, the old year gave way to the new, and I stole the most delicious kiss of my life from Helen's lips.

The more time that Helen and I spent together, the more it seemed that we had everything in common, despite the vast differences in our backgrounds. She was from a middle-class family in the Midwest, and her father, originally from Luxembourg, had graduated from the University of Minnesota; during World War II, he had instructed pilots in climatology. Helen's mother was of Swedish descent. Although she had been a nurse, she later gave up her career to devote her time to raising what would ultimately be six children. They were practicing Catholics, and regular church attendance, devotion to family life, and meals at regular hours were their bedrock foundations.

As time passed, Helen and I grew more and more attached to each other. We spent as much of our free time together as we could and became almost inseparable. But there were complications that we could not ignore. I knew what was going on in Iran because I had stayed in touch with Dr. Bahar Noori, a former colleague. He was now a director in the Ministry of Health, and he anticipated historic changes in the field of health care. The time was ripe for reform, he said, and the expertise I was acquiring in the United States was almost totally nonexistent in Iran. Noori urged me to return home as soon as possible. His words were persuasive. After all, hadn't I always planned to return to Iran when I had acquired the knowledge that I needed to help my country?

But I felt conflicted now because of Helen and stayed awake thinking about the future and my place in it. Should I return to Iran or stay in the United States? At home, my skills were sorely needed, and I would be highly compensated and valued. But what about Iran's corrupt bureaucracy and all its backwardness? What could I accomplish in such an environment? It would be easy to stay in the U.S., have a good job, a high income, and a comfortable life. But if I had really wanted to stay in America, why hadn't I simply continued my path in oral and dental surgery?

I could not forget that I had come to the United States for a specific purpose. I had always intended to return to Iran to improve the country's health care delivery system. I couldn't give up that dream. But what would happen to my relationship with Helen if I went back to Iran? Could I ask her to live in a Third World country? Would she leave her family in Winona, Minnesota, to move halfway around the world to an environment with more social, religious, and human rights differences than she could imagine?

Finally, one night, I poured out my soul to Helen. Torn between returning to Iran or staying in the United States, I asked her a single question: What would happen to us? I emphasized the poverty and cultural differences that existed back home, along with the societal norm that women had fewer rights than their male counterparts. Without flinching, Helen asked, "If the situation is as bad as you say, why must you return home?" Fearing the response of this blue-eyed, blonde Minnesotan, I lowered my head and told her I that had a moral duty and commitment to serve my people.

With directness and honesty, Helen replied, "Then I need to stand by your side and help you honor that commitment."

It was an answer that I never expected. Perhaps I should have trusted her strength of character, but she was an American. How could she imagine how hard it would be to live in Iran? So with great foreboding, I refused her offer and suggested that we split up and see how it went. Helen was reluctant, but she understood it was what I needed to do, so she agreed.

As days turned into weeks, however, I found that what seemed logical and right in theory was difficult in practice. Nothing filled the gap in my life created by Helen's absence. It was intolerable, and on many occasions I fought the temptation to pick up the phone and call her. But it was not my way to go against my word. Sometimes I wished that *she* would put aside our arrangement, but I knew that Helen would never do that. She was too proud and determined. Sometimes I would even go out of my way to walk along her route from home to work, hoping that by chance she might be passing by. I had no such luck. The few times we spoke awkwardly on the phone, we could barely utter any words. And when I tried to start dating again, hoping that it would help me stop thinking of Helen, I found that no other woman appealed to me.

Three months later, when I completed the academic portion of my course, I began my residency at Mount Sinai Hospital in Minneapolis. On the third day of my training, I was walking along a corridor when my eyes glimpsed a familiar sight, a striking woman in a white uniform. I could not believe my eyes; it was Helen, smiling as if nothing had ever happened.

I could barely utter a word. When I told her I was a new resident at the hospital, she said that she was a medical secretary to the Surgery Department's director. Nothing could have made me happier; we were going to work in close proximity for an entire year. It seemed natural for us to have lunch together at the hospital cafeteria, and after only a few minutes of catching up, it was like old times. It would be silly not to see each other, we decided, so that evening we went dancing. Almost immediately after, and without saying anything about it, we were back to our old routine.

Our relationship quickly became more serious. Helen took me home to meet her family, and they instantly made me feel welcome. How could they be so open to and accepting of a person from such a distant culture? Their receptiveness astonished me. I knew that in America, a land of immigrants, no one is really a foreigner, but in my own home country, Helen would be a stranger, and some parts of Iranian society would consider her untouchable. Fanatical Muslims considered all non-Muslims "dirty"; after you touched one of these outsiders, they believed, you had to wash your hands. How could we have a future together in such a repressive country?

I resolved to sit down with Helen and talk about our future in Iran. I could imagine and anticipate what I would probably do when I returned, and I could calculate the kind of life, income, and social standing I could expect. But how would Helen handle the shock of entering such a totally different culture? How could I prepare her? And it would be expensive to live with an American wife, who was used to a higher standard of living. What if my income wasn't enough? For a long time, my trepidation outweighed my hopes.

Finally, I steeled myself to have this difficult discussion. On a warm sunny day, when we were walking along the banks of Lake Minnehaha, I told her, simply, that I was in love with her, that she was my ideal woman, and that I wanted to share the rest of my life with her. Then I reminded her that I needed to return to Tehran, which, as I saw it then, was an impassable obstacle in our path. I no longer thought that I knew what we needed to do, and I asked her to help me solve this problem.

It was the best thing I could have done. Helen said she too was in love, and she told me that she had long wished that I would let her help plan our future together. It was even more heartening to hear her say that she would gladly join me in my crusade to help my countrymen. It had been her original intention to visit developing countries, and she had even thought of joining the new Kennedy Administration program known as the Peace Corps. But now that she had met me and we had fallen in love, she only wanted to join me, make me her husband, serve the people of my country, and make it her adopted home.

Helen's honesty was clear and compelling, and I felt that everything was now falling into place. Her parents applauded our plans, although her father questioned my desire to return home. He believed that America would be a land of opportunity for me. "Everyone has the chance to make a success here," he told me. Why not stay? But I explained that if all the talented people who came to the U.S. decided to remain here, their home countries would continue to be left behind. I wanted to go back to try to make my country more like America, I said. I think he understood.

Later that year, in the summer of 1962, Helen and I married in a small, beautiful wedding ceremony in a Catholic church in Minneapolis. Still, I worried about the future. How would Helen cope with the many difficulties of life in Iran? I described to her what life would be like, but could she really understand what it all meant? I would only know the answer once we got to Tehran.

CHAPTER 9

ODYSSEY TO IRAN

In the United States, we were enjoying a happy life, and within months, Helen announced that she was expecting a baby. To become a father had always been my most cherished wish, and this child would be the sweet fruit of our love and marriage.

We had much to prepare for. We had to make arrangements for our first child and save enough money for the trip back to Iran. Fortunately, when I was about to complete my residency at the hospital, the hospital director asked me to stay on as an assistant. It was a good opportunity, and I agreed. We could use the extra time in the United States to get ready for the trip. With a job, my income also increased substantially, so we would be able to save more. I also happily had more free time to spend with Helen.

When *Now Ruz* again came around, we attended a party organized by the small Iranian community in Minneapolis. Our baby was due at any time, our anticipation was at a high pitch, and right in the middle of the festivities, Helen went into labor. I took her straight to St. Mary's Hospital and, within only an hour, our daughter Lisa was born. I had always wanted my first child to be a daughter, perhaps because I loved my own mother so much, and the baby brought new light and happiness into our lives.

After Lisa was born, Helen and I began serious preparations to move to Iran. I was anxious to see my family and friends, and Helen was excited to begin the next chapter in our life together. Still, though I avoided saying much about it to her, I worried about all the adjustments she would have to make. Was I asking too much of her? Would she be able to adapt?

We left Minnesota in the fall of 1963, in an automobile packed with three suitcases and a world full of hope. On the way to New York, where we'd board an ocean liner, we took a detour to Washington, D.C. Our first goal was to register our marriage at the Iranian Embassy and get an Iranian identification card and passport for Helen. I also wanted to revisit Georgetown and introduce old friends to my new family. A friend in Georgetown threw us a going-away party, and many of my Washington friends tried to convince us to stay in the United States. "Why would you go back?" they demanded to know. "Don't you remember how bad it is?" But Helen's resolve was even stronger than I had expected, and we took their entreaties as gestures of care and kindness.

That evening, I found myself accosted by a young man in an Armani suit, with a white silk scarf draped artistically around his neck. Could this be Abdullah, with a Rolex on one arm and a beautiful blonde on the other? Drinking red wine? I'm not sure how I recognized him, since he bore no resemblance at all to the Abdullah I had once known, with a ragged beard and soiled, ill-fitting clothes. When I declared my amazement that a young man who wanted only to study in Najaf had become a chic socialite, Abdullah grinned and remarked that he had forsaken eternal happiness in the next world for the sweet life on earth. "Apparently, your father knew you better that you knew yourself," I said, and we both laughed.

In New York, we boarded the *Queen Mary,* and after an exciting five-day journey, docked in Cherbourg, France. After visiting the Allied war cemetery in Normandy, where we paid our respects to the liberators of France, we set off for Paris. It was a holiday for us, and as we drove, it seemed like the whole countryside was on holiday with us. When we stopped along the way at a roadside restaurant, a kindly old woman served us lunch and shared her memories of American soldiers during the war. She explained why everyone else seemed to be relaxing and enjoying themselves—it really *was* France's holiday season, the month of August.

Baby Lisa took it all in with amazing flexibility. As for us, we realized quickly that we were no longer in the United States. When we arrived in Paris, we found a small, clean hotel. One of the first things we had to do was take care of Lisa's laundry. Disposable diapers were not yet on the market. In the 1960s, mothers used cotton diapers made by Curity Company. Helen had taken a large supply along, but when they were soiled, she threw them out along the way, thinking that more would be available in Paris. The hotel did not have laundry service, so we spent half a day driving around Paris looking for a Laundromat—only to be told they did not exist in Paris. Helen ended up washing the remaining diapers by hand in the hotel bathtub. "It's like we're already in Iran!" she said.

On the whole, Helen responded to such minor difficulties with the cheerful demeanor I had come to hope and expect from her. I took it as a good sign of things to come. It helped that she was excited to be in France, a place she had dreamed of visiting all her life. I had been to Paris several times and knew my way around the city, so I was able to take my family to all the sights, including the Louvre, the Eiffel Tower, the Seine, the Champs Elysées, and the Latin Quarter. In those days, Europe was as not as developed as the United States in terms of the small conveniences of life, so it occurred to me that the more time we spent in Europe, the easier Helen's adjustment would be when we got to Iran. Everything seemed to fall into place when we met with Hussein, a childhood friend of mine, and his wife, Tahereh. They were planning to leave Paris and return to Tehran by automobile, and they invited us to join them. Not only would that give Helen a chance to see Europe, but it would also give her more time to acclimate to her changing lifestyle. The journey turned out to be a godsend, and Tahereh became one of Helen's guides and a cherished friend.

Since my younger brother, Dariush, was studying in Vienna, we planned our route so that we could visit him—driving through West Germany to Austria, then down through Yugoslavia, Bulgaria, and Turkey. On our first day of travel, it was night when we arrived at the German border. Nothing seemed out of the ordinary, but when German guards with a dog on a leash first approached the car, I noticed that Helen's face grew ashen, and her hands started trembling violently. My first thought was that she might have concealed some kind of contraband without telling me, but when I asked her what the matter was, it turned out to be something completely different. On seeing the German guards, Helen said, all the terrifying war movies and news bulletins she had seen as a young girl during World War II came to her mind. Still, she liked Germany a great deal— observing that, like America, it was filled with hard-working people, though she had never seen so many serious faces on American streets.

After crossing the border, we arrived in Munich. In a beer house where Hitler gave one of his infamous speeches, we drank lager, ate German sausages, and did our best not to think about the tragedy of the Second World War. In Vienna, we spent three days with Dariush, whom I had not seen for six years. The city was a dream come true for Helen, who loved classical music and occasionally played the violin. She had always longed to see one of Vienna's operas, and at last she did. Austria's beautiful parks, public squares, and magnificent statues gave the city a beautiful grandeur, and Helen said she could feel the calm and serenity of its people everywhere.

Driving through Yugoslavia and Bulgaria, however, gave Helen her first experience with totalitarian communism. Both countries were still under the iron fist, and—compared with France, Germany, and Austria—the restaurants, roads, and buildings were of a lower standard. The farther we traveled east, the more the standard of living fell around us. We started seeing things that bothered Helen, such as women doing manual labor, and I could tell that she was beginning to feel nervous in our new surroundings. Helen was ideologically opposed to communist government, and she struggled to understand how people of these countries put up with it. She saw posters and statues of their leaders at every intersection, and she found it disturbing.

We spent only one night in Yugoslavia, then traveled on through Bulgaria to Turkey. Istanbul was a revelation; its historical relics, old mosques, and sultans' palaces were breathtaking. Along the beaches of the Bosporus, there were restaurants, cafes, and teahouses where customers smoked hookahs, and the city's unforgettable sights almost distracted us from its mass poverty and underdevelopment. Most of the villages and cities we passed through didn't have piped drinking water, and public hygiene almost everywhere was appalling. There were no clean public utilities or restrooms, and Helen had a terrible time trying to change Lisa's diapers with the degree of sanitation that she was used to. Thank goodness, Tahereh was there to teach Helen how to use Turkish toilets, as well as other facilities for herself and Lisa. Helen's signs of worry were becoming more and more evident, but she tried to conceal her discomfort and find ways to overcome the shortcomings of the trip.

We spent one night in Istanbul before continuing on. Hussein warned me that from that point on, the condition of the roads would be getting worse, and he urged me to use a great deal of caution when I was driving. I had no choice but to drive slowly. The highway passed through treacherous mountains and was only partly paved. The unlit roads were full of large potholes and places where the asphalt disappeared. With no security, the route was a magnet for smugglers and criminals. Wealthy Iranians often took this road home after buying a car—usually a Mercedes—in Europe and filling it with expensive clothing. Many were robbed before they reached the border.

In those days, car seats for children did not exist, so Helen held Lisa high and tight against her chest during the drive. Helen herself was pale and quiet, with her eyes squeezed shut. When I asked her what was wrong, she said she was afraid that we might have an accident, and she was trying to protect Lisa. I attempted to distract her by talking about other subjects, but Helen could not see how cars could manage on these rundown roads, and she could not relax.

At a brief stop, I suggested to Hussein that perhaps, since darkness was approaching, we should spend the night somewhere along the way. I thought that it would be good for Helen to have some time away from the road and rest up for the long drive ahead. But Hussein said it wouldn't be safe to stop; there was virtually no security in the area, so we would be better off getting through it as soon as possible, since roads and safety would improve as we got closer to Iran. I decided not to tell Helen what Hussein said.

We drove on. Though it was dark, I noticed an almost imperceptible change. The road surface was different—completely black. As we continued, our white car started to be covered with an inky goo, and I quickly realized what had happened. With no warning, we had driven onto a stretch of road that had just been covered with a fresh layer of black tar. There were no lights or road signs, so we continued slowly on the hot, tar-covered road until we reached a village. We briefly pulled off the road, and some villagers almost immediately appeared out of the darkness, offering to wash our vehicle. It was a very profitable scam. After paying them an exorbitant price, our car was finally white again, and we continued on.

Hussein was more familiar with these roads, so he drove faster than we did. The distance between our cars increased until he was no longer in sight. After a few hours of driving in the darkness, however, road conditions improved and, since dawn was approaching, I could drive a bit faster. It was quite light when we saw three men standing at the side of the road ahead of us, dressed in traditional clothing. They signaled for us to pull over, and I automatically started to slow down. As we got closer, however, I noticed that they were all carrying heavy sticks that could be used as weapons. I hit the gas hard. As we passed them, the sound of their clubs pounding the trunk of the car woke Helen and Lisa up with a fright.

"What do you think of Turkey?" I asked Helen, trying to laugh off the incident. A sign indicated that we still had 100 kilometers to go before reaching the Iranian border, but road conditions were much better now, and we could travel quickly. We started talking about everything that we had seen.

Turkey was the first Muslim country that Helen had ever visited, and she was very disappointed with its basic conditions and public services. Restrooms were unsanitary, flies and mosquitoes filled most restaurants, and hotels and public places were dingy and grimy. More than that, she was struck by the squalor that people lived in, practically in the shadow of Istanbul's gorgeous Ottoman palaces. There was no harmony between the hovels of the people and the palaces and mosques of the great. Did the fundamentalist teachings of Islamic mullahs instruct people to hate modernism, she asked? Were political leaders in Turkey incapable or unwilling to upgrade people's standards of living? I replied that she would discover the answer after she lived in Iran for a while. Then, as if on cue, I spotted the Lion and Sun emblem on an Iranian flag fluttering over a small border post in the distance; we had arrived in my homeland.

As we approached Iran's border, I saw an uncomfortable look on Helen's face. I asked her if she was ready to being a new life. She hesitantly replied, "I think so."

The Iranian border guards were pleasant and friendly; after briefly inspecting our car, they welcomed us warmly into the country. To Helen's relief, the roads here were superior to anything we had seen in Turkey. She had kept silent about it, but the conditions in Turkey had made her dread what she might find on the other side of the border. She was happy to see that, when we entered Iran, the highway was better, the small border town of Bazargan seemed cleaner, and the customs officials were very polite and respectful. It didn't take long before Helen began to relax and smile.

When we arrived in the town of Tabriz, Hussein's Uncle Amoghli welcomed us into his home. With traditional Iranian hospitality, he assured us that we would be his honored guests as long as we remained in there. Helen sampled Iranian cuisine for the first time, including Azerbaijani dishes like *badem june khoresht* (eggplant stew), and she enjoyed the public baths, where female masseuses gave customers private scrubs and massages. Iran's customs, traditions, and language were unfamiliar to her, but she told me that she felt like she was with her own family. In the care of these Azerbaijani friends, she felt welcomed and at home, and many of her worries about living in this very different culture almost disappeared.

CHAPTER 10

TEHRAN 1963

When we arrived in Tehran in fall 1963, we rented a three-room apartment just off Pahlavi Avenue, on the second story, overlooking the street. It was right above an apartment where an Iranian surgeon, Mesbah, and his British wife, Pauline, lived with their two small children. Pauline had lived in Iran for three years and was fluent in Farsi. An experienced housewife and former nurse, she quickly became Helen's good friend and guide.

While I was in America, I had kept in touch with the Social Insurance Organization, the state health service where I had worked before. I had also made a point of staying on good terms with a variety of former colleagues. Whenever I came across a medical technique or innovation that could be useful for Iran, I would write a brief account of it and forward it to officials in the medical department. These contacts had led me to think that my old job would be waiting for me upon my return, with a warm reception and challenging position in the SIO. But when I got back to Iran and called them, I discovered that I was not welcomed; in fact, they openly snubbed me. When I met with the head of the organization's health department, he remarked that he was amazed that I would leave a comfortable life and good job in America to return to Iran. A moment later, I found myself outside his office, with no prospects and a blank look on my face.

Surprised and a bit humiliated, I paced the length and breadth of the Social Security building's corridors, trying to plan. The situation in Iran was clearly not what I had expected. The country's economy was in ruins, and the political situation was no better. Corruption was rampant, and the bureaucracy was in utter chaos. Iranians were enduring extreme censorship, imprisonment, torture, and other human rights abuses. The government's security apparatus was increasing its brutality, and the entire nation was growing fed up with its excesses.

Iran's relationship to the United States had also changed considerably. President John F. Kennedy had taken office in 1962. Earlier, as a senator, he had stressed that the United States should not support dictators or other authoritarian third-world leaders, and he had included the Shah, pointedly, in that category. To make matters worse, there were rumors that the Shah had contributed to the campaign of Kennedy's rival, Richard Nixon. Nikita Khrushchev, chairman of the U.S.S.R.'s Council of Ministers, tried to turn the President even further against the Iranian sovereign—boasting to him, at a meeting in Vienna, that the Soviet Union would not have to do much to bring Iran into its orbit. "The Shah thinks his sovereignty was given by God," Khrushchev declared. "He is creating so much discontent in the country that Iran will simply fall into our lap, like an overripe apple."

If the U.S. wanted to keep Iran from falling to the communists, the CIA reported, it would have to achieve fundamental reforms within the country. So President Kennedy assigned a committee of Middle Eastern experts to study the situation. The group proposed three options for improving conditions in Iran. According to the first plan, the Shah would stay in power while carrying out basic reforms. He would appoint credible politicians to top jobs and dismiss all corrupt, unpopular appointees. His family would cease its personal interference in government matters, and Iran's budding middle classes would expand so it could actively engage in the nation's affairs. The committee recommended Dr. Ali Amini, the Minister of Finance who had negotiated the end of the oil nationalization controversy, as a suitable candidate for Prime Minister. Amini had served as envoy to Washington and was well connected in the West. The committee acknowledged, however, that the Shah did not trust him. Amini, moreover, doubted that the Shah would agree to share power with him.

The second option was for the U.S. to facilitate the rise to power of the National Front, the democratic anti-Shah group aligned with Mossadegh. The Administration, however, had been having fruitless talks with National Front members. The third plan was the simplest: if the first two strategies failed, a military coup would replace the Shah with a strong military leader. The Shah was more and more dependent on U.S. assistance and eventually acquiesced to the first option. In 1961, he called on Dr. Amini to form

Negotiations

a new cabinet. Intent on ushering in a new era in Iran, Amini introduced vital reforms: limiting the Shah's power over the army and foreign policy; eliminating many corrupt politicians; preventing members of the royal family from continuing their lucrative, illegal financial dealings; and publicizing the names of officials who had used their positions to make unlawful financial gains—although this list did not include the names of the relatives or close friends of the Shah.

The monarch's associates, however—shadowy power brokers who controlled oil, foreign affairs, and multibillion-dollar military and nuclear purchases—erected barriers to slow Amini's reforms. In short order, politicians and members of the royal family who felt threatened by the winds of change began to plot the Prime Minister's downfall. By the middle of 1962, Amini was a lame duck. Rumors spread about the Shah's unhappiness with Iran's affairs, and the CIA reported that he might have developed a mental disorder, but it was clear that he had no interest in sharing power in a substantive way. Throughout the entire two thousand years of Iran's history, he reminded the CIA, the monarch had been the center of state power; the people of Iran expected the Shah to be their point of reference, and he reiterated his unwillingness to break from tradition. He would rather lose his throne, he said, than stay on and go down in history as a weak monarch.

The CIA tended to agree with the Shah's argument—or believed that removing him would create more problems for the region than it would solve. So as Amini's premiership drew to a close, the U.S. began formulating a new policy of introducing reforms while increasing support for the Shah. By giving the ruler a key role in implementing reform measures, the State Department hoped to keep the government together and give the monarch a stake in the process. The main objective was to convince the Shah to divert public anger from himself and direct it to corrupt aides and ministers. So the U.S. encouraged him to publicly denounce former cabinet ministers and officials in order to save his regime.

The State Department knew that the Shah would never bring his own inner circle and members of his own family to justice, even though they were at the center of Iran's corruption. So the U.S. proposed instead that the Shah sacrifice innocent individuals. Show trials could divert attention; even if corruption charges weren't proved, the public scapegoating of high officials could placate Iran's angry populace.

In March 1962, the Shah accepted the new reform package proposed by the United States, but he made it clear that he would have the final say on who would be the next Prime Minister. Instead of wrestling with someone he couldn't control, he was determined to appoint his own man. When Amini resigned as Prime Minister, the Shah replaced him with his closest and most trusted friend, Amir Assadollah Alam. His family was at the core of the Iran's shadow power, and the Alam family had worked with the British for many decades. Alam had always presented himself as the Shah's most obedient servant, who was willing to kiss his ruler's hands or boots. No sacrifice, Alam professed, was too great for his friend the Shah, and his most cherished wish was to keep the Pahlavi dynasty in perpetual sovereignty. With Alam as Prime Minister, Britain was satisfied, and the U.S. reluctantly accepted the situation.

In his new role, Alam was surrounded and helped by a number of pro-British advisers. Among them was General Karim Ayadi, the Shah's personal physician and constant companion. Ayadi provided basic medical services to the Shah—prescribing his daily does of lemon juice, honey, and vitamin pills. We called him the Pharmaceutical King of Iran, since he controlled all the medical supplies the government purchased and skimmed hundreds of thousand of dollars off that purchasing power. A trusted counselor, Ayadi was perhaps the only person who could see the Shah any time he wanted. I learned firsthand how intimate Ayadi was with the Shah at a meeting I attended, in which the doctor kept his hat on the entire time. I later mentioned it to Ayadi, and he started laughing when he explained the reason. The Shah, he told me, had been thinking about changing the color of his hair and had asked him to try the color on his own hair first. The process had somehow gone wrong, and Ayadi was wearing a hat to conceal the results.

Ayadi parlayed his closeness with the Shah into an appointment as a four-star general in the Iranian armed forces. All procurements for the army, except for armaments, went through Ayadi, and he and his people always took their cut. The Shah also gave Ayadi a monopoly on shrimp fishing in Iran's portion of the Persian Gulf, and Ayadi contracted the work out to a Japanese and Russian firm that paid him handsomely.

Then there was Dr. Manuchehr Eqbal, a French-trained physician who was invited to serve as interior minister in 1946. Tall, dark, and distinguished, Eqbal attracted the attentions of the political elite and, more influentially, the attentions of Princess Ashraf, the Shah's twin sister. Dr. Eqbal knew how to play political games. Thanks to the Shah's patronage, he managed to hold each of the country's top ten highest positions, serving as prime minister and a cabinet minister of every type many times over. Eqbal also served as Governor General of Azerbaijan province and Chancellor of Tehran University and ran an uncountable number of state organizations, including the National Iranian Oil Company, which earned 90 percent of the country's foreign exchange income. Eqbal's slush fund, which he could use as he pleased, was as gigantic as his power of patronage. He once admitted to me that he hadn't spent his own money for such a long time that he couldn't even remember the color of the day's currency.

There was also Jaafar Sharif-Emami, an old-time politician whose loyalty to the Shah kept him in the system for decades. Like Eqbal, he had served in most of the country's top positions, from cabinet minister to prime minister and, finally, as president of the senate. Sharif-Emami was also the president of the Pahlavi Foundation, which managed funds for members of the royal family, and he functioned as a close confidant to most of them. The royal family, in fact, occupied a peculiar place in Iran's government—unofficially running a big chunk of the country's commerce and using positions close to the Shah to snatch up highly lucrative state contracts for cronies and dummy companies.

The Shah's inner circle also included his butler, Hushang Davallu, who cultivated poppy crops and shared the opium he produced with members of Iran's high society. Davallu also received the exclusive right to export Iranian caviar throughout the world, earning him millions of dollars. Serving the Shah, in any capacity, had its rewards.

The greatest power in the Shah's government, however, was held by SAVAK, the state's intelligence and security organization. Established at the height of the Cold War, with U.S. backing, it was designed to stop the expansion of communist ideology in Iran by destroying the Soviet-backed Tudeh Party. The Alam government, however, soon directed SAVAK to jail, torture, and even execute members of the opposition. These repressive acts were soon all too common, and the political atmosphere became deadly quiet. SAVAK began watching people from all walks of life, bugging the homes and offices of ordinary citizens. Conveniently, this aligned with the U.S. policy of eradicating communism in Iran, but there were no checks and balances on what SAVAK could do to people who fell too easily into its clutches. With tens of thousands of detectives and informers, SAVAK quickly became much more than the country's security arm, as vast legal and extra-judicial authority was concentrated in its hands. As I learned more about the underbelly of Iran's politics, I estimated that at least two cabinet members, five ambassadors, and maybe 10 percent of the members of parliament were on the SAVAK payroll. Even Iran's media was penetrated by the SAVAK network.

In practice, however, the mission of "national security" simply masked SAVAK's efforts to gain more power for itself. All candidates for high-ranking positions had to be screened by SAVAK; if there were objections, SAVAK would forward a note saying they were not to be recommended. SAVAK never explained its decisions because it never had to, and its agents were in key positions throughout the government. Anyone deemed by these corrupt and powerfully connected individuals to be a risk or liability would find themselves on SAVAK's murderous black list. If they were close to the Shah or without blemish, SAVAK would work to destroy their characters, spinning extraordinarily powerful campaigns of rumor and innuendo. Its methods of character assassination were so devastating that even strong, decent officials would choose to resign quietly rather than stand and fight.

Only rarely did SAVAK and the Shah come into conflict. Once, the chief of SAVAK's motorcycle escort stopped the car of Princess Ashraf, the Shah's twin sister, while General Teymour Bakhtiar, SAVAK's powerful leader, was driving by. Ashraf subsequently warned her royal brother about Bakhtiar's ambitions; the Shah removed him from his position, and Bakhtiar left Iran and helped conspire to overthrow the Shah's regime. At one point, the U.S. State Department considered Bakhtiar a possible replacement for the Shah, but he eventually aligned with Saddam Hussein and lived—at the Iraqi dictator's invitation—in an Iraqi palace, where he carried on activities against the Shah. The monarch, however, eventually caught up with Bakhtiar. Four SAVAK agents pretended to hijack an airplane and landed on Iraqi soil; when Bakhtiar arrived to greet them, they shot him dead and flew back to Iran.

After Bakhtiar, the Shah named General Nassiri SAVAK's chief. But the most terrifying person in the SAVAK organization was the torturer, Parvis Sabeti. The mere mention of Sabeti's name was enough to frighten millions of people. Nassiri, a military officer with limited education, was hardly qualified for intelligence work. It was Sabeti—an expert in techniques of torture—who worked to establish a reign of terror within Iran. At this, Sabeti proved himself a genius.

With Alam at his side, the Shah was no longer a figurehead. He was now King of Kings and prepared to confront any opposition to his reform measures, even from the clerics and powerful landlords. He began to reinvent the monarchy to make it a modernizing force and sought to curb the old power bases it had long relied on for support. He also began to implement the reform package recommended by the State Department—a wide-ranging set of initiatives that he called the "White Revolution," because no blood, he promised, would be shed. Not only did the Shah propose reforms of the electoral procedure and land tenure system, he also set up a literacy corps, a health corps, and a development corps to help modernize rural areas. He submitted all of these plans to a public referendum, and voters overwhelmingly approved his programs.

Both the Americans and British seemed content with the Shah's performance; for a while, all was well. But mullahs led by the Ayatollah Khomeini began a campaign against the Shah and Alam, claiming that their reforms were against Islamic law. They especially voiced opposition to the land reform program, since they were closely tied to landlords in the countryside. On June 5, 1963, led by Khomeini, the mullahs attempted to overthrow the monarchy for the first time. The commander of the riot police that day was a close friend of Colonel Rasoul. Years later, when Rasoul and I were imprisoned together, he told us what he had heard from that friend:

Demonstrations began on May 29. At first, small groups of demonstrators were reported to be gathering at street corners, chanting slogans against what they called the Shah's anti-Islamic policies. When there was no reaction from the police and security forces, the demonstrators became bolder and their numbers increased. Soon they had organized bands of rioters, inciting the people to rebel against the government.

From there, things only got worse. The security forces shied away from serious confrontation, and the demonstrators resorted to more and more violent tactics. This chaos continued for days, and while the opposition groups got more and more violent, the security forces maintained a low profile.

A massive crowd assembled in South Tehran. Shouting religious slogans against the regime, the crowds waved clenched fists at the security forces, who did nothing. The situation was ominous. Field commanders appealed for permission to deal with the demonstrators as the situation warranted—begging for permission at least to cock their guns in order to defend their positions—but the orders from headquarters kept them at bay.

According to Jafar Sadri—who was then Chief of the General Police Administration and also later imprisoned with us—the situation became so grave that he, the chief of SAVAK, and the Commander of the Armed Forces all went to the Prime Minister's office to raise the alarm.

"We told Premier Alam that the rioters had gotten close enough to the royal palace to scale the walls and swarm onto the palace grounds," Sadri recalled, "and unless the ban was lifted on the army's use of force, we would not be able to stop them. At first, Alam said that His Majesty was absolutely opposed to the army firing on unarmed civilians. But Alam managed to convince the Shah that danger was imminent, and the Shah finally gave orders for us to stop the rioters by any means necessary."

Once the Shah gave Alam full executive power to suppress Ayatollah Khomeini's uprising, things quickly came to a head. Units of the armed forces and riot police confronted the mob. When the shoot-to-kill orders finally came, according to Colonel Rasoul, the security forces blocked several thoroughfares leading to Jaleh Square in downtown Tehran, where most of the demonstrators had gathered. Once they had boxed the core group of the rioters in and around that square, the security forces started firing. They heaped the corpses of the dead on army trucks, took them to a place out of town—close to the Kavir Desert in central Iran—and buried them in mass, unmarked graves.

The massacre succeeded in silencing the mullahs and their cronies. SAVAK suppressed the news, and nothing was published about the incident. The international media also kept quiet about it; I wondered why the BBC and *New York Times* did not cover the story. Human rights organizations overlooked the incident, and the U.S. State Department and British Foreign Office had nothing to say. All was quiet on the Iranian front, as far as the world was concerned. Everyone agreed that, to maintain stability in the Middle East, the slaughter of a few religious fanatics was not too high a price.

Now, with the opposition crushed, the Alam government acquired extraordinary power. The Prime Minister became the highest commander in the hierarchy of Iranian corruption. His friends were given top positions of influence, with full control of means to amass unprecedented wealth.

CHAPTER 11

INSIDERS AND OUTSIDERS

Prime Minister Alam had reshuffled the cabinet, and the changes had an impact on Iran's health care system. For years, health services and medical education in Iran had been based on the French model. Their new leaders, under Alam, had deep reservations about graduates of American universities, whom they called "Massachusettia." After I spent an afternoon consulting with friends in various health organizations and hospitals, I learned that all the important positions in governmental health organizations and university medical faculties were only being allocated to Iranian graduates of French-speaking medical schools in Europe. These new officials were extremely jealous of the privileges they had acquired, and many drew government salaries while spending most of their time in their profitable private practices.

In Iran's medical schools, some surgeons and professors had not been in an operating room for years; others had never treated any patients at all. Many physicians, perhaps a third, were political appointees and delegated their responsibilities to subordinates as much as possible. Standards were very low, compared to what I'd seen in the United States. Almost no one in Iran did original research, and medical textbooks were Persian translations of outdated French texts. Course curricula were prepared, by inexperienced assistants, from lectures given in past years, and both faculties and students were ignorant of the tremendous new technological advances.

Medical school departments were chaired by unqualified professors, but better qualified doctors who had graduate degrees from prestigious American universities were unable to find jobs. In the early 1950s, American hospitals had been in dire need of young medical residents, and many fresh Iranian medical school graduates had been glad to take well-paying jobs in American hospitals. Soon, 60 percent of Tehran's annual med school graduates found their way to America. Few returned to Iran, and those who did came back with high hopes, but they faced strong resistance from the status quo. Some qualified specialists could only find jobs in provincial areas, despite the fact that their skills and abilities could only be fully utilized in Tehran. As a result, these physicians returned to the United States and resumed their high-income jobs and comfortable lifestyles. Those who were tenacious enough to stay on survived mostly by opening up private practices. They soon became well known for their skills and knowledge and, over time, were warmly received by the general public. But there were few of them, and medical conditions in the country remained grim.

As I learned about the employment situation, I began to lose hope. The Director General of the National Insurance Organization had said he would consider my request, but I wasn't optimistic that he would give me a job. So one day, I visited an American-trained plastic surgeon, Dr. Manucher Shahgoli, in a rented building on France Avenue, where he had opened the fifty-bed Pars Hospital. I was impressed: in sharp contrast to university hospitals, Pars had all the equipment it needed, an excellent nursing staff, and a team of recently returned physicians from the U.S. who were performing medical procedures that were unknown elsewhere in Iran. In a short period of time, Pars had become the Mayo Clinic of the country, a place where patients who had been diagnosed as incurable in other hospitals would find help and hope.

Dr. Shahgoli told me that trying to work within the medical school system was pointless. University hospitals were so outdated, poorly maintained, and poorly equipped, with such unqualified personnel, that it was better to start from scratch. And since there was a clear demand for modern, well-equipped hospitals, he had surmised that it might be possible to set up a well-equipped facility on a small scale if he could raise the necessary funds outside the university bureaucracy. Such a hospital, equipped with the latest medical equipment and qualified personnel, could be highly successful.

As we sipped coffee in his office, I told Dr. Shahgoli my situation. After some small talk, he asked me what I thought about Pars hospital. With complete honesty, I told him how impressed I was and that establishing this kind of facility in Tehran, with all the problems, was simply a miracle.

"You don't need to say that," Shahgoli laughed. "But managing this hospital," he added, "is a technical task, and it needs someone with the right training. The job," he told me, "is yours for the asking." I gladly accepted.

Once I had started working with Dr. Shahgoli, and Helen and I were well established in our new home, it was time, I thought, to take my new family to northern Iran to meet the rest of my relatives. My mother lived by herself in our old house in Sari, and she and my grandmother welcomed my American bride and our baby with wide open arms. Even without being able to communicate verbally, Helen and my mother had no trouble conveying their love and affection for each other.

My grandmother welcomed Helen in the Mazandarani dialect, but it was the language of the kitchen that brought them together. Grandma was a good cook, and she and Helen spent hours in the kitchen preparing indigenous dishes. I still remember the *sak-ghalieh* they prepared, mixing pheasant and duck in a garlic and sour orange and garlic sauce. To our relief, too, we learned that my grandmother was modern-minded: in preparing our bedroom, she had pushed the twin beds together.

Her home was an old-fashioned Persian house. It had a cold storage room in the basement and both an old-style kitchen, with a charcoal-fired oven, and more modern cooking facilities. The past and future seemed to come together on our visit. As the scent of orange blossoms wafted through the air, I watched Lisa discover my old play areas, and when Helen and I picked oranges in the orchard, it was like watching my own childhood over again. We had originally intended to spend only two days in Sari, but we stayed a week. To my delight, Helen became completely enamored with Mazandaran and its people, and we were reluctant to leave.

When we got back to Tehran, it turned out, we had some adjustments to make. My sister had sent a maid back with us, and she was a great help with Lisa and domestic work. Helen, however, had difficulty with the idea of a live-in maid; the notion seemed strange to a person of her upbringing, and she valued our privacy. The maid had nowhere else to go, however, so Helen eventually accepted that live-in domestic help was the only option. Without help, she knew, it would have been difficult to keep the house together.

My professional situation was changing, too. While I was still working at Pars hospital, the Social Security Organization finally sent me a letter offering me a position as "adviser in health management." I had almost lost hope by that point, and while I never discovered why they suddenly offered me a job, I was happy to accept, especially since it was a position with no real authority or responsibility. Being an "adviser" simply meant that you earned a salary but didn't come to work, so I could accept it without giving up my position at Pars hospital.

When I told a friend who was a surgeon about my new position, he laughed and told me a story. A man took his dog to a vet, he said, because it was crazy about females; it would spend day and night chasing after stray bitches. After the vet had the animal castrated, the man's mind was at rest. But after four months, the man returned to the vet and complained that, while the dog had been fine for the first three months, he had fallen into his old ways. The vet smiled. "This time," he explained, "your dog is only acting as an adviser!"

As Helen became more and more adjusted to life in Tehran, she made many friends among Americans living there. She was also getting better acquainted with the Iranian language and culture. After she enrolled in a Persian class at Tehran University, we worked together at home to build her vocabulary and confidence. Since she missed being in a professional working environment, she found employment at an IBM corporate office that needed English-speaking staff. Helen had some trouble with "Tehran tummy," as the Americans called the regular bouts of food poisoning that plagued foreigners, and she lost fifteen pounds in the first year. But she was getting used to things.

She had also taken a fancy to the way shopping was done in Tehran, after my sister gave her a lesson in the art of bargaining, called *chaneh*. Helen liked the challenge of the negotiations, as well as the rewards of getting cheaper prices, and liked to brag when she managed to purchase something less expensively than her friends. One day, she proudly told me that she had bought a twenty-rial bottle of milk for eighteen rials. This was quite an accomplishment, I said, since a government company with fixed prices supplied the milk. I later questioned the grocer on this point. He shook his head and smiled. "You mean that foreign lady?" he said. "I tried to convince her that the price of milk was fixed, but she wouldn't accept it. She wouldn't stop trying to bargain with me, and eventually she wore me down. 'Since you don't understand what I'm saying,' I told her, 'Pay me eighteen rials and be done with it!'"

As our life in Tehran came together, however, the political climate was disintegrated. Iran's epidemic of graft and corruption was reaching its peak. With the grotesque spectacle of staged parliamentary elections, the royal family's ham-fisted wheeling and dealing, and the culture of favoritism and subservience to power, the conditions in the country were reaching a crisis.

CHAPTER 12

ASSASSINATION OF THE PRIME MINISTER

By now, the U.S. had lost confidence in Alam's ability to control Iran's affairs. By cutting off aid, it pressured the Shah to ask for Alam's resignation. As his replacement, the monarch selected Hassan Ali Mansour, the well-educated son of a former Prime Minister under Reza Shah. Hassan Ali had been involved in politics from an early age, but his prominence came from a political movement called the "Center of Advancement," which he had formed with Amir Abbas Hoveyda, Dr. Shahgoli, and other graduates of foreign universities. That movement later became the nucleus of the New Iran political party.

With Alam's removal, Britain's influence over Iran's political and economic affairs quickly declined. The Shah moved slowly to appoint Mansour, however, and Anglophile forces in Iran almost immediately launched a smear campaign against him. When the Shah traveled to Switzerland to ski, Mansour worried that British officials would derail his appointment. So he telegrammed the Shah and convinced him to issue a declaration from Switzerland naming him Prime Minister and to sign the document promptly on his return.

The struggle over Mansour's appointment exposed the battle being waged between the British and Americans for influence in Iran. Mansour, however, was relatively independent. Though he was accused of being appointed by the American Embassy and CIA, he filled his cabinet with fresh faces, including technocrats who had been educated in Europe and the United States. He appointed Amir Abbas Hoveyda as Minister of Finance, and together they initiated a variety of development plans to improve society in Iran. Fighting corruption became one of Mansour's priorities. Corrupt officials were sacked, and the royal family's interference in government affairs ground to a halt.

Mansour's core policies for a democratic Iran involved a two-party system, laying the foundations for both the *New Iran* and *People's* political parties. He worked to give Iran's judiciary independence from political meddling and bolster the constitutional power of the Supreme Court. While the Shah remained commander-in-chief of the armed forces, Mansour worked to prevent government interference in the electoral process and ordered members of the royal family to stay out of day-to-day government business. All these fundamental changes spoke well for Mansour's government, but many Iranians worried that they were setting the stage for confrontations with entrenched insiders. A prominent journalist warned that Mansour was a time bomb, and all of Tehran expected an explosive conflict.

America's influence in Iran was gaining momentum, and British colonial tendencies were on the decline. Still, old political hands doubted that the British would leave Iran's political arena; close one door to the British, and they would come in through another. That was true. The mullahs, old allies of Britain's secret service, proved to be the undoing of Mansour's government. After a propaganda campaign attacked his promotion of Western modernity, a seventeen-year-old with a picture of Khomeini in his pocket shot the Prime Minister Mansour in front of the Parliament building.

Hoveyda and Dr. Shahgoli rushed him to Pars Hospital. Hoveyda, appointed caretaker by the Shah, carried out the most urgent duties of office from his friend's bedside. He kept the Shah regularly informed about the Prime Minister's health. Despite round-the-clock efforts by the medical team, however, Mansour went to his grave with his vision for a modern Iran only a dream.

Eventually, the assassin confessed to killing Mansour because the Prime Minister had insulted Khomeini. The killer was condemned to death, and his two accomplices were imprisoned for life. The rumor mill, however, tried to implicate the Shah in Mansour's death. At the time, many Iranians believed that. Years later, however—after the revolution—it was clear that the real players in this affair were Seidali Andarzgou and Akbar Rafsanjani, who would later become Iran's president. Khomeini richly rewarded both of them for leading the conspiracy against Mansour.

CHAPTER 13

THE SHAH AND HIS PARALLEL GOVERNMENTS

Soon after Mansour's death, the Shah permanently made Hoveyda his new Prime Minister. As Hoveyda told Dr. Shahgoli, my trusted friend, he learned of his appointment in an unexpected way:

> The Shah was angry and restless, pacing the length of his office at the Marble Palace. Suddenly, he stopped and put his penetrating glare on me. "I have chosen you to be the Prime Minister," the Shah said, without hesitation. "Prepare the government's plan for continuation and prepare yourself to carry out your duties."...I was summoned to the Marble palace, and while I anticipated the Shah's intentions I was shocked by the abruptness. It was as if I was receiving an imperial command, to be obeyed and carried out without question. At first, I was at a loss for words. But I had serious reservations, and I had to say something.
>
> "Your Majesty, I have been away from Iran for many years, and many of the country's problems are somewhat unfamiliar to me. Maybe I'm not qualified to take over the position in these circumstances. Perhaps it is not in the country's best interests to have me at the head of the line."
>
> The Shah barely registered my words. While standing at the window with his back to me, he said, easily, "None of that matters. We will instruct you in how to carry out your duties." He turned and pierced me with his eyes. "After all, you will not *really* be at the head of the line."

Hoveyda was an intelligent man and widely regarded by his peers as an intellectual. He had spent most of his youth in Lebanon. After completing service in the Iranian army and State Department, he had followed the diplomatic channels through London, Paris, Zurich, Geneva, and Istanbul. He spoke seven languages and was known to be a careful conversationalist—polite, courteous, and a good listener. As a young diplomat in Europe, he was known for reciting poetry. He was popular with artists and writers, whom he made a point of befriending. In Hoveyda's younger days, he had experimented with socialist ideas, but in his maturity, all his friends and associates knew him to be a committed and determined democrat. None of us believed he would submit to a dictatorial regime, and we understood why he had hesitated to assume the position of Prime Minister. But we also knew that the Shah had no intention of being upstaged.

At the start of his premiership, Hoveyda enlisted the cooperation of his reform-minded friends and hoped to continue the strides Mansour had taken toward a more open political environment. But he was well aware that the Shah would not put up with a Prime Minister who questioned the monarch's constitutional status as head of government. Hoveyda believed, nevertheless, that he could work within the limitations of the Shah's constitutional powers. As the Shah's chief executive, he thought, he would be able to use the aura of royal supremacy to maintain stability in Iran while developing government plans and reforms. Hoveyda and his cabinet were responsible for education, the economy, science, technology and health and welfare. They were known as technocrats who were trying to advance the modernization of Iran. Hoveyda led with integrity and ran a legitimate government controlled by law.

Underneath the veneer of this legal government, however, was a shadow power led by Alam and his chosen political cronies. The Shah had appointed Alam as his new Minister of Court, reporting only to him and creating a divided government. This parallel government structure was in charge of oil, foreign affairs, and multibillion-dollar military and nuclear purchases. Alam's power brokers engaged in corruption, embezzlement, oppression of the Iranian people, and human rights violations facilitated by SAVAK, the ruthless Iranian Secret Service.

Hoveyda and Alam both reported to the Shah and enjoyed his patronage, though they were political rivals heading warring factions, and they despised each other. The Shah was well aware of what was going on and encouraged their conflict, keeping them in balance, despite the fact that the U.S. and Britain were unhappy with this dual system.

Hoveyda's critics thought he was ambitious, playing on the Shah's massive ego to secure his position. But to his friends, Hoveyda was at worst a dreamer whose faith in the Shah's "Great Civilization" was so strong that it blinded him to the forces that would bring him down. He was convinced that with sufficient time and opportunity, Iranian technocrats would be able to solve Iran's problems. By mobilizing enough of the country's talent, Hoveyda believed he would be able develop Iran's natural resources. He enlisted the services of every skilled Iranian he could find, especially those who had acquired their expertise in industrialized countries. Increasing numbers of Iranians abroad accepted his encouragement to return home and put their knowledge to good use. People could also see that more and more cabinet ministers and high-ranking officials were coming from middle-class backgrounds instead of hereditary wealth. And as all of us became aware that the regime was willing to reward talent and expertise, rather than confine government to the thousand families who had run Iran for centuries, we began to have more hope for the future.

CHAPTER 14

PURGING THE PARASITES

In our personal family life, too, things were getting better. Thanks to the varied sources of income I had managed to cobble together, we were now doing financially well enough that Helen could plan to return to the U.S. with Lisa for a short family visit. As we prepared for their trip, we were happy to get another piece of welcome news: we would soon have a new addition to our family.

One day, however, a chance observation by the Shah put my life on a completely different track. As he was flying low over the city of Isfahan, on his way to Shiraz, he noticed a tall new building that was unfamiliar to him. He asked what it was, and a minister told him that the building, which the Social Insurance Organization (SIO) had completed a year before, would be a new hospital, big enough for five hundred beds. Some problems had delayed the hospital's opening, he said, but he reassured the Shah that it would be ready for its first patients within a year.

The Shah refused to accept the minister's explanation—remarking angrily that, with such an acute shortage of hospital beds in the country, it was obscene for a hospital to be left empty because of organizational incompetence. With imperial gravity, he declared that he planned to inaugurate the hospital on his next visit to Isfahan. It was an indirect ultimatum, but the minister clearly understood the Shah's order.

Since the Shah was scheduled to visit Isfahan in three months, the minister quickly contacted the chairman of the SIO's board and told him of the ruler's decision. When the Shah spoke in such tones, government machinery always swung into action, but more than determination was required in this case. The old hospital and a new, modern facility were completely different institutions, and medical authorities lacked the skills to run the new hospital the Shah demanded. The SIO's task was to close this gap within three months, and no one was optimistic that it could be done.

The old two-story hospital was a converted residential building with no elevators. Rooms on the ground floor had doors opening onto a central courtyard, and medical personnel simply moved patients between sterilized operating rooms, across the open-air plaza, without regard for infection. With no radiology unit or laboratory, critical tests had to be performed outside the hospital. The facility had no filing system to keep track of patients' records. A sheet of paper was simply nailed to every occupied bed-frame. Three qualified nurses were responsible for patient care, but in practice, in-patients were cared for by a spouse or relative who stayed at the hospital to see to their needs.

The SIO's top medical management recommended hiring a consultant from abroad, but the plan was rejected, since it would take too much time. So the chairman of the SIO board consulted with Dr. Shahgoli, who had been appointed Minister of Health because of his success with Pars Hospital. Shahgoli was quick to suggest my name; "the only man for the job is already on your payroll, and you aren't using him," he said. "If you're not careful, he'll return to the United States before you can contact him."

The chairman asked me to come to an emergency meeting, and when I met with him, he got right to the point: could I get the new hospital running in three months? It was an intimidating prospect, and it was obvious that the big shots were worried about their positions. I said I needed a week to study the matter before I could give him a firm answer, but he took my response as a definite yes.

Since time was of the essence, my plan was to keep the old hospital operating while we trained staff to get the new hospital up and running. As it became operational, we would transfer staff over to the new facilities. At zero hour, we would close the old building down and move all the in-patients and staff to the new hospital.

When I first set foot in the new facility, I thought I was back in the United States. The operating rooms I visited featured the most modern equipment, and there were up-to-date laboratories, a pathology department, a morgue, and other necessary services. The emergency and trauma center was well-equipped, and there were modern kitchen and laundry facilities. As

I inspected the hospital, something very telling also caught my eye. Almost every piece of equipment was identified by a tag written in English. Most of these items were completely new to Iran, and there were still no Persian equivalents for words like "Intensive Care Unit," "Recovery Room," "Medical Records Room," "Morgue," or "Central Supply."

In those days, many qualified Iranians were looking for jobs in modern hospitals, so a professional staff of physicians and nurses was not hard to assemble. Ironically, however, recruiting non-medical and auxiliary personnel was the biggest headache. Iran had no school to train medical records librarians, dietitians, technicians to work with modern medical equipment, or laundry staff and cooks to work with automatic machines. Often, I had to train new recruits myself. Since there were no manuals in the Persian language, we had to laboriously translate everything for the many employees who didn't know enough English. In some cases, I personally translated handbooks into Persian myself and demonstrated how to operate the equipment.

It was a grueling time. But despite the difficulties, my dedicated staff had no intention of falling behind, and Reza Pahlavi Hospital, named after the monarch's father, was ready a day ahead of schedule. The opening ceremonies were attended by many top officials and dignitaries and presided over by the Shah himself. I personally had mixed emotions about him. There is no doubt that he did many positive things including pushing for a modern Iran. On the other hand he ignored human rights and freedom for the people. He surrounded himself with a group of sycophants and had little connection with ordinary people. He didn't understand how they lived or their ideas. It was well known that the Shah was afraid to speak to the masses. I wasn't sure if this was because of his fears or those of the people around him.

The hospital's inauguration gave me an opportunity to arrange for some of the staff to speak to the Shah directly. I instructed the happy doctors and nurses I selected that they could ask the ruler questions but needed to avoid politics. Then, two hours before the event, a group of men showed up to check security and protocol. The director of security said that no questions were to be asked of the Shah. If the monarch asked a question, we should simply answer it, he told us; otherwise, there could be consequences.

On the day of the grand opening, the Shah seemed happy and within his element. Although his original itinerary had called for an hour-long tour, he took three full hours to inspect every corner of the vast medical complex. He wanted to learn everything related to the operation, and I did my best to respond to each of his royal inquiries about the functions of specific equipment and the staff's background and specializations. There were memorable moments. The hospital's urologist, a young, American-trained physician with a sense of humor, asked me to bring the Shah to his Urology Department. When we arrived, the doctor introduced himself to His Majesty and showed him a large jar filled with liquid and an object. He asked the Shah what he thought it was, and the monarch guessed that it was a large chicken egg. The doctor corrected him, explaining that it was the kidney stone of a sixty-year-old man. The ruler smiled and seemed satisfied, and the exchange ended without incident.

At the end of the tour, the Shah was filled with enthusiasm. We then had tea together. The monarch carefully drank his tea from a thermos—because he was convinced that someone would try to poison him—and asked me about my own background and education. As he concluded the visit, he declared approvingly, "It is a very good hospital." Before he departed, he took out a gold fountain pen to sign the visitors' book and handed it to me as a gift.

The next day, the hospital opened for business, and I had a front-row seat for the media blitz ignited by the hospital's inauguration. In a city with mosques and royal palaces dating back to the fourteenth century, it became a prime tourist attraction; people lined up to walk its halls and see twentieth-century medical technology. Even though the complex was now fully operational, I couldn't leave Isfahan for six months, until it was set to operate for the long term, but I had no complaints. My reputation was skyrocketing, and when I finally came back to Tehran, I was showered with job offers from Iran's most prestigious medical institutions. Only a week after my return, I was appointed Director of Hospitals for the SIO, with twelve facilities under my direct supervision.

When Helen returned from her trip to the United States, I was delighted—and a bit surprised—to learn that she was happy to return to the challenges of Iranian life. We began to look forward to a bright future that seemed more attainable. We felt optimistic. My prospects were encouraging, and the future of the country seemed more promising than it had at any time in my own memory.

My first project in my new position was to increase the efficiency of Iran's hospitals. Although the SIO was under pressure to expand coverage to government workers, there weren't nearly enough doctors or facilities to cope with existing patients. When we first analyzed the problem, we thought that opening new clinics and increasing the availability of outpatient service could help close the gap. But on closer examination, we realized that demand for hospital services would far outstrip our ability to supply them. We could improve clinical services and make them more accessible, but as we increased the number of patients, we would also increase the number of diagnoses and fall further behind in treatment. From a big-picture perspective, clinical expansion would further stretch Iran's overburdened facilities. As a short-term solution, we began converting residential and office buildings into hospitals. The shortage of beds, however, was a more fundamental issue that had to be addressed in creative ways.

The problem, I felt, was the underutilization of hospital beds. In those days, the phrase "occupancy rate" had never been used in Iran, and data analysis explained why the country couldn't catch up. One patient in Iranian hospitals occupied a bed for an average of twenty days. This was less than the thirty-three day average of university hospitals, but far more than in private institutions, like Pars Hospital, where patients occupied beds for less than five days on average. The hospital occupancy standard in the United States was about six days. In other words, to treat the same illness, Iran's hospital was using roughly four times as many resources as Pars or a comparable American hospital. The problem was not a shortage of beds, but inadequate utilization and management of those beds.

I submitted a comprehensive plan to the Board of Directors, proposing a new statistically tracked, professional system to improve efficiency. I promised that if the plan was implemented, the average occupancy period would be cut in half, effectively doubling hospital capacity. The plan was accepted, and my good friend Dr. Moe, who had returned to Iran from Minnesota, played a vital role in implementing the new system. Moe had also set up a private obstetrics and gynecology practice in Tehran, which was soon helpful to us as well. Early one morning, Helen told me that our second child was on the way. I rushed her to the hospital where Moe was practicing, and the delivery went smoothly. As it happened, there was a shortage of nurses that day, so I ended up scrubbing in to help Moe deliver our second child, our beautiful new daughter Cathy.

More changes soon followed. My efficiency plan was first implemented as a pilot project in a single hospital. When the average occupancy rate dropped by half, to ten days, the board appointed me Director General for the SIO's

Health Department. This was a great promotion, to one of the top five health-care management positions in Iran. The job would demand managerial skills and political savvy, but in those days I had little sense of what I was getting into, so I accepted it with relish and quickly got down to business.

I almost immediately noticed, to my surprise, how many "ghost employees" were on the payroll. Euphemistically known as "absentee employees," they were people who, on paper, had a variety of skills and drew handsome salaries but didn't actually seem to *do* anything. Some of the highest paid served as "advisers to the Director General," but none of their names were familiar to me, and I certainly wasn't getting advice from them. These were not minor sinecures; in addition to high salaries, these "advisers" also enjoyed perks, including cars and drivers. When I started talking about turning off the tap, friends quickly let me know that this would be dangerous; by changing the status quo, I'd risk my career. A few self-appointed "well-wishers" made a special point of telling me that if I valued my job, I shouldn't talk about upsetting the apple cart.

As a result, I understood clearly that any changes I made would have consequences. Some "absentee employees" had been hired because of recommendations from higher up—by SAVAK, senators, and members of the Majlis (the parliament), as well as the royal family. The more I thought about it, however, the more determined I became to end this practice. My first order of business had to be purging the parasites from a department mired in corruption. If I wanted to bring real improvement to the country's health-care delivery system, there was no alternative.

My intention in returning to Iran was to revolutionize the backward medical health care system of the country. Millions of Iranians suffered from the inefficiencies of the present system. I understood the depth of the problems and, with my recent training in the U.S., I knew what strategies to follow. This was the time for action, not surrender to the entrenched patterns. I had no worries about losing the job. I had two offers in hand from major private hospitals in Iran, with higher pay, and I could always return to the U.S. for greater health care opportunities, including a new oral surgery practice.

So straightaway, I abolished the organizational positions that were held by freeloaders. Almost immediately, I was bombarded with protests, verbal abuse, negative newspaper articles, and parliamentary protests. It was my first encounter with this kind of politics, so I had to feel my way through it. Still, by restructuring management systems, we significantly improved the quality of services. At a time when most governmental organizations were suffering under heavy budget restraints, our organization was accumulating large reserve funds.

Unfortunately, those surpluses began to attract attention. At the time, the Shah was busy modernizing the armed forces. Although he had allocated sizable budgetary resources to the military, corrupt elements within its hierarchy were not satisfied and wanted to appropriate the SIO's reserves. When the Shah indirectly suggested that those monies could be reallocated, the SIO chairman ignored him, reasoning that because the SIO had collected the funds from workers' wages to provide retirement pay and health benefits, it couldn't simply be allocated elsewhere. When the chairman of the board of the SIO refused to loan the money to the Armed Forces, the decision had grave consequences, almost immediately. The Imperial Inspectorate Organization, a watchdog group connected to the Shah, had been created to penalize those who refused to play ball. An irate general claimed that our agency had misused funds. The SIO then singled out the chairman and me and began investigating our business and threatening us. The general said that he was the eyes and ears of his majesty the "Shahanshah," and if he decided, no rule or law could stop him. The investigative team scrutinized files and audited accounts, questioning every employee they could. It was obvious that they were fishing for something that could incriminate us. When they were unable to find anything, they left the investigation indefinitely open, keeping us in limbo with our salaries frozen, and prevented us from leaving the country for any reason.

In a way, it was a stalemate. But I had learned enough about politics at this level to see that it would be a losing hand in the long run. It wasn't long before the SIO's chairman was replaced and returned to teaching at the Tehran University of Law. I was replaced, too, but managed to parley my success into a management position at Pars Hospital. Just like that, I was out of government and happy to be back in the private sector.

Previously, as a member of Dr. Shahgoli's team, I had initiated a low-interest loan plan for physicians who were interested in establishing new, modern hospitals. The plan was successful, and within two years, ten new, well-equipped hospitals were established in Tehran and provincial cities. Thanks to the loans, several graduates of American universities had set up a two-hundred-bed hospital with outpatient clinics in the capital. The building, named "The Tehran Clinic," was completed amid much fanfare. For another year, however, disagreements among the partners kept the hospital from opening. Because of my success in Isfahan, I was asked to serve as the hospital's executive director after I left government.

This position was ideal for me. I enjoyed working in an environment of my own choosing. More than the comfortable income, I also liked the authority to put my ideas into practice. It was not long before the Tehran Clinic was accepting patients and providing quality medical services. Being out of government, away from politics and bureaucracy, I was once again happy and hopeful about the future.

Helen by now was working with the United Nations Development Program in Tehran, as executive secretary to the Director of Economics. Lisa and Cathy were enrolled in the Community School of Tehran, which taught an international curriculum based on the American system. Although they were taught in English, they also studied Farsi three hours a day. By then, I had managed to build a comfortable home for our family in the Farmanieh district, an upper-end neighborhood in Tehran with morning views of the white, snow-capped peaks of the mighty Damavand Summit, the tallest mountain in Iran and the highest volcano in all of Asia. We seemed assured of a comfortable, happy family life in Iran.

Then one day, unexpectedly, Dr. Shahgoli, the Minister of Health, asked me to come to his office to consult about a complicated situation regarding the Government Employees Health Insurance system (GEIC). The program, which was both under budget and poorly managed, had to provide medical insurance to two million civil employees and their families. The situation had reached a crisis level. "By the end of the current month," he told me, "it won't even be able to pay the wages and salaries of its employees." It was hardly news that the system was going bankrupt; its resources were far too limited to cope with demand, and very few civil servants even bothered to apply to it for medical help.

Dr. Shahgoli wanted to investigate and conduct a far-reaching study that would yield specific tactical recommendations. I agreed to help. After I spent a week inspecting and going over the paperwork, I discovered that only about a third of GEIC employees even reported to work, following the pattern for most governmental organizations. My study controversially recommended that the existing department be closed down and replaced by an efficient system. Instead of continuing with all the freeloaders and incompetent staff, I proposed a clean start and a system of outsourcing in which the GEIC would contract out medical services to the private sector.

I felt good about these recommendations, and I thought that my responsibility would end there. But a week later, Dr. Shahgoli surprised me at home with a surprising proposition. I was the only one, he said, who could clean up this den of corruption, and he would be grateful if I would help. I faced a dilemma. Just a year earlier, I had freed myself from the clutches of government employment and settled into a comfortable life in the private sector. I was reluctant to put my head back in the lion's mouth.

Dr. Shahgoli told me that he understood my reluctance. He had had a front-row seat when the Imperial Inspectorate had savaged my reputation and impugned my character, simply because I had done my job. But he insisted that things were changing and Iran was on the road toward development. "Your country needs you," he urged. "You have the ability to be of great service to your country, and this is your chance. And this time, you will have the support of the government. The Shah himself will issue a royal command recognizing your services." When I asked about the case against me, which was still pending, Dr. Shahgoli answered that, if I accepted, he would ask the Imperial Inspectorate to offer evidence of the charges or dismiss them. If the Inspectorate still hesitated to clear my name, he said, he would take the matter to the Shah. I agreed, and it wasn't long before the Imperial Inspectorate conceded that no charges were pending and summarily closed the file. The general who had led the attack against me was dismissed, leading me to believe that perhaps things *had* changed.

My first order of business was to clean house. After uniformly dismissing all the absentee employees, I annulled all the contracts with hospitals, service providers, and physicians linked to corruption and initiated new contracts with reputable hospitals and doctors. I didn't fully understand, even then, how my actions would threaten Iran's Executive Committee or foresee the political consequences that they would have.

CHAPTER 15

ROYAL TREATMENT

By 1974, after an unprecedented jump in the price of crude oil, Iran's national budget had tripled, and the Ministry of Health launched an aggressive plan to build sixteen large hospitals and hundreds of clinics. For Dr. Shahgoli and those of us on his team, this was a dream come true; we had always had a plan, but never the finances. The billions of dollars these construction projects would cost, however, attracted wheeler-dealers salivating for a piece of the pie. Iranian experts visited American and European cities to study specific aspects of development, and international companies began to roll out the red carpet for Iran's new *nouveau riche* clientele. Marketing agents began visiting Tehran regularly to promote their products and develop new lines of business. Meanwhile, Iran's shadow power swung into action, and Dr. Shahgoli's hard line on corruption at the Ministry of Health provoked a counterreaction.

Under pressure, the Shah replaced Shahgoli with Dr. Anushisrvan Puyan. A graduate of Paris Medical School, Puyan was associated with powerful cliques. Sociable and elegant, he always liked to be called professor, in keeping with French custom. While Puyan was in Paris, he had become an integral part of the international jet set and was an ideal host for Alam and the royal family on their frequent trips to Paris. This friendship led him to be tapped, on his return to Iran, as dean of Tehran's Melli Medical School. In less than a year, Puyan was promoted to chancellor of the university. But his association with powerful interests was soon more important than his work. As a shrewd politician, he knew how to lobby hard for advancement.

Now, as Iran's new Minister of Health, Puyan devoted all his attention to pharmaceutical affairs and hospital construction, without bothering to acquaint himself with the ministry's organizational chart. Issuing permits to import pharmaceuticals into Iran was the main cash cow for the ministry's corrupt bureaucrats, since new drugs needed permits to be imported for the first time. The bribe rate was between $200,000 and $300,000 per item. Puyan kept things simple, demanding a flat 10 percent cut off the top as his personal share. He also took responsibility for hospital construction projects, opening lines of communication with international dealers and promoters who had extensive experience in setting up turn-key construction deals for rich Arab countries. Since Iran lacked the necessary resources to build modern hospitals, Puyan argued, it was necessary to make arrangements with European firms. He made frequent trips to London and Paris and formed a British advisory group that, predictably, selected three contractors: one British, one French, and one from the United States.

Hoveyda took advantage of the cabinet reshuffle to move Dr. Shahgoli to the Ministry of Higher Education and Science. At the same time, he promoted Dr. Sheikh to head the newly established Ministry of Social Welfare. Dr. Sheikh asked me to be his second in command at the ministry. I was presented to the Shah, who said to me, "The country is on the threshold of great developments, and you have taken heavy burdens on your shoulders in accepting this charge. Since everything necessary to carry out your duties will be provided, there can be no excuse for failure."

There was no ambiguity about the urgency and gravity of this royal decree. But how seriously would the Shah stand by his rhetoric if we came into conflict with the shadow power? As it turned out, it didn't take long to find out. As Puyan prepared construction contracts with the three foreign companies for approval, Prime Minister Hoveyda grew increasingly suspicious of his actions. But, keeping in mind Puyan's direct connection to the Shah, he decided to present the contracts to the cabinet and urge further study. We were given a copy of the proposed contracts, and Hoveyda charged us to study them and submit our views.

Very quickly, Dr. Sheikh and I realized what was going on. The contracts specified that each hospital bed would cost three times the prevailing price, and the total cost was double that of a modern hospital of similar size and construction within our ministry. In contrast to our plans, which specified top-of-the-line equipment, the contractors' plans were maddeningly vague. As soon as Hoveyda read our report, he had an audience with the Shah and convinced him that such important contracts required further study. In the meantime, he ordered that the Puyan project contracts be placed on hold.

The delay caused havoc in Tehran, London, and Paris. Faced with this unforeseen situation, Puyan was extremely agitated and under pressure from his overseas connections to solve the problem. Prime Minister Hoveyda told me that the British Ambassador, Sir Anthony Parsons, assailed him and demanded to know what was going on with the hospital project. "You have taken away our sugar and pharmaceutical business," he charged. "You have given us no quota in your arms purchases. And now you stop this contract? It seems like you are telling us to pack up and leave."

Of course, the British had no intention of leaving Iran. Instead, it was Hoveyda whose position, day by day was becoming less secure. As the conflict heated up, the switchboards between Tehran and London lit up with frantic telephone calls trying to salvage the deal. Then Barbara Castle, secretary of Britain's Department of Health and Social Services, made a personal trip to Tehran to show her government's interest.

I was relaxing at home one evening when Dr. Sheikh called to tell me that we needed to meet with Secretary Castle at the Prime Minister's residence. I could tell from his voice that it was a serious matter. The residence was the former palace of the Shah's brother, which he sold to the government. The gathering took place on a patio overlooking a beautifully manicured garden. Minister Castle was an attractive woman in her mid-fifties with an easy smile. Her prime reason for coming to Iran was to get an understanding of why trade between Iran and Britain had declined. I was introduced to Minister Castle as the Iranian official who had to be convinced that Iran should go with Britain's prices for building twelve six-hundred-bed hospitals, worth many billions of dollars.

At the meeting, we compared our facts and figures with those in the contract. Minister Castle firmly assured us that the fairness of the prices had already been confirmed by British officials and reflected the cost standards prevailing in Britain. If I traveled to London, she suggested, I could meet with British specialists and receive additional briefings, which would clear away all misunderstandings.

After some tense negotiations, we agreed that I would travel to England with a team of experts to try to resolve the disagreement. I was beginning to worry that I would be crushed between the mountains these people were moving to salvage the deal; after all, I'd been in this position before and had learned that the shadow power could ruin an honest person. Would I be punished for doing my job again?

Dr. Sheikh did his best to reassure me that Hoveyda and the rest of the cabinet were opposed to the consortium contract. Trying to scuttle a multibillion-dollar deal, he conceded, was no small matter, however, and it would upset a lot of people of great influence. Still, he assured me that if we could muster convincing evidence that the deal was misbegotten from the start, it would be possible to derail it. Together we selected two experts in engineering and architectural contracts who would join me on the trip to England. With barely time to say good-bye to Helen and our family, I took off.

At Heathrow Airport, the British Chief of Protocol welcomed us with a reception. Since our arrival coincided with the inaugural flight of the Concord—the first supersonic passenger jet—from Paris to London, he also invited us to view the ceremonial launching. I'll never forget his words as he watched the Concord take off: "Damn the Americans!"

Our British hosts offered us accommodations at one of the government's official guesthouses, but we preferred to stay at a hotel that our own government had booked. The next morning, we called on Minister Castle. After the usual pleasantries, she assured us that her government attached a great deal of importance to its dealings with Iran and spoke fondly of more than a century of "relations." I didn't tell her what I thought of that historical relationship and let her go on. "We are always interested in further cooperating with you in cultural, economic, and scientific fields," the Minister explained, "so this contractual agreement is of special importance to us. We would like to address and remove any obstacles in the way of this agreement."

Once we got down to details, the British experts presented the same list of cost factors that we had seen in the original contract. Compared to costs of labor and materials in Iran, the British cost standards were outrageously high. The prices of supplies, labor, engineering, and architecture were much less in Iran than in England, but on this point we could not make ourselves understood. Finally, we agreed to make a site visit to a model hospital, and our hosts clearly expected that it would persuade us to agree to the contract. After traveling 200 miles to York in the north of England, however, we saw a newly built hospital that was not very impressive. It was a fine hospital, but the quality of the equipment did not match the standards that the London experts claimed they would provide. In fact, after discussing the matter with York city councilors in charge of the project, we discovered that there were substantial cost disputes between the contractors and the city council. The visit was not proceeding according to our hosts' expectations, and they were becoming frustrated with my refusal to back down.

After we left York, we were invited to a dinner at an exclusive club in the London suburbs. There, a smartly dressed master steward led us into a dimly lit room, where three distinguished looking English gentlemen and three chic middle-aged women were waiting to meet us. We were somewhat intimidated at being introduced to this group of aristocrats, and at first we kept mostly silent. A few drinks, however, melted the icy atmosphere. Lady K. spoke of the Shah's intelligence and the beauty of northern Iran. I returned the compliment and spoke about the charms of London, Churchill's powerful personality, and the achievements of British industry, especially the Concord. One of the three men was so familiar with top Iranian officials that he referred to them by their first names. The group complimented Hoveyda's talents and Empress Farah's beauty, but also made specific reference to improvements in public health and the sudden rise in the price of crude oil, which had made them possible. The conversation was inconsequential, but we were clearly trying to size each other up.

After dinner, we were escorted into a luxuriously furnished library, where the chitchat continued. Then, at a certain point, Lord K. took me by the elbow and led me to a quiet corner of the room. Warming his brandy snifter in the palm of his hand, he lightly raised the subject of our visit for the first time. "So," he said, "What do you think? I mean, regarding the contract for these hospitals?" Before I could reply, he added, "For reasons not apparent to us, your government has halted the execution of this contract. We spent a great deal of time and sustained heavy expenses in drawing up a contract we thought would be acceptable to both sides. Since the contract's terms were so carefully studied and had already been agreed upon by both parties, we were a bit puzzled that your government scrapped it. It doesn't seem to us like fair commercial practice."

I answered carefully. As far as I was aware, I explained, the contract was still going through preliminary stages of the official approval process and was still far from complete. The government of Iran had never given its final approval, so there seemed to be no reason to call it a binding contract. As for the question of expenses, I added, very carefully, that the contract seemed to be a standard architectural plan, with a routine list of medical equipment and mechanical installations. The preparation of such a contract could hardly, in my professional opinion, have entailed significant expense.

His Lordship avoided my attempt to make the issue purely professional and vaguely, but significantly, alluded to the politics behind the matter. Such contracts, he said, were more than simple business deals, and one had to consider the bilateral political relationship. In Anglo-Iranian relations, he assured me, economic matters were vitally important in strengthening political ties. In the context of vigorous, international commercial rivalries, he explained delicately, nations face a complex set of circumstances. To meet the challenges posed by these complications, one has to mobilize various forces and sustain considerable expense.

I didn't try to argue with him. Instead, I said firmly that such political matters were far beyond the scope of my authority. "We have been commissioned to complete a professional study of the proposed contract," I told him, and I repeated my opinion that the quoted prices were, in our opinion, higher than the prevailing norm. As I began to clarify the issues for him, he interrupted me, saying that our brandy snifters needed to be refilled. He was obviously unhappy with the direction the conversation was taking, so he changed the subject. It appeared to him, he added, that they had been negotiating with the wrong party. When I told him that the proper authority was the Minister of Health, he retorted that the consortium had already undertaken extensive talks with the minister. Since he now realized the minister lacked authority to finalize the deal, our conversation came to an uncomfortable end.

As my colleagues and I prepared to leave, Lord K. called me over again. This time, he put all his cards on the table. Without mincing his words, he said that the consortium had spent close to $3.5 million to get the contract to its present stage, and that they were prepared to spend more to remove all obstacles. "If you or anybody you might care to introduce to us to can give us guidance in this respect," he said, "it will be worth your while."

I have never been rich. Moments like these came often in my professional life, but I never felt the urge to take advantage of them. Perhaps I was afraid of the consequences, but I would rather think that it was in my true nature to be honest, that I had been raised to stay on the straight path. Perhaps the fact that my uncle took advantage of my mother had an impact on me. In any case, I told Lord K. that I was in no position to help, and that spending more to get the contract executed would accomplish nothing. If they adjusted their quoted prices, I suggested, they might still have a chance of getting the contract accepted, but I refused to take personal responsibility for anything or allow him to find any way to "lubricate" the deal.

For the rest of the evening, he tried to get the names from me of those in Iran who were opposed to the deal, but I made sure that no information passed my lips. In turn, I tried to learn the names of the parties who were intent on pushing the deal through, but he refused to tell me anything about the foreign parties involved. It was, he said, contrary to professional ethics to divulge that kind of information. But the names Shapour, Puyan, and Alam reoccurred enough times for me to take note. When we finally departed, he suggested, weakly, that I should "take off my dark glasses" when preparing the report and give it a positive slant. I don't think he expected me to do that, though.

On the way back to our hotel, my colleagues and I discussed the substance of my talks with our hosts. They were worried and alluded to stories of British trickery, so I decided to allay their fears and fly back to Tehran the next morning. When we bade farewell to Minister Castle, we were cordial, thanking her for her warm hospitality and useful information. She had, of course, been apprised of the breakdown in negotiations, so she conveyed her regard for Hoveyda with a certain coldness, stating only that she yet hoped our trip would yield positive results.

Back in Tehran, before I began drafting my report, I met with Dr. Sheikh and briefed him fully on our sojourn in England. Then we met with Hoveyda at his residence, where I gave him the gist of the report I proposed to write. He nodded, then laughed. He had not been aware, he joked, that the Alam clan had lowered its rates of bribery so steeply!

On Hoveyda's instructions, I said nothing about bribery in my report. But when Hoveyda submitted the report to the Shah, he told him verbally what I had uncovered, and I later learned that the Shah had been furious. In his memoirs, Alam recalled being interrogated by the Shah on this matter. "When His Majesty questioned me about the embezzlement," Alam wrote, "I was extremely worried and spent an agonizing night beforehand." It seems that Alam gave the Shah his word that he would investigate the issue and submit a full report. The long and short of it was that he arranged for a sum of almost $3 million to be returned from his personal bank account.

A key player in all these deals was Shapour Reporter, known as the head of the British intelligence service (MI6) in Iran, as his father had been before him. He acted as the principle go-between for many large-scale contracts between the government of Iran and top British companies. Reporter had gained the exclusive rights to import sugar for a close friend of the Shah, and he worked to steer huge urban reconstruction projects and arms manufacturing contracts to British companies. In every case, all the parties got very lucrative deals at the expense of the government. Although he was a British subject, Reporter thought of Alam's house as his own, often played cards with members of the Alam family, and was as their confidant. He had greased the wheels of Puyan's deal with his own hands.

Dr. Sheikh and I knew that our work would make us the targets of powerful individuals and their friends in SAVAK. Sure enough, one day in 1975, Hoveyda summoned us to his office. Before we had even walked in the door, he berated us, taking us to task for our lack of respect toward the nation and its dignitaries.

"How dare you show disrespect to the nation's most esteemed personalities?" he shouted. Then he pushed a button on a tape recorder on his desk, and Dr. Sheikh and I were astounded to hear a recording of a telephone conversation we had had several days before. SAVAK had bugged our telephones, it seemed, and recorded our friendly, off-the-cuff conversation. We had been talking about the Dr. Eqbal, a leader of the shadow power. After honoring him with several expletives, we had speculated why he was condoning corruption in his department. Hoveyda, still shouting angrily, informed us that Dr. Eqbal had gotten hold of the tape through SAVAK and had sent it to His Majesty, complaining that he had been sworn at and insulted.

I tried to explain, but Hoveyda gestured for us to keep quiet and pointed his finger toward a chandelier above, while he continued shouting at us. Even the Prime Minister's office was bugged! As he continued to heap displeasure on us, he ushered us courteously out of his office, all the while loudly declaring that he would figure out how to punish us later. The words were for the benefit of SAVAK agents who were listening in. As we reached the threshold, he whispered into Dr. Sheikh's ear: "I'll see you two for dinner on Wednesday at my mother's place."

Hoveyda used to visit his mother for dinner each Wednesday night, and when Dr. Sheikh and I met him there, he took us to the courtyard without a word. SAVAK had bugged his mother's house, too, he said. He urged us always to take extra care when talking about people in high places, since SAVAK had planted bugging devices almost everywhere in clocks, flower-pots, and telephones. He also warned us that our drivers, close associates, and secretaries would all be under pressure to report our every move, meeting, and conversation. Even the distant fruit peddler outside our home turned out to be a SAVAK informant.

Later, we learned more about SAVAK's activities. Thousands of people spent their lives listening to conversations and collecting data. It wasn't only treason or espionage they were looking for—it was opportunities for black-mail. Their snooping gave SAVAK agents information they could use to serve their own interests instead of the nation's. While the urban guerrillas of Fadaee Khalq and other extremist religious groups were training in terrorist camps in Libya, Palestine, Syria, and Yemen, SAVAK agents were spending their time and money abroad in the cabarets and casinos of London, Paris, Rome, Washington, Berlin, and Tokyo.

I had several personal encounters with SAVAK agents. Once, Dr. Sheikh and I went with two other Iranian physicians to the annual conference of the World Health Organization in Geneva, where we stayed in a villa rented by the Iranian government. Two SAVAK agents had been assigned to guard and shadow us, but the day we arrived they disappeared, and we didn't see them again.

Things were more serious, however, when the driver of Parviz Sabeti's wife shot an innocent man, and I became embroiled in the cover-up. The incident occurred at the Charles Jourdan boutique in downtown Tehran, when I was running the Tehran Clinic. Sabeti's wife arrived to do some shopping, and after somehow managing to misplace her handbag, she accused a young woman, who was buying shoes for her wedding, of having stolen it. When her fiancé protested at the insult to his bride-to-be, the driver drew his revolver and, without a word, shot the young man in the head.

He was brought to the Tehran Clinic Emergency Room and died two hours later. Almost immediately, SAVAK agents showed up and ordered everyone to keep silent about the incident. When an agent appeared with a message from Sabeti, demanding that I keep the news from reaching the public, I held my tongue. Even if I had wanted to keep it secret, it was not within the realm of possibility. News of the tragedy could not to be contained, and it was soon common knowledge throughout the city. That was the first time I came into conflict with SAVAK, and it foreshadowed a great many future problems.

CHAPTER 16

LACK OF MEDICAL EMERGENCY SYSTEM

In 1976, a new cabinet reshuffle pushed Puyan out of the cabinet and merged the Ministries of Health and Social Security into a new agency, headed by Dr. Sheikh. I was reappointed as his Vice Minister. The shakeup had been an embarrassing defeat for the shadow power, and we had already managed to get in the bad graces of many of the major players. And since we were inheriting a corrupt, incompetent organization, we realized it would be difficult to get anything done without stepping on more toes and making more enemies. SAVAK, that powerful bully of the shadow power, was up in arms against our promotions, but Hoveyda ignored its warnings. It was an unprecedented move to disregard SAVAK's objections, but once Hoveyda presented us to the Shah, we were the new Minister and Vice-Minister of Health and Welfare.

Iran in those days suffered from shortages of adequate health facilities and medical manpower; most statistics showed us having only about one-fifth the coverage that was normal in developed countries. Other studies suggested the situation was far worse, with 75 percent of doctors concentrated in large cities and a quarter of all specialists located in the capital of Tehran. People in the sixty thousand villages scattered throughout the country were basically deprived of health care. Those in desperate need of medical services had to cross the primitive, badly maintained roads between isolated villages and the cities.

Most Iranian physicians were paid a government salary. We discovered that while salaried doctors were paid for eight hours of work, their actual government work totaled only two to four hours per day—although in their private practices, however, their effective work rate was twelve hours a day.

Iran's salary system kept the efficiency of governmental health services at an abysmal level, while substantially increasing physicians' income. It was ripe for reform, so Dr. Sheikh and I introduced a new fee-for-service system, which substantially increased the volume and efficiency of their work. Twelve hundred Iranian physicians, who had been trained and living in the U.S. and Europe, were attracted to the new payment system and returned to Iran.

The next problem was hiring enough physicians to fill positions in outlying areas. We hoped that constructing modern hospital facilities, improving working conditions, and increasing legitimate physician income would be sufficient to attract Iranian physicians working abroad, who could bring with them knowledge of advanced medical procedures and technology. Still, even in the best case scenario, there would not be enough doctors to fill the gaps. So we hire fifteen hundred foreign doctors from countries that were producing more graduates than their medical systems could absorb—using Iran's oil wealth to draw physicians from places like India, Pakistan, and the Philippines. The "brain drain" phenomenon was common for developed countries with strong economies and good social possibilities, and we were now able to make use of it ourselves. Since Indian and Pakistani doctors were often familiar with the Persian culture, a short, intensive course in Farsi and local customs was enough to prepare them to be sent off to small villages in mountainous or remote regions.

We knew that in inaccessible hamlets, where doctors were reluctant to live, local manpower could provide medical first aid, which was better than nothing and could be a lifesaver in certain cases. So we worked to select young men and women who could read and write and inaugurated intensive courses to train them to provide basic services in their communities. In the first year, we trained ten thousand people throughout the country.

In one village in Fars Province, a farmer dug a well for drinking water, assisted only by his four children, and prepared a room in his mud-brick dwelling to be used as a medical clinic. The day we went to his village to inaugurate the clinic, the hard-working, suntanned farmer shed tears of joy. He thanked me for a job well done, and I had a very hard time reminding him that he had accomplished most of the work himself.

In Zanjan Province, training local people was also of great benefit. Three villages there were all served by the same open-ditch water supply which came from the mountains that served for both drinking water and sewage disposal. The doctor in a local clinic told me that each summer, up to thirty children died from diarrhea and food poisoning in surrounding villages. With the assistance of a young aide, however, the number of deaths had drastically declined. The aide had collected enough money to construct a septic sewage well. After training people to boil their drinking water and wash their hands, he managed to greatly reduce the incidence of sickness in these villages. The cost of training these young men and women was relatively insignificant, but their heroic efforts dramatically improved the quality of life.

Another problem we needed to solve was that emergency medical services were nonexistent. Hospitals and clinics might have an old, rundown white van with the word "Emergency" written on both sides. Their untrained drivers mainly used them to deliver messages and everything but patients. People who needed emergency care had to use any form of transportation they could find to get to the hospital, and far too many of them died before they got there.

In Tehran, I took personal charge of establishing a program of emergency technician training. I also procured ambulances that met international standards, equipped with radiotelephones. By calling the three-digit emergency telephone number 123, residents could now request emergency medical aid; within three minutes of a call, help would be on the way. This free emergency service was greeted with great enthusiasm by the general public, and decades later it is still considered to be one of the most widely appreciated services established by the former regime.

We also clamped down on corruption and double dipping. Some doctors, for example, became senators or congressmen while keeping their salaried position at government hospitals or universities. We notified them to select one position. These strategies created powerful enemies for us, including pharmaceutical companies and their middlemen; influential physicians who had lost their high incomes and prestigious positions; and the wheeler-dealers who found Ministry of Health contracts blocked. I was well aware of the deep-rooted corruption and power of these groups but hardly expected the fallout, which ranged from private death threats to public attacks by SAVAK and members of Parliament. I remained steadfast, but Dr. Sheikh and I wondered how long the situation might last. What would happen if the shadow power decided to take action in earnest?

For the most part, though, my days were busy with the odds and ends of government work. In one of my first days at the Ministry of Health, for example, I received an order from the Shah's office to address the problem of stray dogs in Tehran. The city had approximately two hundred thousand wild canines, and the mayor was unable to do anything about them. By calling the dogs a public health nuisance, they managed to make it our problem. I was shocked; nothing I had ever done had prepared me for this kind of work.

I first contacted officials of the Sanitation Department. They told me that the municipality had traditionally killed stray dogs by throwing poisoned meat into the streets. Things had changed, however, when one of Princess Shams's dogs died from eating the meat. She pushed the municipality to change its procedure, so it started rounding the dogs up and putting them to sleep. Each dog had a bounty of nearly two dollars, and thousands of dogs were delivered on a daily basis. Still, the dog population seemed to remain constant.

As I studied the problem, I discovered that dog-pound officials were selling impounded dogs to street dealers for a dollar and then, at the government's expense, buying the animals back. It was a thriving trade in wild dogs that made everyone happy, until the scheme was discovered. In the end, the Ministry of Health hired sharp shooters, who first anesthetized the dogs, and then put them to sleep humanely.

CHAPTER 17

THE GREAT CIVILIZATION

President Richard Nixon's close friendship with the Shah gave Iran tremendous advantages at the beginning of the 1970s. In the years since the Kennedy Administration, the words "democracy" and "human rights" were little more than slogans, and realists like Nixon's Secretary of State, Henry Kissinger, had pushed them aside in favor of close engagement with the Shah. In 1971, the British ended their protectorate presence in the Persian Gulf, withdrawing their forces, and Nixon—against Britain's and Saudi Arabia's wishes—agreed that Iranian forces should fill the power vacuum. Selling Iran unlimited military equipment, planes, and ships, Nixon encouraged the Shah to become the region's decisive power strategically, militarily, and politically. The Shah was quick to show his strength. Soon after, Iran swiftly and decisively recaptured the three islands of the Greater and Lesser Tombs and Abu Musa, giving notice of Iran's new status to all other Persian Gulf states.

Dreams of reviving the Iranian Empire began to consume the Shah's mind. He organized a lavish extravaganza celebrating Iran's twenty-five-century imperial monarchy and invited the world's heads of state to the ruins of Persepolis, the ancient, illustrious palace of Cyrus the Great. In the Shah's mind, Iran was at the threshold of what he termed "The Great Civilization." That was previously his name for the White Revolution, but much had changed since those early days. His program of modernization had initially been led by people like Hoveyda—selfless policymakers who were willing to stand up to landowners and the powerful in the name of reform. In those days, the Shah was a democrat and a reformer. But by the 1970s, the shadow power and American encouragement had inflated his massive ego.

convincing him to create bigger and more extravagant expressions of his own glory. "The Great Civilization" now signified huge events and building projects that, instead of enriching the country, lined the pockets of the corrupt. The bigger the Shah got, the more wealth went to the shadow power, and the more confused he became about the purpose of his rule.

In 1973, however, American politics were shaken to their roots by the Watergate scandal, and the aftershocks were sharply felt in Tehran. When the American people chose Jimmy Carter as president in 1974, they put their faith in a man who promised to restore America's greatness by putting aside the ideas of the past, placing democracy and human rights first, and limiting the power of the CIA. As Carter populated the State Department with his own people, a very different policy emerged toward Iran. With his appointment of Secretary of State Cyrus Vance and Deputy Secretary of State Warren Christopher, the State Department became a magnet for misguided and inexperienced liberal activists who were schooled in textbooks and idealist theories. In the meantime, the Shah had squandered much of his popularity among American politicians and officials, and Iranian students in the U.S. were becoming trusted sources of information for the U.S. State Department and Senate.

Nixon's Ambassador to Iran, Richard Helms, had been appointed in 1973, but he had been called back to Washington, D.C., for the Watergate investigation, so the U.S. embassy in Iran had been functioning without a head for quite a while. Carter's people opted to clean house completely, assigning an entirely new group of people to the embassy and taking a much harder line against their former partners in the Shah's government. Meanwhile, human rights activists in the U.S. disseminated exaggerated reports of torture and political detention in the Shah's jails. The American press followed suit and began reporting extensively on corruption and fraud in the Iranian government. Congress scrutinized sales of arms to Iran much more closely, and demonstrations against the Shah's regime, no matter how small, attracted widespread coverage in American media.

The Shah was deeply concerned by the sudden about-face of the United States. To deal with the uproar in the press, he began making efforts towards reform. Under Hoveyda's guidance, the modernization of Iran's infrastructure began progressing rapidly, and the economy began booming from an influx of oil revenue. The uncontrolled injection of huge sums of money into the Iranian monetary system, however, created a problem. Iranian economists noted that middlemen, foreign and domestic, were not sitting idle. Every day, people with friendly ties to the imperial court used their connections to introduce new projects to the Shah.

Iran's military expenses were estimated to be about 12 percent of its GDP—three to four times that of Britain or France. When the armed forces recommended projects to the government, no one dared to say no. Their confusing, mismanaged projects, however, had a negative effect on the country's larger development plans and drained Iran's monetary reserves. To complicate matters further, Hoveyda's government had no authority over SAVAK's activities or those of the National Iranian Oil Company. The Plan and Budget Organization had to prepare the nation's annual budget without even knowing how much revenue was actually coming from oil exports, while the Atomic Energy division carried out its activities with only the Shah's supervision. The projects and entities not under official government control were ballooning in size and became a growing source of the shadow power's wealth and influence.

Meanwhile, to deal with the bad press he was getting, the Shah ordered Hoveyda to prepare a report on the conditions of political prisoners in SAVAK jails, which he could then use. SAVAK claimed that there were no more than three thousand political prisoners in Iran and that they were never mistreated or tortured. Hoveyda, however, had doubts about those claims. He advised the Shah that if His Majesty thought the information presented by SAVAK was reliable, the most convincing approach would be to allow international agencies to visit Iranian prisons and ascertain the truth for themselves.

After consulting with SAVAK's chief, General Nassiri, the Shah gave the go-ahead, and Hoveyda called Dr. Sheikh and me to a meeting in his office. He began to explain the situation and formally requested that we visit the prisons to find out if SAVAK's report was accurate. He emphasized that prison officials and SAVAK had already received specific orders to facilitate our visits and give us their full cooperation.

Dr. Sheikh and I exchanged worried glances. Hoveyda was well aware that SAVAK harbored deep grudges against both of us. Why was he trying to involve us in this dangerous game? Everyone in Iran knew that, under Parviz Sabeti, torture had become SAVAK's main tool for interrogation. Hoveyda and General Ayadi, the Shah's physician and closest companion, knew this as well as anyone. They must also have known that our report would catch SAVAK in a compromising position and that we would face stiff retaliation for our involvement.

Quick on his feet, Dr. Sheikh mildly pointed out that SAVAK had never trusted the two of us, calling us the "adventurous pair." A report from us might seem like a political ploy and do more harm than good. Perhaps, he suggested, such an important duty should be entrusted to doctors who held no official government positions and had made no enemies. Hoveyda promptly agreed. After asking us to nominate suitable candidates for the job, he asked General Ayadi to appoint someone from the Armed Forces whom he trusted to take part in the mission.

We left Hoveyda's office with mixed feelings. I was nervous, of course; both of us knew we were putting our heads in the lion's mouth. But we also trusted Hoveyda. However treacherous the assignment might be, we knew that he would have carefully calculated the risks and wouldn't put us in danger without good reason. The results were a foregone conclusion, of course; everyone knew that SAVAK was engaging in torture. If Hoveyda was asking us to put together the report, we assumed it was time to reveal that secret to the world. I don't know how much the Shah really knew about what was going on, or how much he wanted to know. My guess is that Hoveyda made the risky assumption that the Shah really wanted the facts to come out, and that it was an important enough opportunity to risk our lives. While it might seem that he was putting us in harm's way and taking the high road himself, his reputation was our ace in the hole. If Hoveyda got in trouble, we would all be in trouble. By keeping his own hands clean, however, he would have power to protect us.

Dr. Sheikh and I chose three physicians of integrity whom we guessed would be courageous enough to handle such a sensitive job, and we sent them off to complete their investigation. As expected, the group's reports starkly contradicted SAVAK's claims on almost every point. After noting the ways that SAVAK had tried to hamper their investigation, their final report was damning and thorough. Based on visits and interviews with over three thousand political prisoners, they showed that beatings and mental torture had been daily occurrences until six months prior to the investigation. After that date, physical torture had ceased, but SAVAK was still using techniques of psychological torture.

When they submitted their report to Hoveyda, he carefully passed it along to the Shah, unopened and in its original envelope. General Ayadi was present in the room as a witness. Hoveyda wanted neither the Shah nor SAVAK to suspect his involvement in the report. Since Ayadi was one of the Shahs' most trusted men, keeping him in the loop could help shield the Prime Minister from the fallout. I kept a copy of the report in my own safe, although I didn't think about it much at the time.

As we had expected, reaction was swift. Sabeti sent us indirect word that reporting on SAVAK's use of torture was playing with fire and that there would be repercussions. Attacks began in media outlets controlled by SAVAK, and the agency spread false news through rumors in countries with censored news media. The bigger the lies that SAVAK circulated, the faster they spread. I was rumored to be an American intelligence agent making vast sums of money from corrupt contract awards. Even Helen was tarred by SAVAK's smear campaign. One newspaper stated that her father was former Ambassador and CIA head Richard Helms, and another claimed that she was Helms's secretary. Helen had never even worked at the American embassy.

Despite these attacks, Helen was enjoying her happiest, most rewarding years in Iran. When our son Cyrus was born in August 1969, Helen had quit her job at the United Nations and started involving herself in charity work for disabled orphans. Set up by the Tehran Municipality, the center was badly managed and short of funds, with inadequate facilities and poorly trained nurses. There were many tasks that desperately needed attention. Since there was no one to do them, Helen set up a system of volunteers. She presumed that people would do a better job if they worked from the heart instead of for money, and she especially tried to attract educated Iranian women who had little to do. She also personally took care of Amir, a frail, blind, disabled six-year-old boy. They bonded immediately, and Helen was so fond of him that she used to count the hours until she could visit him. She would often find him sitting near the door of his room, and when he heard her voice, he would squeal with happiness. As Helen spoke to him in Farsi, Amir would move his small hands over her face and stroke her long blond hair. She did not know how long he had been at the orphanage, but she did know that he could occasionally become angry and violent. On one of her weekly visits, Helen went to his room and found him lying down with both wrists restrained by cotton cloths. When she released the restraints, Amir hugged her and took her hand as they walked out to the playground. Only once was he aggressive toward Helen. They were walking back to his room, and Amir didn't want to go in, and he bit her arm in his frustration. Still, she often told me that the best part of her day was finding Amir sitting on the steps at the front door, eagerly awaiting her arrival.

On a larger level, however, conditions in Iran were reaching a breaking point. By 1975, the country's annual oil income was more than twenty-one billion, up from less than three billion dollars in 1973, but its relations with the West had disintegrated. The Shah wasn't satisfied with the nation's immense wealth. Behind everything that happened in the Middle East and all the countries and kings in the region, he saw the powerful hand of the Western oil companies. Who could blame him for that belief? After all, his father's abdication from, the coup that overthrew Dr. Mossadegh, and his own ascension to power had all been at least partially engineered by the oil lobbies. The Shah's father had given him a piece of advice that he always carried close to his heart: beware of oil and the British. And so, behind every development in the region, the Shah saw the hidden agenda of the oil companies and their patron, the British government.

The Shah knew that oil was a vital commodity, but the West had kept its price as low as drinking water, and he was determined to change that. As his hubris grew and he gained confidence in his power, he challenged the oil companies directly. In a show of force, he invited the major oil producers of the world to participate, with the Iranian parliament, in raising the price charged for oil that they exported to the West. He convinced most oil-producing countries to cooperate, but the industrial countries quickly protested. Oil and gas powered the world's economy, they argued, and any sudden increase in petroleum prices would upset the system, leading to economic bankruptcy around the world.

On their frequent trips to Tehran, President Ford's Secretary of State Henry Kissinger and Vice-President Nelson Rockefeller tried, in a friendly manner, to warn the Shah about the risks of his oil policy. But the Shah disregarded the Western powers' demands and continued his hard-line stance. Ignoring economic forecasts, he let himself believe that the increase in price would merely cause an insignificant uptick in the global inflation rate.

In September 1975, after Kissinger's shuttle diplomacy failed to keep the Shah from raising oil prices, President Ford grew fed up and sent a strongly worded, threatening letter to the Shah warning him against further price increases. He reminded the Shah of the consequences that inflation would have on American public opinion and the possible repercussions that Iran could face from an angry Senate. In his response, however, the Shah sharply rebuked President Ford. He argued that the price of American goods sold to Iran had increased by 30 percent over the same period, so Iran had no choice but to raise the price that it charged America for oil. From that point on, the Shah disregarded calls and letters from the French President, the German Chancellor, the British Prime Minister, and the Japanese Prime Minister, each of whom asked the Shah not to raise oil prices.

Even King Khaled of Saudi Arabia, in what he called "a brotherly fashion," tried to warn the Shah of the consequences his actions would have on oil-producing nations like Iran and Saudi Arabia. But with his ego unchecked, his view of the world was distorted. In an interview with a Reuters correspondent, the Shah stated that "oil can be used as a political weapon," and he even suggested that Organization of Petroleum Exporting Countries (OPEC) could sell its oil to the Soviets. These declarations were reckless and dangerous.

In 1976, Ford's Treasury Secretary Bill Simon and Secretary of Defense Donald Rumsfeld viciously went after the Shah. Simon—who once called the ruler "a mad man"— arranged an anti-Iranian deal with King Khaled of Saudi Arabia. It succeeded beyond their expectations.

In December 1976, when OPEC met at Doha in Qatar, the Saudis blocked the oil-price increase supported by the Shah. In addition, Saudi Arabia increased its own oil production from 8.2 to 11.8 million barrels a day and flooded the market with cheap oil. When the Shah handed the U.S. government a long shopping list of military equipment, moreover, he was startled to discover that the fighter jets, battle cruisers, submarines, tanks, radar systems, and long-range rockets he desired were not forthcoming. The U.S. had always welcomed arms sales to Iran, especially during Nixon's presidency, but political differences between the two countries had reached a breaking point. Democrats in Congress had never been fond of the Shah and mistrusted his motives, especially since he was purchasing the most advanced military equipment in the world.

The Shah reacted in a harsh, confrontational manner. "We have no choice but to procure our requirements from new sources," he declared. "We take orders from no one and are under no one's influence." His insistence on establishing atomic energy facilities and secret negotiations with South Africa and Australia over the purchase of uranium only increased American suspicions and made the situation worse. Rumsfeld's Pentagon then deliberately inflated the cost of American weapons sold to Iran, jacking up Iran's payments to the United States, in some cases, by 80 percent.

The Shah was checkmated. Iran's oil production plunged 38 per cent. The country had a 30 percent inflation rate, and national income plunged by a third. Iran's economy was in crisis. The country could no longer rely on an inexhaustible supply of oil revenues to keep things together. Unprecedented inflation was causing the price of goods and services to rise uncontrollably, while foreign oil companies were reducing the volume of oil purchases from Iran as part of a concerted campaign. As revenues decreased, the costs of large infrastructure projects spiraled higher and higher.

The chaos took its toll on Hoveyda. To those who knew him well, he was an optimist full of hope for the future, but now his friends seemed to be looking at a different man. Hoveyda appeared more and more care-worn, ground down by the burdens of his office and his enemies' attacks. When Dr. Shahgoli, one of his close friends, visited him at home one day, he found Hoveyda a shadow of his former self. He always wore an orchid boutonnière that his wife, an artistic and engaging woman, pinned on his breast pocket every morning. According to Shahgoli, however, Hoveyda was now so sad that even the orchid on his breast looked like it was limp and dying. After a drink, the Prime Minister said that he worried about the country's economy and that the blessing of oil wealth was turning into a curse. Thieves, like termites, were eating away at the very foundation of the country's infrastructure. Dr. Shahgoli said he had never seen Hoveyda so depressed and asked whether he believed it was time to resign. Hoveyda only shook his head; he was so deeply involved that he couldn't even contemplate such a step.

Hoveyda was not the only official feeling the strain. One night, Dr. Sheikh and I took refuge in a hot sauna. I was feeling tired and depressed, and Dr. Sheikh was in no better shape. We both felt like fish swimming against the current. Finally, I told him that I had decided to return to the private sector in Iran or go back to the United States before I ran out of steam. I felt that the structure of the government was shaky, including Hoveyda himself. Many of my friends in high positions were anticipating changes. I was confident of my decision, but I didn't have the courage to tell Hoveyda. Anyone who received an order from the Shah need the Shah's approval to resign. After everything he'd been through, how could I ask him for permission to quit now?

Dr. Sheikh saw that I was serious about my decision, so he took it on himself to meet with Hoveyda and discuss my case. To my surprise, Hoveyda didn't oppose my request, and he volunteered to discuss the matter with the Shah. But now was not the best time, he cautioned; I should wait a few months and, in the meantime, continue my regular duties.

About two months later, a colonel from the Special Imperial Office sent word that Hoveyda wanted to meet with me. Early the next morning, I found a man who was about forty years old waiting for me at my office. He looked like a young businessman, but he said he was an officer, serving directly under General Fardoust, who carried out His Majesty's orders in special situations. As we chatted, he told me some cloak-and-dagger stories about past assignments. The tales sounded like they were from a spy novel, but I had no doubt that they were true.

"I've been investigating you for about eight weeks now," he said casually. His office, he informed me, had scrutinized everything about my life and work, up to the present date, and he began telling me details of my family and professional life. Politely, he described my time in the United States, my friends in the past and present, parties and government meetings I had attended, the balances of my bank accounts, and the names of my enemies. I sat there, astonished, as he listed—carefully and with great precision—details of practically every move I had made in the past decade. The effort and manpower expended to collect all this information had been prodigious.

When he was sure that he had gained my full attention, he pulled notes from his briefcase and began interrogating me about international drug companies, the U.S. Food and Drug Administration, our problems with discontented physicians, and suspicions regarding our contract with Ross Perot's Electronic Data Systems Company. We talked about new hospital construction in the abstract and particular contacts I had with Pars Hospital and the Tehran Clinic. The officer was especially concerned about the potential misuse of funds and illegitimate contacts, but I had nothing to hide and told him so. When we were finished, I commented that I was certain that nothing I'd said was new to him. "You have so many details in your briefcase," I said, "that I'm sure the answers to all your questions are already at your fingertips. Whatever your findings are, I accept them."

With a small smile, he said my guess might be correct, but that it was his duty to meet with me and include my responses in his report. I was glad he had done so, I explicitly told him, because I saw the hand of SAVAK in each of the issues he had raised. Behind every question he was prompted to ask, I could imagine the lies that were being told about me. I was very familiar with them through SAVAK's personal vendetta against me, and I didn't have to guess.

I was also familiar with the Iranian bureaucracy and prepared to defend myself. Long ago, I had started keeping a personal archive, creating a copy of every document pertaining to every deal or contract in which I was involved. After explaining this to the young officer, I offered him copies of any documents he would need, and we spent a few minutes combing through file cabinets for the appropriate paperwork.

About two weeks later, Prime Minister Hoveyda met with the Shah on the Kish Island, and His Majesty ordered General Fardoust to read out the results of my interrogation. The Special Imperial Office, Fardoust said, had found all allegations against me to be without merit and categorically rejected them. Dr. Aram, the report stated, was a capable and brave member of the government. The Shah then directed Fardoust to prevent Dr. Eqbal or SAVAK from interfering in the workings of the Health Ministry.

Hoveyda congratulated me with the good news. General Fardoust sent me a personal message, asking to be informed if SAVAK caused any problems for me. There were no more complaints from Dr. Eqbal, and a SAVAK agent even visited me at my office one day to convey Parviz Sabeti's message of congratulation. But he also, ominously, mentioned on his way out that my file at SAVAK was still open. I sat in my office for a long time afterwards, mulling that over.

At a reception later that month, I had a chance to thank Hoveyda for supporting his subordinates, something that was all too rare. He smiled somewhat wearily and told me that it was not so difficult to support me.

"You are like a basketball," he said. "The harder they hit you, the higher you seem to fly!"

Hearing these words, from a man like Hoveyda, was almost worth the trouble.

CHAPTER 18

DIPLOMATIC DELUSIONS

By time President Jimmy Carter took office in 1977, the United States had a totally changed diplomatic posture toward Iran. Instead of the close relationship President Nixon had established with the Shah, the Carter Administration, especially the President's new envoy to Iran, was impatient for change and had a negative, cynical perspective toward the Shah.

In 1973, President Nixon had appointed Richard Helms U.S. ambassador to Iran. Helms, the former director of the CIA, was an experienced diplomat who knew the region well, respected its people, and strove to understand them. He had been the Shah's schoolmate in Switzerland and had wide social contacts in Tehran, and his desire to know the country through its people served him well. Helen and I knew Helms and his wife, Cynthia, socially, and he worked hard to get to know as many people as possible in the capital.

President Jimmy Carter, however, replaced Helms with William Sullivan, whose approach to Iran could not have been more different. Sullivan saw the country through dark glasses, as the Farsi proverb goes: no matter where he looked, he only saw the worst in everything. His biased point of view was evident throughout his book, *Mission to Iran*, from its distorted facts and mangled Iranian history to his distaste for the country and its population. Although Sullivan was a career diplomat, he had never anticipated being sent to Iran and didn't welcome the assignment. After serving in Laos and the Philippines, where he had gained a taste for "adventurous" diplomacy, he expected to be sent to Mexico and was greatly disappointed when he was posted to Tehran instead. Even so, with only the most elementary information about the country, he arrived in Iran full of preconceived notions and a desire to create sweeping changes in a nation that he hardly understood.

Of course, Sullivan was not the only American diplomat who was out of his depth. Not one American at the U.S. Embassy in Tehran knew Farsi, so their contacts with Iranians were limited to a handful of people who spoke English. Sullivan refused to consult with the former embassy staff; as a result, in contrast with Helms, he had only a limited perspective on the country. Since he socialized only with the few English-speaking Iranian families, he had a view of the Iranian people that was confined to the smallest subset of Western-educated, liberal-minded individuals. That, perhaps, had a great deal to do with his misconceptions about the Ayatollah Khomeini and his intentions.

Sullivan also drew much closer than Helms to Britain's ambassador to Iran, Anthony Parsons. Parsons was fluent in Farsi, and because of his long service in various Middle Eastern countries, he was friendly with many prominent politicians in the region. Sullivan relied on Parsons for information on the politics and sensitivities of Iran, and he and Parsons became something of a united front in advising the Shah. So obvious was their connection that the Shah himself sent Sullivan a message, through one of the ambassador's friends within the government, warning the "honored U.S. Ambassador" not to follow so closely in the footsteps of the British, who "had mobilized the mullahs" with "devastating results for our country," the Shah cautioned. "Don't make the same mistake again!"

But Sullivan ignored the Shah's advice. Instead, he spent a great deal of time trying to undermine what he viewed as wrongheaded strategies that the architects of Iran's new economy were trying to put in place. Sullivan wanted human rights established in Iran, immediately and without delay, and he worked with the British to set aside the policies of engagement that men like Richard Helms had tried to use to reform the country. In theory, nothing had changed: Helms and Sullivan would have agreed that their ultimate goal was a stable, democratic Iran. But Sullivan didn't want to wait for progress or listen to anyone in the current regime. Instead of trying to reform the regime itself, he worked against it. He was happy to establish links with groups that opposed the Shah, regardless of their politics. As this shift in U.S. policy grew obvious, anti-regime activities became more open, and the political situation grew more explosive.

In June 1977, Cyrus Vance, America's new Secretary of State, arrived in Tehran—not to confer with the Shah, but to inform him of changes in the U.S. government's policies on Iran. To convince people that a new era had begun, he called for Hoveyda's ouster and demanded that the country's politics and economy become more open. If Vance and Sullivan had understood Iran better, they might have realized that Hoveyda was one of the few people in the regime who was working for the very goals they were espousing. But they were following plans cooked up by think tanks in Washington and by men in the State Department who knew only what their ideology told them.

Years later, John Stemple, then the highest ranking official in the U.S. embassy, wrote that the plans U.S. diplomats received from think tanks were more based on slogans and sentiment than on local context. Everyone agreed about Iran's long-term importance, but the neophytes in the State Department demanded speedy change, without understanding the possibility for revolution. Blinded by their theories and ignorant of the reality on the ground, they struck at Hoveyda, one of the only allies they had, if they had known it.

As Sullivan became more extreme in his demands, the Shah walked a fine line, attempting to placate him and trying to pursue Hoveyda's vision. In an annual speech he gave during the anniversary celebration of Iran's Constitution, the Shah promised in his annual speech that, while new changes and developments were underway, he had not and would not bow to American pressure. "For us," he said, "democracy is not an imported commodity. Freedom will only come in its Iranian context." But there was no Iranian democracy under the Shah.

The monarch was still relying on Hoveyda and Alam. But the day after his annual speech, Hoveyda presented his formal resignation as Prime Minister. The Shah quickly replaced him with Jamshid Amuzegar and named Hoveyda Minister to the Imperial Court, replacing Alam, who was then lying on his deathbed in a Paris hospital. When Alam learned about his dismissal, he was greatly hurt and reportedly complained that the Shah should have dismissed him while he was in Tehran. "He could have consulted with me on my replacement," he said, "even if it was just a formality." But Alam was loyal to the end and wrote a few confidential letters to the Shah warning him of the many threats to his throne, particularly from Britain. The Shah disregarded his letters.

Amuzegar was appointed Prime Minister at a critical time in Iran's history. Although he was a proficient technocrat known for his honesty and integrity, political experts never considered him a particularly clever politician. Unfortunately, events proved them more or less right. Amuzegar became Iran's Prime Minister as the country was plunging into an ocean of trouble, and he was not experienced enough to keep the ship of state from sinking.

In London, Paris, Palestine, and especially in Najaf, Khomeini was suddenly taking on a new role and importance. With calculated cunning, he claimed the leadership of "all Iranian freedom seekers" and made common cause with the Shah's secular opposition. The ayatollah declared that, "in order to destroy the foundations of despotism and political oppression, I shall fight until the Shah's cruel regime is destroyed."

The British were already secretly working to destabilize the regime. When the American government openly pressured Iran to loosen its political controls, the resulting chaos in the regime provided the perfect nesting ground for Khomeini's activities. The opposition groups were isolated and dispersed, with many commanders and few foot soldiers. When Khomeini entered the political fray with the support of his religious guerillas, they were able to take charge of the primary anti-regime campaign. Khomeini's commanders, however, hid the true nature of the Islamic Republic—its religious fanaticism, decadence, and superstition—under their turbans. When Khomeini managed to draw hundreds of thousands of religious fanatics onto the streets of Tehran, the media began calling him the "World Leader of the Shia" and gave his activities twenty-four-hour-hour coverage. Liberal and human rights activists were deceived by his slogans and followed him like sheep, bleating his praises.

Perhaps moderate Grand Ayatollahs like Shariatmadari, Milani, or Golpayegani could have played a constructive role in keeping Khomeini's revolutionary fire from engulfing the nation. But one of Amuzegar's first actions in office was to cut the monthly allowances that Hoveyda had been paying these clerics for years, alienating the very people who could have been key allies. Amuzegar seemed not to understand what he had done and explicitly rejected any possibility of making common cause with Islamic leaders. "The era of reactionary mullahs is over," he said, "and Iran has adopted a new path, running in opposition to them." They were laudable words, in a way, but he lacked the political skill to make them a reality.

Amuzegar announced that his mission would be to open up Iran's political climate and bring the government closer to the people. But in these efforts, he completely failed. He rarely mixed with ordinary people and, fearful of confronting the political chaos that was engulfing the country, avoided addressing the widening gulf between the Shah and the opposition.

Dr. Sheikh and I remained in Amuzegar's cabinet, but our relationship with him was always cold and indifferent. Anything requiring the Prime Minister's approval was likely be left undone. The budget was a problem, and all the passion from the Hoveyda days, however hard-fought and frustrated, had vanished from our daily activities. Instead of facing the growing crisis, everyone simply waited for the government to do something—even those who were in the government themselves. Despite Amuzegar's experience in economics, his limited efforts to restrain inflation were fruitless, so prices soared. Farmers in rural areas were forced to migrate to large cities in search of work, but the lack of jobs only encouraged them to join the growing demonstrations.

Amuzegar, meanwhile, lacked the power or influence to control the many expensive projects that his office was supposedly supervising. In a much-publicized speech, he announced the establishment of a commission consisting of the Shah; Moeinian, his personal secretary; and General Fardoust, a trusted confident of the monarch, nicknamed the Shah's shadow. The commission was charged with investigating and prosecuting influential people who had misappropriated government funds. But while its work was broadcast live on radio and television, it quickly turned into a ridiculous sideshow, with no obvious purpose other than to discredit Prime Minister Hoveyda and his team. People knew who the corrupt officials were, and there was a glaring absence of any of the big names in this carefully staged political drama. In the end, the whole soap opera came to a grand finale without convicting a single person. The process had a demoralizing effect on public opinion, which now understood that the government was not interested in frying the big fish.

Ambassador Sullivan claimed that Hoveyda's ouster was the direct result of his own activities and reported to the State Department that Amuzegar's appointment was a good sign. Amuzegar was an "able and positive" man, he said, but under the direct guidance of the U.S. State Department's undersecretaries, Sullivan pursued a vast, subversive program to promote "liberalization" by working with opposition groups. He boldly contacting a variety of dissident organizations so openly that most of the details were reported in the media.

During the fall of 1977, President Jimmy Carter made a state visit to Iran. In his speech at the banquet held in his honor, he paid tribute to the Shah's efforts, which had, as he put it, made Iran "an island of stability in a turbulent Middle East." Such rhetoric led the Shah to conclude that Carter was endorsing his leadership in Iran and that the Americans would continue to give him a free hand in running the affairs of his country. It was a dangerous misperception.

The U.S. State Department was unhappy with the President's compliments to the Shah and redoubled its efforts to indicate its concerns with the monarch. Somewhat unexpectedly, SAVAK, at the same time, seemed to be applying the brakes to its ongoing crackdown on opposition forces, leading the regime's opponents to intensify their activities at the worst possible moment for the Shah.

In those days, the Ayatollah Khomeini, in exile in Najaf, Iraq, issued a powerfully worded statement accusing the Shah of being responsible for the death of his eldest son, Haj Mustafa. Predictably, an angry Shah instructed Hoveyda to prepare a media counterattack against Khomeini and have it printed in the newspapers. When Hoveyda penned a very balanced, measured response to Khomeini's tirade, however, the Shah's pride was not assuaged, and he ordered another bureaucrat from the Imperial Court to write a more forceful, insulting article. It was sent to the *Etelaat* newspaper to be printed in place of Hoveyda's, but the newspaper's editorial board declined to publish it, arguing that such a loaded attack on Khomeini would only provoke the public. The authorities, however, put such intense pressure on the editorial staff that the article appeared under the fictitious byline "Ahmad Rashidi Motlaq." Khomeini's supporters exploited the situation masterfully. The article, as predicted, led to widespread demonstrations against the Shah and Iran's monarchy. Demonstrations against the regime intensified, and it became increasingly common for civil servants to go out on strike in protest.

Though he held a key position, Hoveyda had, for all intents and purposes, been pushed aside. Against him was assembled a coalition of the Empress Farah, SAVAK, Prime Minister Amuzegar, and Ambassador Sullivan. All his efforts in his new position to clean up the Court only made the powerful elements around the Shah furious. Hoveyda pleaded with the Shah that the anticorruption campaign had to begin from His Majesty's own household, arguing that he had to deal decisively with the corrupt practices of his brothers and sisters and other relatives. The Shah, however, ignored all his requests. He even refused to sign rules and criteria that he had instructed Hoveyda to draft for dealing with conflicts of interest.

In February 1978, I traveled to Washington, D.C., as a member of the Joint Economic Committee of Iran-America, and the reception we received from our American counterparts was surprisingly cold. While the U.S. State Department didn't want our meeting covered by the media, I tried to make good use of the opportunity by negotiating with both the University of Pennsylvania and the University of Minnesota to promote the exchange of professors and students between our two countries.

One day, Cyrus Vance organized a working lunch in his office for the Iranian delegation. Ardeshir Zahedi—who had been ambassador to the U.S. when I was at Georgetown—was again Iran's Ambassador and attended the luncheon. I was seated next to Deputy Secretary of State Warren Christopher, who had just returned from a meeting with the Senate. He told me about the difficulties the Administration had dealing with Congress and, grinning sarcastically, quipped that we Iranians were lucky not to have such problems. Halfway through the meeting, a man entered the room and handed a file folder to Christopher, who examined it briefly and handed it back. It must have been important. After a moment's pause, he looked at me and asked my opinion of the Islamic *mujahedin*. "The Shah thinks they are just communists dressed up in Islamic garb," Christopher said. "But our experts think Islamic ideology couldn't ever coexist with communism."

I gave him the most diplomatic answer I could. "With the extensive information that you have," I said sarcastically, "I am sure you know better." I understood the gist of his question. The U.S. State Department was still dancing around the idea of supporting fundamentalist Muslims in Afghanistan, using them as proxies against the Soviet communists. Yet for all its sophistication, the intelligence service could not fathom that these fanatical Islamists posed the greater threat to American capitalism. It was a perilous misunderstanding.

CHAPTER 19

JIHAD

Islamic *jihad* was founded in earnest in 1979 when Muslims went to war against the Soviets in Afghanistan. Using British colonial tactics, with the help of the Saudis, the United States used Islamic fanaticism to mobilize the Afghan people against the Soviet materialists in their midst. In the short run, the Afghani victory was an embarrassing defeat for the Soviet Union, and its retreat was viewed as a mighty victory for democracy. But in the long term, the victory these Muslim fanatics won in defeating a mighty superpower only spurred them on to greater ambitions. After the war in Afghanistan, they rejected peaceful coexistence with the West and began to challenge the superiority of the western world.

The Soviet Union carefully noted how successfully capitalist governments fueled religious bigotry to fight communism. If the resentments of religious fanatics could be used against communists, why not use these same fanatics to attack capitalist governments? And so the Middle Eastern communist parties, changing their tactics, suddenly made a 180-degree turn from their scornful opposition to religion and adopted the guise of devotion to Islam.

In Iran, Dr. Ali Shariati was the first ideologist to reconcile religion with politics, mixing socialist thought with religious principles in ways that attracted youths worried about their future and eager to acquire knowledge. His books, especially *Marxism and Other Western Fallacies*, found many enthusiasts. Though he was opposed to fanatical groups and armed guerillas, he helped clear the way for organizations like *Fadaee* and *Mojahedin Khalgh* by transforming Shiism and anti-imperialism into political theology. Led by people like Dr. Shariati, the Communist Party set aside its ideological differences with religion and joined with Khomeini.

In a communist magazine in the Soviet Union, Iraj Eskandari, the Tudeh Party's veteran leader, wrote that Tudeh welcomed the religious campaign against the Shah and that the Shia clerics were a progressive force. Intellectuals, students, and all who were eager for freedom became Khomeini's obedient followers. Viewing religion as merely a means to obtain their freedom, they believed Khomeini's promises that the clerics would go to Qom after the Shah's downfall and not interfere with running the country.

When these groups first took up *jihad* against the Americans, their activities were insignificant. *Mojahedin Khalgh*, for example, was founded in 1962 as a vanguard terrorist group, but it wasn't until years later, when it began incorporating religious beliefs into its communist framework, that it became a potent political force. Pursuing political violence under the twin banners of religion and the fight against global oppression, the *mojahedin* trained terrorists in Palestinian, Libyan, Lebanese, and Syrian camps. After 1972, when Khomeini announced that it was the duty of all good Muslims to help the *mojahedin*, states like Libya provided millions of dollars to the group, and bazaar merchants in Iran volunteered financial support. My old friend Qotbzadeh was instrumental in engineering the group's rise, even though he was neither religious nor communist. By the mid-1970s, Islamic fanatacism, terrorism, and anti-western, anti-capitalist ideology had fused into a powerful and fearsome political force.

Its immediate target was the Shah's regime, supported and advised by western leaders. Henry Kissinger met with the Shah three separate times. Ronald Reagan, even before he ran for president, visited Tehran and was a guest of Ardeshir Zahedi, staying at his personal residence. He was ostensibly on a fact-finding mission, but he also came to give the Shah his support. Margaret Thatcher and David Rockefeller, president of Chase Manhattan Bank, both spent several days in Tehran and tried to brief the Shah on the devastating consequences that increasing the price of crude oil would have on the economies of industrialized countries. Their aim was to persuade the Shah not to insist on further price increases at OPEC and to dissuade him from trying to acquire more modern, sophisticated military arms.

These first-rate world statesmen never hesitated to advise the Shah about the growing political crisis in Iran. But he paid no attention to their counsel and failed to adopt the policies that they suggested. Conceited and demanding, the Shah was adamant in his desire for a powerful army and rising oil revenues, which had been flat in recent years. He also ignored those who urged him to adopt a Western-style democracy, believing that such a mode of government in Iran would lead to chaos.

Meanwhile, the political tide within Iran began to turn. In 1978, after the Shah removed General Nassiri as head of SAVAK and replaced him with General Nasser Moghadam, the pressure on the press eased to such an extent that some newspapers openly began supporting opposition groups. Some even printed the slogans chanted by Khomeini supporters. Respect for opposition parties was demonstrated in Parliament too, and its members began to criticize and even defame Hoveyda and his colleagues. These attacks became so virulent that it was clear that SAVAK's position had shifted. It was now aligning more with the opposition and quietly edging farther away from the Shah's government.

In increasing clashes with the opposition, the Shah always seemed to be the loser. He would resist reasonable terms in negotiations and then, under pressure, give in, accepting far less favorable conditions. He dragged his feet in making decisions until the best opportunities passed and he had no choice but to surrender. Increasing internal pressure gradually mellowed his resistance to outside influence. By then, however, because of his regime's lack of respect toward the religious establishment, it was no longer possible to stop Khomeini.

CHAPTER 20

OPERATION SCAPEGOAT

On August 19, 1978, the Rex movie theater in the southern Iranian city of Abadan was set on fire It was a barbaric act; more than five hundred innocent people were locked inside and burned alive. The newspapers were filled with the story, and people's faith in the government was rocked to the core. Many turned to another kind of faith. Before long, it was clear that the cinema fire was part of a larger, fast-spreading inferno. Political violence had been increasing for a long time, but suddenly Iranians understood that standing innocently on the sidelines was no guarantee of safety. While the crisis continued, no one was secure any longer.

Suspicion immediately fell on SAVAK, and people cried out for justice. In Najaf, however, Iraqi leader Saddam Hussein had kept a careful watch on Khomeini, and when his men turned up news that a man named Abdul Reza Ashour was responsible, they arrested him. Under "interrogation," Ashour confessed everything. But when he was extradited to Tehran, the city attorney in charge of his case released him within days and ordered the court's records sealed.

We now know more about what really happened. Since the intelligence gathered by Saddam's men would have clearly implicated Khomeini and his deputies, it is likely that the mullahs threatened the attorney: if he didn't release their man, they would have him killed. Days after Ashour returned to Iraq, Khomeini gave him a huge reception and declared that the Rex Cinema fire was a praiseworthy act, the "destruction of a rotten center of anti-Islamic culture." Setting fires at cinemas was part of Khomeini's larger strategy—

to make people afraid of things that he and other extremists declared were against Islam.

In Iran, however, everyone thought at the time that SAVAK was responsible, so when the opposition claimed that the government had been behind the fire, they easily believed it. Even the head of the U.S. Embassy's Intelligence division started asking questions about the government's hand in the affair. Sullivan, of course, knew better; he would have been informed if the fire had been SAVAK's doing. But he, too, was happy to blame the regime, and he carefully finessed the truth. He reported to Washington that "the people" blamed SAVAK, but he knew better.

The Rex Cinema fire was a tipping point. It created the "critical mass" of Iranians' anger and loss of faith in their government. Rioters chanted "Death to the Shah!" in the streets, and security forces clashed with violent mobs in Tabriz and Qom. In the face of this politically motivated violence, the government declared martial law across the country, and in Qazvin, Mashhad, Shiraz, Zanjan, and Kerman, angry protestors demanded the resignation of Prime Minister Amuzegar and his government.

The Shah, confused and depressed, refused to respond forcefully. He also refused to yield to any of the opposition's demands or hand powers to anyone else. While the Shah vacillated, Amuzegar deferred to the monarch's indecisiveness and did nothing. By August, however, he had had enough, and he resigned.

The Shah asked Jaafar Sharif-Emami to form a new cabinet, which would be called the "Government of National Reconciliation." Sharif-Emami, however, was one of the primary pillars of corruption in the country. No one with the slightest understanding of Iranian politics could fail to marvel that he was named the architect of reform. Sharif-Emami understood this better than anyone, but, as he told a friend, he would try to accomplish the impossible by accommodation, compromise, deals, and sacrifice.

First, Sharif-Emami tried to pose as an Islamic figure, stressing his family ties with Ayatollahs. He even struck up a dialogue with the religious reactionary bloc and made great efforts to back away from positions that were unpopular with the mullahs. He changed the Iranian calendar—which had begun with the Persian Empire of Cyrus the Great—to the Islamic calendar, putting Iran in step with the rest of the Muslim world. Then he ordered the closure of the country's gambling establishments and casinos, despite the fact that he had earlier helped the Pahlavi foundation gain a license to run the casinos. Finally, he declared that his government's top priority would be adherence to Islamic traditions, a move that was widely viewed as Islamic "window dressing."

The first few days of Sharif-Emami's premiership passed with no major incidents, and he began to hope that his political patchwork was paying dividends. Sullivan even reported to the State Department that Sharif-Emami's appointment was a good choice and crowed that his programs were already silencing Khomeini's tirades. Events, however, were still playing themselves out.

Several weeks after the new government was formed, Hoveyda tendered his resignation as Minister of the Imperial Court. He finally surrendered to the relentless campaign of opposition that the empress, SAVAK, and Sullivan had mounted against him. They were all uncomfortable with his power and proximity to the Shah. But Hoveyda, too, was unhappy in his role at the Imperial Court; he thought he was wasting his time there and believed that he would sooner or later be taken down. He hoped that his enemies would be satisfied with his resignation. As it turned out, however, nothing short of exile could ensure his safety.

In the meantime, the honeymoon was ending between Sharif-Emami's cabinet and the opposition groups. Khomeini's supporters had been biding their time while they gauged the resolve of the new government. It didn't take them long to realize the new cabinet's impotence, and their guerrilla units were soon on the streets again.

On October 4, 1978, Khomeini left Iraq for Kuwait, carrying an Iranian passport in the name of Ruhollah Mostafavi. He was not permitted to enter Kuwait, however, and had to return to Iraq. Sharif-Emami, meanwhile, successfully pressured the Iraqi government to expel Khomeini, while ensuring that France would accept the Ayatollah's request for admittance. So on October 7, Khomeini moved to Paris, where he found the world's media hanging on his every word. Suddenly, an unknown mullah from Iraq became a daily news item. From his Parisian center, he began plotting to overthrow the Shah and seize the nation of Iran as his domain.

In Iran, bearded, chanting men and black chador-draped women were waiting for Khomeini's order to strike. The grand Islamic festival of the *Eid e Fetr*, at the end of Ramadan, was the day of reckoning. Festival prayers are usually held that day in open spaces at the edges of towns, but the mullahs turned that religious event into a show of force to intimidate the Shah and impress the masses. A crowd of more than a million assembled at a designated place to give their *Fetr* prayers. As the commander of the Imperial Helicopters took the Shah up in the air to observe the prayer area, the monarch clearly saw how the people had responded to Khomeini's call. "For the first time," the commander later recounted, "I could see signs of fear on His Majesty's face."

The more the regime showed its indecision, the more Khomeini upped the stakes and violence. His followers engineered widespread strikes and forced government offices to close. In response, Sharif-Emami appealed to the "Sources of Emulation"—senior clerics whose precepts are accepted without question—as well as elders from the religious establishment in Qom, Najaf, Mashhad, and Karbala, to no avail. No one, not even the highest-ranking theologians, was willing to stand up to Khomeini and his supporters. The Communists, the Tudeh Party, the National Front, and even liberal intellectuals were intimidated.

Until then, the very heart of Shia tradition was that the faith had a diverse multiplicity of leaders. But as Khomeini's authority grew, he was presented as an infallible being guided by regular divine visitations. The BBC began calling him "Leader of the Shia Muslims of the World," and conspiracy theorists began blaming the British for again foisting reactionary Islam on Iran.

The Shah's advisers, however, did nothing to slow Khomeini's rise. In fact, with deluded faith in their own power, they accelerated the regime's decline. Everyone—from Prime Minister Sharif-Emami and his cabinet to the Empress Farah and the chief of SAVAK—struggled to convince the populace that those responsible for human rights violations would be brought to justice. By this time, the public had heard so many lies from the government that it looked on the regime's claims with extreme skepticism. When Sharif-Emami declared that the government's new slogan would be "Swift Justice for Corruption," we Iranians, among ourselves, called it "Operation Scapegoat." We knew that Prime Minister Emami himself was the ultimate symbol of corruption.

By that time, even his administration knew that the only way it could extract itself from the quagmire would be to set up some kind of public tribunal. In theory, this would raise citizens' confidence by bringing corrupt former officials to justice. But everyone—opposition groups, ordinary people, and top-ranking officials—knew how unlikely that would be. The people most guilty of corruption were those powerful politicians and businessmen who supported the Shah's iron-fisted rule and suppression of the people's rights. Would these men voluntarily expose themselves to popular justice and place themselves in the hands of people's tribunals? Anyone who knew anything about the way things worked in Iran laughed at the idea.

When foreign advisers suggested bringing a host of sacrificial lambs to trial, the Shah jumped at the plan. By blaming selected officials and businessmen in public show trials, he hoped the public would forgive the regimes' misdeeds. In this circus of justice, the innocence or guilt of the victims would be totally irrelevant. The regime would be able to engineer the spectacle, as well as whatever outcome it chose, and take revenge on former officials who were out of favor.

The scapegoat ploy began almost immediately. New cabinet members started launching relentless attacks on Hoveyda and top officials in his former cabinet—demanding their arrest on charges of corruption, followed by summary trials and immediate sentencing. When the Prime Minister presented the Shah with a proposal to follow through on these demands, however, the monarch hesitated at first—asking what charges were to be raised and suggesting that the Ministry of Justice gather evidence before officially charging the former ministers. "Your Majesty," Sharif-Emami suggested, "instead of trying them on charges of embezzlement, charge them with trampling upon the law." The Shah was again reluctant, however, reminding Sharif-Emami that any transgressions against the law would implicate the regime. "What could Hoveyda have done without my orders or blessing?" the Shah asked.

"Your Majesty," Sharif-Emami replied, "the law of the Constitution dictates that the sovereign is above responsibility. Only Hoveyda will stand accused." Still, the Shah declined to order the arrests.

As the scapegoating conspiracy was taking form, opposition forces intensified their attacks. Demonstrations and rioting gave way to armed assaults on police stations, and the list of murdered police officer rose steadily. Acts of arson became common. When the Prime Minister asked the Majlis to declare martial law in eleven cities, no one but the government paid attention. To the opposition, it didn't matter if the authorities issued strongly worded communiqués, since SAVAK's response was mild and ineffectual. Every day, scores of people were killed and injured, and the media's inflammatory reporting helped fuel the chaos. The newspapers even exaggerated the casualties, a gesture of sympathy with the opposition that played an instrumental role in fanning anti-regime feelings among the general public.

In a report on the Iranian crisis, Cyrus Vance stated that "the demonstrations of the summer of 1978, in particular the bloody clashes, fully illustrated the Shah's indecision. From that date onwards, new views were expressed with regard to the Shah in the White House. Personally I was strongly in favor of a political solution involving efforts to keep the Shah on his throne as a Constitutional Monarch if at all possible. But also without him." National Security Adviser Zbigniew Brzezinski, on the other hand, firmly believed that political stability in Iran could only come if the Shah weathered the storm and remained in power, and he was willing to engineer a military coup to ensure that result, if it became necessary.

When Vance and Brzezinski presented their opposing views to President Carter, it was still unclear which policy the U.S. government would back. But in a telephone call to the Shah, lasting about one and half-hours, President Carter urged him to take every measure to maintain the stability and security of his country. The Shah emerged from the conversation with Carter reassured that America was on his side. Sullivan, however, advised him that it was Carter's style to blow hot and cold and continued to advise against any direct action. Still, the Shah had been swayed, and he finally yielded to the pressure to arrest Hoveyda and other former top government officials. After allowing Sharif-Emami to submit a list of names prepared by Parviz Sabeti, the Shah struck out Hoveyda's name but allowed his prime minister to go ahead with the arrests, while cautioning him against rushing into things. The genie was now out of the bottle.

Sharif-Emami's plans were anything but judicious. The people on the list—mostly Hoveyda's colleagues—were to be arrested under Article 5 of the martial law, which waived any requirements that charges be substantiated by evidence or a court warrant. In "Operation Scapegoat," the sacrificial lambs were culled from the herd—men who had served their country with such distinction that they earned the enmity of the shadow power. Not one of the chief members of that powerful group was on the list; at the most, only a few of their underlings were offered for sacrifice.

Almost immediately, rumors began to circulate in the capital, and important officials or businessmen connected with the government began examining their options. The savvier ones sensed what was coming and didn't wait for the midnight knock on their doors. Before long, the exodus was in full swing. Private citizens were transferring many billions of U.S. dollars out of Iran, and airlines reported that all seats to major European and American destinations were booked for weeks.

I hadn't paid much attention to the rumors. One day, however, I got a call from General Mehdi Rahimi, the martial law commander and a close friend of mine. I should probably leave the country, he advised, even if it was just a precaution. I was astounded.

"I have never misappropriated any public funds," I protested. "I've never been a torturer or involved with criminals. I haven't even amassed any wealth. So why should I have to flee my homeland?"

CHAPTER 21

LAMBS TO THE SLAUGHTER

These, of course, were the wrong questions to ask, as I found out soon enough. On the morning of September 8, 1978, I was working at my office at the Imperial Medical Center when my secretary took a call from my eleven-year-old daughter Cathy. Her voice was shaking, and as soon as I heard her words, my heart seemed to stop. "What has happened?" I choked out. "Where is your mother?"

Helen and the children had been alone in the house. Someone had rung the doorbell, and when Helen opened the door, she found a middle-aged man in a dark suit. He had asked to see me, and Helen told him politely that I wasn't home. On his insistence, she said I had already left for work. He then wanted to use our telephone. Helen refused, but told him that there was a public telephone booth at the end of the block. He left, but only momentarily. Once again, the doorbell rang, and to Helen's surprise, she saw the same man on the doorstep. Now, however, there was another man with him, also dressed in a dark suit. He immediately put his foot in the door and pushed it open. Both men came in, brandishing revolvers. They pulled the telephone cord and began searching the house for me. When they realized I wasn't there, they stood in the hallway and didn't leave. When Helen asked them, "Who are you? What do you want?" they replied that they were from SAVAK. At that moment, Helen glanced at the framed document on the wall where they were standing. It was a beautiful copy of the Declaration of Independence, which she had recently hung in honor of its bicentennial anniversary. Her knees shaking with fear, she tried to keep calm while she served them tea. Meanwhile, unbeknownst to Helen, Cathy noticed that the agents weren't paying attention to her. She managed to get out onto the balcony and jumped to the garden level, where she raced to a telephone in the basement laundry room. She had written my new office telephone number on her hand and called me at once.

"They are after you!" Cathy warned me. "They searched the house and demanded your office address. Mom told them she doesn't know where you are, so they're waiting for you to come home. What should we do?"

I tried to ease Cathy's anxiety by maintaining my confidence. Laughing out loud, I told her that she, her mother, and her sister and brother shouldn't worry. There was obviously some kind of misunderstanding. Cathy should give the men my telephone number and tell them to call me. Then we'd straighten everything out, I reassured her.

I said goodbye to Cathy and hung up. Minutes layer, two SAVAK agents arrived at my office, blindfolded me, and took me to a prison, which I eventually learned was the Anti-Sabotage Committee's detention center. I was held for two weeks in a tiny, lightless cell, with hardly any food or contact with other humans. I was terrified, cut off from my family and any news outside the steel door of that coffinlike cell, with only two ragged blankets for warmth. As I heard the screams of tortured prisoners, I had no idea what was happening to my country, or what my fate would be.

Soon, however, other officials were seized as part of "Operation Scapegoat" and brought to that horrifying place, including Dr. Sheik; Reza Neqabat, former undersecretary of health; Mansour Rouhani, former agriculture minister; Fereidoun Mahdavi, former commerce minister; and Colonel Rasoul, a union leader and former police officer. We were moved into a crowded communal cell, and every day we would discuss news from the outside and pool our intimate knowledge of Iran's politics and the hidden machinations of the shadow power.

And then, one day, two weeks after I arrived, despite the wretchedness of our condition, there was a ray of sunlight. Officials informed our relatives that one member of each prisoner's family could visit us in prison. I waited impatiently, pacing like a death-row inmate before the last visit. Finally, in a small room, under the watch of a brooding SAVAK officer, my eyes met Helen's again, and we embraced. There was a lump in my throat, but I held her close and showered her with kisses. She wore a lovely cotton lilac dress that she knew I liked. She put on a brave face, but anyone could see the dejection in her sad eyes and her pale complexion. Wiping away tears, she asked me question after question, which I tried to answer in ways that would assuage her fears.

Was I being held in a shared cell or in solitary confinement? Was I being interrogated? How long would I be held, she asked. There were also practical issues. What should she do if my monthly salary check was not deposited? She felt weak and helpless and prayed for the strength to get through this. My father had died when he was only seven, and I had had assumed responsibility at an early age. I was a self-made man with a strong constitution, characteristics she had always admired. Not it was her time to be strong and stay positive for the sake of our family.

All things considered, I told her, my circumstances were not that bad. I had not been formally charged with anything. Several friends and colleagues were in custody with me, and we were able to spend this difficult time together. But I worried about the children. They were too young to understand what was happening, and I wondered how they were handling the news of my incarceration. But Helen told me that they were bearing up quite well, and she took, from inside her handbag, a piece of paper on which each of the children had written a few lines. When she tried to hand it to me, the SAVAK guard viciously snatched it from her, but after reading my children's words, he relented and placed the letter in my hands. It was a gift from the heavens. Through it, I could "see" my children and their bright faces, and they warmed my heart.

Helen told me that the children understood what was happening; at school, bad news circulated fast, and in those days, even school children had a keen interest in current events. When the kids heard things at school, they would talk about it with their mother when they came home, and Helen knew how to handle the situation. Without flinching, she helped them understand the harsh reality, while instilling confidence and optimism for the future.

I felt like a different person after I spoke with Helen, and I started to hope that our family would weather this storm. Helen was a good Catholic with strong convictions, and I felt warmed and heartened by her faith. She was absolutely sure that I would emerge from prison unscathed and that justice would eventually prevail. Being who she was, she could not think otherwise; as she told me, an innocent person might be taken to the gallows, but God would not let him be hanged.

I tried to share her optimism, but I knew that this was a different environment from the democratic life she had grown up with, where people had rights that the government respected. This much was certain—I could always trust her to be there for me and for the children. While I was locked up, she would be able to take care of life on the outside.

At this first meeting, we talked about our dwindling cash reserves and how to manage the family's daily expenses. I suggested that she take the children to the United States to be with her parents, but she refused to leave me behind, saying her fate was interwoven with mine. I desperately wanted my family to be safe but, selfishly, I was glad that they were nearby. I was extremely anxious and had a difficult time sleeping. What was going to happen to Helen and our children? How was I going to provide for them? How were they going to live? Our house in Tehran and villa in the Caspian Sea had been confiscated by the government.

Before the guards brought our brief meeting to a close, I urged Helen to try to speak with General Fardoust, the Shah's powerful confident. Fardoust came from an ordinary family, but he had shown great promise as a youth. The Shah's father had selected him as a companion for his son, to keep him connected to the common folk, so Fardoust lived with the Shah throughout his childhood, going with him to school in Switzerland and serving with him in the army. He had once promised that he would protect me against SAVAK—and Sabeti in particular—if anything happened. I had no reason to think that he would not be as good as his word, and I asked Helen to try to see him.

Too soon, however, the SAVAK official informed us that our visiting time was over and escorted Helen out of the room. It was difficult to control the tears rolling down my cheeks; my dread of returning to the hole into which I had been cast was indescribable, but seeing Helen again gave me new courage. Later that day, Dr. Sheikh observed that our relatives' visits had brought smiles back to our faces. Shoja, as his friends called him, was always cheerful, and his strength and support on the inside was almost as important as my family on the outside. Behind bars, we had a lot to talk about and the time to do it.

On Dr. Sheikh's birthday, with a little work, we managed to have a small party. I told Helen what we were planning, and on her next visit, she casually warned me to be careful with the bag of clean laundry she had brought me.

Suspecting that she was telling me something important, I opened the bag to find, nestled among the clothes, a bottle of Hennessy Cognac.

That night, after lights out, we toasted Shoja in style. By candlelight, we filled eggshell cups from breakfast with the cognac and listened to a tape by Parisa, an Iranian singer, that Mansour Rouhani had smuggled in. Rouhani recited a poem from Hafez, and Shoja recited a poem that his wife had written for him. When he was too emotional to continue, I finished the recital for him.

Three weeks passed between Helen's first visit and her second, and I wrote brief letters for each of the children for her to bring back to them. Words seemed insufficient; there was so much I wanted to tell them, but it was so difficult to find a way to express my sentiment. My children represented precious hope for the future, so I urged them to develop the will to resist injustice and the patience necessary to survive in the face of adversity. I asked them to make life easier for their mother and expressed cautious hope that our paths would cross again.

This time, when Helen visited, she was in higher spirits. Hoveyda had sent me a message, through her, predicting that these unhappy days would soon be over and that normalcy would again return. He knew that we were honest individuals who had served our country, and he promised to support us with all the power at his disposal. He had been offered a position abroad as an ambassador, but he had turned it down so he could remain in Iran and put up a fierce struggle to ensure the truth would be told. His friends had faithfully served their country, and now it was his turn to serve us.

General Fardoust had been similarly reassuring and optimistic, telling her that this struggle portended positive changes for the country and its people. Referring to our cases, he said that his office, the Imperial Inspectorate, had carried out an investigation that showed that Dr. Sheikh and I were honest, hard-working individuals, with impeccable records. Be patient and hope for the best, he urged her. He even went so far as to pay our monthly salaries out of his own office fund for the next two months.

At their meeting, Fardoust had also said something extraordinary. He had always been renowned for his reserve, and it was not his style to discuss sensitive issues casually. But he told Helen that a number of army officers, indifferent to the fate of the country, were planning a military coup. He said that he was focused on stopping them, and I have no doubt that the plotters' failure had a great deal to do with the General's efforts.

As Fardoust later admitted when Khomeini arrested him, he had been collaborating with British intelligence. In the turmoil of the revolution, he played a leading role in maneuvering the Iranian Armed Forces into finally surrendering to the mullahs. Fardoust always remained one of the Shah's most trusted advisors, one of the few whom power had not corrupted. Fardoust never changed, but the Shah had changed and become a dictator, a womanizer, and a leader starving for power. Fardoust detested the parties and debauchery of palace life, and there was no love lost between him and the other members of the royal family. But the Shah always kept Fardoust close, regardless.

While we remained captive and powerless to help ourselves, our families struggled to get us released and make our lives easier. They sought help from anybody in a position of authority and worked to publicize the miserable conditions of our detention. Somehow, their efforts began to bear fruit. One day, the new chief of SAVAK, General Moghadam, paid us a visit. Almost overnight, our living conditions began improving. The prison guards suddenly treated us with respect, we were transferred to new quarters, and the prison infirmary was cleaned and refurnished as a place where we could meet outside our cells. We were permitted to play backgammon and chess, and the tight control the guards had wielded over our movements loosened up.

All of us wondered at these improvements and felt a ray of hope that the political climate might be changing. Then General Moghadam paid us a second visit. This time, however, Parviz Sabeti walked beside him like a shadow. Talking to each of us in turn, Moghadam was polite, smiled a great deal, and assured us that things were looking up for us. "His Imperial Majesty was very unhappy to hear what has been happening to you here," he told us. "He has dispatched me to act swiftly to make your stay more tolerable."

After he had spoken to most of us informally, he dramatically put on his official SAVAK chief's cap and addressed us as a group. "On behalf of SAVAK," Moghadam said, "I apologize for the inconvenience we have caused. From now on, you are our guests, not our prisoners. I have therefore instructed the officials to do whatever is in their power to provide for your comfort and welfare. His Majesty has graciously asked me to convey to you a message: he still regards you as servants of the country and the crown, but since the country is going through difficult times, he has been forced to keep you in prison for awhile, in everyone's best interest—yours included. When the storm has subsided, things will return to normal." He paused dramatically, then said grandly, "His majesty has also asked me to convey to you his deepest appreciation. He will never forget the sacrifices that you are making for the good of the country."

The Shah's message delighted everyone, some of us more than others. A few of us believed him, but others did not. Rouhani, who was well known for his royalist passions, stood up and, after announcing that he spoke for the rest of us, requested that General Moghadam convey a message to the Shah. "Please give our assurances to His Majesty," he declared "that we all stand ready to sacrifice everything for the good of the nation and for the crown." At these words, my jaw dropped, but Rouhani wasn't finished. "If the monarchy's survival can be assured by sending us to the firing squad, then we are ready even for that ultimate sacrifice."

Rouhani's impromptu speech came as a shock. I was bewildered, to put it mildly. I stayed silent but wanted to shout at him, "Speak for yourself! Would you really offer up our lives in such a conspiracy?" The practice of blaming innocent people, making them sacrificial lambs to save a corrupt regime, was morally reprehensible. The public knew exactly who was responsible; the names of the torturers were common knowledge, and the culprits were living it up in Paris, London, Geneva, and New York. The smug expression on Sabeti's face was enough to make me vomit. His eyes glistened at seeing us in prison uniforms, and the pleasure he took in his revenge was enough to refute Moghadam's words. I'm sure he was delighted to hear that his victims were now lining up to be sent to the slaughterhouse. I was in a rage, but Dr. Sheikh cautioned me to remain silent.

Still, I couldn't deny that it felt good to be treated more humanely. The prison authorities now allowed us to have weekly visits, and we were permitted to receive current news via radio and newspapers, as well as from our families when they came to see us. To my delight, my children were even allowed to visit. It had been thirty-one days since I had seen them, and it seemed like years. The night before they visited for the first time, I was unable to sleep. I tossed and turned. What should I tell them? What should I ask? I had to remind myself to hide my anger and grief and to say nothing that might disturb or frighten them.

The next afternoon, when they ran into my arms, I couldn't even try to hold back tears. My eldest daughter, Lisa, then fourteen, controlled her feelings with great effort; I could see that she had risen to the challenge and was taking care of the others like a responsible adult. Lisa was serious and careful, and her mother told me what a big help she was. At school, she had always been a leader, and now my heart swelled with pride. When Lisa asked me what she could do to help, I told her how proud I was to see what an immense support she was for her mother and me. "I expect you to be strong, to study hard and to help your mother," I told her, "and I know you will."

Eleven-year-old Cathy said very little. She was a sensitive, tender child, with a world of sentiment and kindness in her eyes. She sat watching me with a sad smile on her lips. There was depth in Cathy, and she kept asking questions about my stay in prison. "Do they hurt you?" she asked, with a piercing look in her eyes. "Can you sleep? How long do you have to stay in prison?" Her anger was obvious, and though I tried hard to change the conversation, it was useless. Lisa, on the other hand, managed to hide her anxiety and sorrow until the last minute. When it was time to leave, a tear rolled down her cheek, and she asked, suddenly and urgently, "What will happen to you, Daddy?" I told her not to worry and that I would soon be joining them, but the disbelief in her eyes was unmistakable. It broke my heart.

Cyrus was only seven, and the fear and confusion on his innocent face were the worst of all. He couldn't keep his eyes off the armed guards, and his questions cut me to the bone. "What do they want from you?" he asked. "Why do they have guns?" I told him that the guns were for our protection, but he wasn't satisfied. "Why don't you come home, Daddy? There are bad people here." I could only tell him that I was there for a special job and that we would all be back together soon. I told him he was the man of the house for the time being and urged him to take care of his mother and sisters. Very seriously, he replied, "Yes, Dad!"

CHAPTER 22

INSIDE INFORMATION

Deprived of his two trusted friends, Alam and Hoveyda, the Shah was now almost completely alone. His wife, Farah, and her associates continued to influence him, giving the monarch empty advice and wild theories while warning him not to take strong actions against his opponents. His most trusted advisors now, however, were British Ambassador Anthony Parson and U.S. Ambassador William Sullivan.

Both had been pressing the Shah to open up Iran's political arena and release all political prisoners. There were many in SAVAK's jails, of course, but the prisons were also filled with dangerous Islamic extremists. Sullivan and Parsons refused to make any distinctions, hammering away at the Shah to release them all. And so, when the monarch finally relented and opened their doors, almost four hundred of the most hardened and deadly terrorists walked free in the streets.

In prison, Colonel Rasoul was livid; he had been personally involved and shot in the course of arresting some of these criminals. When he read their names in the newspaper, he threw it against the wall. Violence in the streets will go through the roof, he predicted; these were experienced terrorists, trained in camps in Palestine, Yemen, and Lebanon.

All too soon, his guess proved correct. With these murderers back on the street, the level of violence escalated almost immediately. In addition to waves of strikes, the government was now facing open terrorist attacks on a daily basis, and the streets were seething with mob violence. At the same time, Sharif-Emami's decision to arrest faithful officials while releasing terrorist thugs sent a clear message to anyone who might harbor the least thought of standing by the regime. Those who still could left the country immediately. Everyone else now knew to keep clear of the regime, and many joined the opposition without hesitation.

Parsons and Sullivan counseled the Shah daily, ostensibly with Iran's welfare in mind. The U.S. and British governments, however, refused to sell tear gas, plastic bullets, or any other kind of riot control equipment to Iran. Instead, the soldiers enforcing martial law in Iran were provincial youths without riot-control gear or any kind of training. The only thing they knew how to use was deadly force, and that was precisely what they were not permitted to use. Even as Sullivan and Parsons demanded that the Shah control the violence and placate the opposition, they refused to give him the means to do it. And the violence grew.

Khomeini's power increased as the armed forces' morale and effectiveness dwindled. At the same time, more mujahedeen were being trained in terrorist camps in Lebanon, Yemen, Libya, and Palestine. SAVAK was indifferent, focusing on scapegoating high-profile officials, while opposition activities grew bolder. The days when the words "Death to the Shah" were treasonous were long past; now it was dangerous to say, "Long Live the Shah!"

In prison, our helplessness made us dependent on the news. Our eyes and ears were glued to television, radio, and newspaper reports, desperately searching for signs of our impending release. The somber truth was always there, however, too terrible to say out loud: no matter who won, we were all doomed. The Shah had put us in prison; we knew better than to expect mercy from SAVAK; and Khomeini's lieutenants were unlikely to be sympathetic. Within the walls of that wretched prison, we had no choice but to wait and see which side came to get us first.

One day we heard that Rahim Ali Khorram would be joining us. An illiterate man who spoke Azari and barely knew any Farsi, Khorram was quite a character. He had started out in life as a laborer, pouring asphalt, and now he was the biggest contractor in Iran. A vigorous nationalist, he always claimed that he kept his assets in Iran. While his compatriots were sending their money to American, French, and Swiss banks, Khorram bought Iranian property and businesses, from a casino on the Caspian seashore and an amusement park on the Karaj highway to low-income housing in Tehran. He was proud of his roots. He kept an old pair of shoes on his fine, inlaid mahogany desk to show visitors; he had walked to Tehran in those shoes, he would say, and they kept him in contact with the earth that he came from.

Khorram had close contacts in SAVAK, and they had tipped him off that he was going to be arrested. He had escaped to Pakistan and, once there, visited General Nassiri—the former SAVAK chief, now Iran's ambassador—to ask his advice. Nassiri ordered Khorram to return to Iran and give himself up, so that any misunderstanding could be cleared up quickly. The embassy arranged for a plane to fly him back, but SAVAK agents were waiting for Khorram at the Iranian airport, and they arrested him.

I was present when he was brought into prison. When Khorram was handing his clothes to the guards, the jailer pulled an enormous wad of foreign bills out of one of his pockets, staring at it in disbelief. Since Khorram was illiterate, the duty officer asked me to help him count the money. Together, we sorted out almost ninety thousand dollars in German marks, British pounds, and American bills.

Some of my fellow inmates objected to Khorram's presence, saying that if we mixed with "criminals" like him, we would look like criminals too. I wasn't convinced. People had always been less than generous with Khorram, accusing him of succeeding through intimidation or nepotism. But to me, he was a bit of a wonder. None of his friends ever visited him, but I was addicted to his wild stories, and we helped each other pass long hours in prison. I read newspapers to Khorram, since he wanted to know what the press printed about him. He would go into rages when he heard that members of Parliament were speaking out against him, exclaiming, "You have no idea how much money these bastards have gotten from me!"

I also helped Khorram with his opium addiction. Since he didn't have access to the drug in prison, he was in bad shape, and his pitiful moans in the middle of the night were enough to touch even the cruelest hearts. With the help of Khorram's sizable "donations" to the guards, I asked Dr. Sheikh to intervene, prescribing Methadone pills that helped him weather the withdrawal. Khorram eventually used his wealth to get opium smuggled inside.

He always mentioned his special respect for and trust in General Nassiri and believed that the former SAVAK chief would set him free sooner or later. I don't think his faith ever wavered, but when we were eventually transferred to the Army Engineers barracks, Khorram was sent to Qasr Prison. I never saw him again, and he was later executed.

In my prison life, visits from my loved ones were my happiest moments. Still, the jailers did everything they could to pollute this comfort. The prison governor would sit majestically behind his desk, watching our visits with nauseating smugness. Whenever he shook my hand, he delighted in squeezing my fingers so hard that I thought he'd crush them. With a smile, he would ask me, "God willing, are you enjoying your stay?"

One day, my daughter Cathy told me that a desperate man holding a newborn child was standing outside the prison gates. His wife, the child's mother, was in jail, and the baby was refusing to take milk from another woman. The father begged to be allowed to bring his child to the mother before it starved, but the officer in charge refused to give him permission to visit. Could I pull some strings? Cathy asked me. Was there anything I could do to help?

She and I went to the warden. I encouraged Cathy to ask him herself, believing that no one could refuse the simple mercy that a little girl asked. But the warden only sneered and put his face so close to my daughter that his foul breath, reeking of onions, made her recoil. "You can tell that son of a bitch," he said, "that if he wants to help his baby, he should give us the information we need." The sight of Cathy pleading with this heartless monster broke my heart, and I led her away from the brute as quickly as I could.

Lying in bed that night, I thought about what Cathy had told me. An innocent child, desperate to suckle her mother, was going to lose her life in this clash with inhuman jailers. What effect would that kind of brutality have on Cathy's mind?

The uncertainty began to get to me. After five months in prison, thoughts of my family no longer comforted me, and the days ahead seemed bleaker and bleaker. Anger and hatred built up inside me, and I started to fear that I would do something dangerous out of desperation. My friends soon sensed that I was sinking into a dark place and came to my rescue. Fereidoun Mahdavi was the first to speak with me, and I will always be indebted to that good man. Mansour Rouhani would try to lift my spirits by reading me poetry by Hafez. He also arranged exercise programs that strengthened my physical and mental condition. For an hour every day, we would run around the circular corridors "like the mill-stone horses of old," Rouhani used to say. We would jog in pairs, and as we lost ourselves in conversation, we almost forgot that we were imprisoned, running with a serenity that was indescribable. One night, I looked up and saw the moon. As I stared at it with joy, I remembered Neil Armstrong's great steps, that giant moment in human history. Khomeini's fanatics claimed that they could see their master's face in the moon, but I saw nothing then, and I see nothing now.

Mahdavi, meanwhile, started organizing discussions to keep our minds agile and active. Our sessions soon included many long-time government officials and others with close ties to revolutionary leaders. As a result, we were in a unique position, able to gather information from both sides. I took notes at these meetings, and initially, a SAVAK agent was present at all of them—most likely to ensure that we weren't doing anything suspicious. He eventually stopped attending, probably because he thought we were visionary idlers. A high-ranking SAVAK officer, however, joined us for two of our sessions. We were gratified that someone in such a sensitive job, at such a critical time, would spend a few of his spare hours at our gatherings, and he admitted that our discussions were quite instructive for him. Despite his high rank, he confided, higher-ups tended to keep their subordinates uninformed, so we knew much more about was going on than he did. Within SAVAK, in fact, divisions were forming between those who were loyal to the Shah and those who had allied with the opposition; long-time officers were being pushed out of the loop.

Reliable sources informed us that Sullivan and his people were negotiating with the leadership of opposition groups, including the National Front and the Freedom Movement. Stemple, the U.S. embassy's political agent in Tehran, had told his superiors that these opposition leaders were promising electoral victory within six month after the political arena was opened up. But these leaders—including Dr. Sanjabi, Dariush Frouhar, Dr. Bakhtiar, and Bazargan—represented scattered and diffuse constituencies that were not well organized, united, or politically powerful. The groups couldn't reach any agreement among themselves, so it was obvious that they were not organizing the demonstrations, setting the fires, or carrying out the assassinations. People like Sullivan who believed that these groups were orchestrating events were wasting precious time and misleading the State Department. Khomeini himself was the only one with the power to order riots, assassinations, and bombings, but neither the Shah nor Sullivan were willing to accept this fact.

The plundering and arson of cinemas and banks continued, and attacks on police stations and increasing street violence showed the uselessness of Iran's martial law. While we rotted in jail, two hundred more guerrillas were released from prison, free to cause more murder and mayhem. Parsons and Sullivan were urging the Shah to be as lenient as possible, and SAVAK quietly undermined efforts to keep terrorists off the street. Almost no one was arrested any more; even those accused of murder or bombings were released from custody in less than twenty-four hours. Sharif-Emami's government was disintegrating. Every move it made to neutralize the violence made the situation worse. The regime's attempts to liberalize the political arena only added to the chaos and confusion. The government announced that the salaries of strikers would continue to be paid, so the strikes doubled in frequency. And as the Shah became more and more indecisive, agents of his own government started turning against him.

In September, the Iranian Ambassador to the United States, Ardeshir Zahedi, returned to Iran, hoping to spur the Shah into taking action. With all his close connections to top American officials, Zahedi was in the best position to interpret behind-the-scenes negotiations between the Carter administration and key senators and advise the Shah on how to work with them. He also firmly believed that the best way to proceed was to institute law and order by force and only then to open up a free political arena. Nevertheless, although Zahedi was the Shah's son-in-law, rumors spread that he had come to Iran to organize a military coup. It was not such a farfetched idea, since years earlier he had been involved in the coup against Mossadegh.

The Shah, meanwhile, was so deeply under the influence of Sullivan, Parsons, and Queen Farah that he refused to take Zahedi's advice seriously. Daryoush Homayon, Zahedi's brother-in-law, was in our prison group and told us that Sullivan was even manipulating communications between the Shah and President Carter. When Zahedi told the Shah that he had received a telephone call from Carter urging the monarch to take action, Sullivan argued that this was only diplomatic posturing; the State Department and U.S. Senate, he claimed, opposed the use of force in resolving the crisis. Why, Sullivan asked, hadn't the President sent a letter, which was an undeniable indication of seriousness? But when President Carter did send a handwritten letter, Sullivan persuaded the Shah not to take that seriously either. The monarch, in fact, was so convinced that Sullivan and Parsons spoke for their governments, and was so intimidated by them, that he ordered Zahedi to tell Sullivan personally that he rejected the President's proposal and irrevocably opposed using military force against his opponents.

On October 16, 1978, the Shah appointed Aligholi Ardalan Court Minister. Ardalan been away from the political scene for many years, and he was perplexed at the state of affairs he found on his return. "Why is it," he asked the Shah, "that even though all the opposition's demands have been met, violence hasn't decreased? You've arrested corrupt government officials, you've released political prisoners, there's freedom of the press now, and the political process has been opened up to all parties. Shouldn't the opposition, in return, be bringing back calm and order and preparing for free elections?" Ardalan shook his head. "If the only result of this liberalization is more terrorist activity, more bombing, more arson, and assassination, then I feel sorry for this country and its people."

The Shah took Ardalan's words seriously enough to try to negotiate a coalition government with the opposition. He invited some of the country's most sincere elder statesmen to discuss the matter, but he ultimately rejected all of their suggestions. The Shah was still unwilling to give up significant power, especially over the armed forces.

Khomeini, in any case, did not support a coalition, and it was on his orders that chaos and anarchy were overtaking the country. Anyone with eyes could see that there were only two viable solutions. Either a powerful central government would take strong action to bring order to the streets, or the Prime Minister would allow the military to surrender and Khomeini to take over the country and execute the monarch and those close to him. Neither option was appealing, but the Shah's vacillation and self-delusions were leading Iran into the worst of all possible crises. Ignoring the handwriting on the wall, the Shah impotently witnessed the inevitable decline of his regime. As an American journalist observed, "Ministers and other high-ranking officials are dazed and paralyzed, pacing back and forth behind draped windows. It's like they're waiting for a Robespierre to appear and send them all to the guillotine."

One day, as the Shah was stepping out of his car, three top commanders of the armed forces fell at his feet, begging him to take radical action to save the country. And, initially, their appeal spurred the monarch into action. He summoned General Oveisi and instructed him to prepare himself to be Prime Minister of a military government. Oveisi would have been the right choice. He was a rough, unforgiving military man who would have done whatever was necessary to assert control. Zahedi and Brzezinski supported the plan, and Oveisi, with a group of elite military officers, started organizing a military coup code-named "Operation Khash." The plan was to sweep up the clerics and leadership of Khomeini's group, as well as anarchists in the streets, and imprison them in the city of Khash. With its majority Sunni population, Khomeini would find few Shia followers there. Many pundits believed that this plan could succeed.

But Farah opposed the decision and lobbied vigorously against it. The "compassionate" ambassadors, too, wore the Shah down with their friendly persuasion and veiled threats. Fardoust and Moghadam also voiced their opposition to the proposal, but it was ultimately Farah who succeeded in dissuading her husband from the decision. Instead, in one more last-minute compromise, the Shah brought Sharif-Emami's government to an end. He named General Azhari prime minister and asked him to form a new cabinet that was partly civilian and partly military. Under Farah's supervision, the Shah read a prepared speech to the nation, broadcast live on radio and television, essentially abdicating his remaining moral authority. On television in the prison, we watched him say that he had "heard the sound of your revolution," and he accepted it as an act against corruption and oppression. He then took an oath that the mistakes of the past would not be repeated. After conceding that strikes were an acceptable reaction to his regime's corruption, he informed the nation that the new government would be only provisional.

The Shah's authority was devastated by this display. Everyone could see that he spoke from a position of weakness. The distress in his trembling voice, tearful eyes, and pleas for forgiveness were not at all what people expected of their omnipotent ruler. The Shah's repentance destroyed any semblance of authority he might have had. It drove away military commanders like General Oveisi, and the public lost hope when they saw their monarch in such a depressed, unreliable state of mind.

Azhari's new government made waves. He claimed that it would not be a military regime, but he was an experienced general, and many Iranians wondered if he would draw a hard line. In the end, Azhari was not allowed to use military force, but he lacked the managerial expertise to run a civilian government. When he promised to restore calm to the cities and issued threatening declarations, the opposition disregarded him and intensified their terrorist activities. The crisis continued.

Farah, SAVAK, and the ambassadors again urged the Shah to avert calamity by scapegoating former officials. It would be easy to arrest men who had left the government and whose loyalty left them defenseless, so prison officials told us to prepare for additional "guests." Soon, more high-level officials—generals, senators, and cabinet ministers—joined us as inmates. Most were downcast and despondent. But Gholam Rerza Kianpour, the former Minister of Justice, arrived with a mocking smile on his face. He explained that he had walked into prison under his own power.

"I was sitting at home drinking tea," he told us, "when I heard my arrest being announced on television and radio. I immediately called SAVAK and told them that if it was their intention to arrest me, I was going to pack my bags myself. I am not the kind of person who runs away!"

SAVAK's propaganda machine again made a lot of noise about the arrest of "The Corrupt Agents of Oppression," promising speedy trials and punishment. But the numbers of detainees they reported—more than a thousand—was much more than the current prison could hold, so we prepared to move, and one day, after a couple of weeks, the guards loaded us all into a bus. There were no windows, but I could glimpse the outside world through a crack in the door, and the sight of people moving in the streets tugged at my heart. I envied their freedom and would have given almost anything to be one of them. I saw a laborer throwing bricks up to a master mason, and I imagined myself in his shoes; for a moment, I could almost feel the grit of the masonry and the wind in my face. Too quickly, though, the bus came to a halt. We had arrived at another cage, a prison inside the Army Engineers' garrison.

The thought of being imprisoned again made me feel suffocated, like walls were closing in. I felt disoriented, and our new surroundings were more claustrophobic than our old quarters. Our prison was a two-story building. The soldier's dormitories were located on the ground floor, and we were housed on the west wing of the first floor, with the military prisoners in the east wing. The areas between the two wings were allocated for the use of prison officers and SAVAK agents, as well as toilets, bathrooms, and food pantries. At that time the jail also held eight hundred to a thousand armed forces technicians, called *homafars*, who were supporters of Khomeini.

Here, our tiny cells faced onto a narrow corridor shadowed by towering walls. A small window near the ceiling let in the smallest slivers of light, and for the first few days, we were constantly kept locked inside our cells. The policy was eventually relaxed, however, and we were ultimately allowed to mingle in the corridor during the day and only locked inside our solitary cells at night.

In general, however, our situation was an improvement. Two soldiers were tasked with looking after our needs, and they stayed with us constantly during the day, cleaning and carrying out errands for us—buying newspapers, bringing us food, and delivering messages. We got to know one of them quite well—a smiling Kurdish soldier named Panjali. A kind and simple soul, he was always ready to help us any way he could.

Over the next few weeks, more cabinet ministers joined us, along with a variety of businessmen and a former police chief. The new inmates included Iraj Vahidi, Minister of Water & Electricity; Manouchehr Azmoun, Minister of Labor; Manouchehr Taslimi, Minister of Commerce; Manhouchehr Piruz, Governor of Shiraz; Gholam Reza Kianpour, Minister of Justice; and Azim Valian, Governor of Khorasan. Later, Houshang Nahavandi, Minister of Housing and Development, and Majid Majidi, Director of Plan Organization, were arrested by Prime Minister Bakhtiar and imprisoned with us. I was surprised to see how many of these men, when they entered the jail, calmly acted like they were going on vacation, confident that their detention would be temporary and the situation would soon settle down to normal. They were naïve.

Those of us who had been imprisoned for some time looked forward to tapping these new sources of information, expecting that they would energize our discussions. We were disappointed. The new detainees arrived with so much hope and in such high spirits that they preferred to chat privately in groups of twos and threes and never joined us. Later, as they inevitably became depressed by the reality of their situation, they would become silent, going off into corners by themselves and showing less interest than ever in our discussions. In this atmosphere of gloom, our own enthusiasm cooled, and our discussions and debates became less frequent.

Eventually, however, the new inmates opted to join our sessions. These men had all played a creative role in the foundation of modern and progressive Iran—witnessing its successes and failures, its deviations and treacheries, and its constructive and destructive policies. As I took notes at these meetings, it was obvious that the insights they shared were vital to the true history of the revolution. I began hiding them and secretly passing them to Helen for safekeeping.

Helen and I drove through Europe to Iran in this Chevy Impala

Helen and I on the Danube River Bridge

Lisa and Helen's first visit to my hometown, Sari

Reza Shah Pahlavi, at the hospital dedication in Mashad, Iran

Helen, Lisa, and baby Cathy

*Cyrus sending me off before my
meeting with the Shah*

Helen and her father enjoying tea, Persian style

**Lisa, Cathy, and Cyrus
before the Revolution**

برای دستگیری ۱۸ عامل رژیم سابق به دادسرای انقلاب کمک کنید

List of officials with a death sentence wanted by the Islamic Revolutionary Guard, Dr. Aram (bottom left)

Reunited at last

Celebrating with my beautiful family

CHAPTER 23

BLOODED TIGER

Just before to the January 1979 G-8 meeting in Guadeloupe, Carter commissioned George Ball, a career diplomat with a wide knowledge of the Middle East, to produce a report on the situation in Iran. Ball reported that the days of the Shah's absolute rule had come to an end, but he confused Carter by suggesting a long list of possible outcomes. The Pentagon and Iranian Armed Forces, Ball said, preferred a constitutional monarchy in which the Shah would reign but not rule, with a coalition government in charge of the country's affairs. There was also the possibility of a regency; the Shah would either be deposed or abdicate in favor of his son, leaving the country in the hands of a mixed ruling council. The report also discussed the establishment of a republic. Dr. Amini or Dr. Sanjabi would lead the country as president, finding some way to come to terms with the Islamists and the armed forces and making maximum use of educated technocrats to ensure the nation's progress. If such a republic did not survive, Ball noted, the establishment of an Islamic Republic would be inevitable. Iran's modernization would cease, but the country's armed forces would almost certainly bring down such a regime. If the present chaos continued, he predicted, the armed forces would take matters into their own hands.

Carter left for the G-8 as bewildered as before about the Iranian situation. Meanwhile, other world leaders were far ahead of him in their plans. Two weeks before the conference, France's Ministry of Foreign Affairs had asked Sadeq Qotbzadeh, my old friend from Georgetown, to prepare a report outlining the type of government that Khomeini would put in place if he gained power. The French were supposedly opposed to Khomeini, but they were negotiating directly with his chief lieutenant.

Qotbzadeh had come a long way since I knew him in the United States. He and Dr. Yazdi were among Khomeini's top deputies, widely referred to as his "two sons." With other key liaisons, they made the revolution possible by serving as Khomeini's bridges to the outside world. Yazdi was Khomeini's connection to the United States, while Qotbzadeh was his link to Libya, the Palestinian leader Arafat, and terrorist groups. Ayatollah Beheshti and Ayatollah Rafsanjani were his connections to the British.

After all, Khomeini was not only physically located in Najaf, but his worldview was also sharply limited by his fundamentalist outlook. He spoke only Farsi and Arabic and only knew what his own twisted version of Shiism told him. Qotbzadeh and Dr. Yazdi, on the other hand, knew English and French. With their understanding of international politics and contacts in the West, they became indispensable to Khomeini's diplomatic efforts. Even more importantly, perhaps, their contacts with Libya and Palestine made it possible for trained guerillas, the foot soldiers of the revolution, to come to Iran and fight in Khomeini's name.

Qotbzadeh promised the French that Khomeini wanted to put in place a republic based on democratic principles and the observance of human rights. The government, he said, would maintain good relations with the West and respect Iran's prior commitments. Current oil contracts would be honored and Islam and communism, he promised, could never coexist in Iran. Moreover, he insisted that Khomeini and the mullahs planned to confine their activities to religious matters; after the Shah was gone, he said, they would refrain from interfering in state affairs.

France had long reconciled itself to the Shah's removal, and Qotbzadeh understood that the West was mostly concerned about what type of regime would replace him. His discussions with France convinced Qotbzadeh that Khomeini could be accepted by the West if he made the right promises. So Qotbzadeh made them. He believed what he was saying, because he misinterpreted Khomeini's goals. Like most of the mullah's secular supporters in the opposition, Qotbzadeh believed in democracy and that he was fighting for his country's freedom. Like so many others, he eventually paid the ultimate price for misjudging Khomeini.

Qotbzadeh prepared the report which the French foreign ministry had commissioned. The ministry, in fact, helped him write it, then presented it to the French president, Valery Giscard D'Estaing. Giscard D'Estaing took the report seriously and shared it with West German Chancellor Helmut Schmitt as well as British Prime Minister James Callaghan. Callaghan was delighted. Giscard D'Estaing argued that Khomeini now represented the majority of Iranians and that it would be in the interest of the G-8 to end their support for the Shah. Qotbzadeh's report was treated as gospel truth. On the basis of that pack of lies, France, West Germany, and Britain agreed to a common course, and the West found itself supporting an implacable enemy. At the G-8 meeting, Giscard D'Estaing worked vehemently to persuade Jimmy Carter to go along. After a series of private sessions with each of his three counterparts, Carter let himself be swayed and agreed to stop supporting the Shah.

Iranians will never forget what Giscard D'Estaing and James Callaghan did, for it was only with their help that Iran was able to travel a hundred years into the past. Britain, France, and West Germany laid the foundation for Khomeini's rise and were indirectly responsible for the atrocities that followed.

In Iran, the Shah was being abandoned by almost every political force in the country. While we were in prison, two or three individuals in our group received daily information from their contacts in the Prime Minister's office or from other government officials, and two frequently obtained information from leaders of the revolutionary National Front and Khomeini's people. We also knew from the information we gleaned from TV, radio, and newspapers that nothing General Azhari did to quell the mass uprisings was successful. When he called for a moratorium on violence so tat the two sides could negotiate, Khomeini mocked him. "A blooded tiger," he responded, "doesn't let his dying prey go, so why should I? And while a tiger that tastes its own blood only fights all the harder, neither do the prey have any need to negotiate. The time for talking is over."

The regime was no longer able to govern. *"Allah O Akbar"* was chanted from rooftop to rooftop, and fear and dread pervaded the police and security forces. The Shah began to feel the walls close in. He asked Anthony Parsons to use his influence with the mullahs and try to reason with them, but Parsons claimed that he, like all previous British ambassadors, had to refrain from meddling in state affairs. The truth was that Britain had always been in contact with the mullahs, and the Shah knew that. Parsons was telling him that he would be on his own.

Despite it all, Ardalan, the new Minister of the Imperial Court, tried to convince the Shah to delegate authority to a Regency Council of seasoned, respected politicians as a last-ditch effort to reform the government, but the monarch refused. No Shah had ever relinquished command of the military, and he knew that he would be finished if he lost control of the armed forces. In retrospect, he might have been right, and a Regency Council might not have been enough to save him. But it was the last possible chance that the Shah had to retain power. When he turned it down, the end was inevitable.

Farah realized that the Shah was not going to remain in power. She suggested that he resign so that their son would become Shah; since the boy was not yet of legal age to rule, she would then become the regent in power. The Shah refused. Farah then urged him to ask her relative Shapour Bakhtiar to form a new reform government. The Shah accepted this plan, but it was too late.

Bakhtiar, whose father was the head of the Bakhtiari tribe, was one of the secular leaders of the National Front, which opposed the regime, and he had never been sympathetic to the mullahs. Perhaps because he was opposed to the clergy, the Shah thought that he would be able to accomplish something with the remaining nationalists who hadn't signed on with Khomeini. But when Bakhtiar accepted the Shah's charge, the National Front's central committee almost immediately turned their backs on him and strongly condemned him for joining the Shah's regime. The Shah hoped Bakhtiar would be able to build a bridge to the secular opposition, but Bakhtiar instead found himself alienated from those allies and the head of a government that he had worked for years to overthrow.

It wasn't surprising that Bakhtiar had so little success. When he presented a strongly worded bill to Parliament, ordering a new wave of arrests of former government officials, he managed to scare off any loyal officials who remained. As a result, his cabinet was a motley crew of inexperienced figures, with little or no public support and no chance of functioning effectively in turbulent times.

In this intractable situation, Bakhtiar did two things that would ensure his government's failure. First, he ordered SAVAK to disband—a command that was far beyond his ability to enforce. Since only the few remaining loyal elements in SAVAK had any intention of obeying his order, it had the effect of pushing the rest of the intelligence service into open revolt. Secondly,

Bakhtiar forced the Shah to leave the country without receiving the ruler's authority to control the military.

By that time, the Shah was sick, nearly dying, and had long lost any hope for his continued rule. He was only too happy to go and had been begging Sullivan to help him leave the country. Bakhtiar's government announced that the Shah would be leaving on vacation, but no one believed it. Everyone, even the Shah, knew that he would never return. After approval from Parliament, the Shah and his family left Iran almost immediately. Bakhtiar, some political supporters, and various high-ranking commanders of the armed forces were present to see him off—some kissing his hand and all showing the highest possible respect. The streets that day were filled with an outpouring of jubilation. The Shah's departure was seen as an auspicious event, as if it would solve everything.

But with the Shah went Iran's last sign of stability. When he departed—with his german shepherds and a jar of Iranian soil in his hand—he did so without delegating a successor as Commander-in-Chief. He left the armed forces on the verge of disintegration and Bakhtiar without the support of the only power in the country that could still stand up to the opposition. The country was split wide open, ripe for the picking. No one ever doubted Bakhtiar's patriotism or courage, but only a miracle could have saved him. He entered the political arena unarmed and unprepared, and the miracles were all on the other side.

Now Khomeini could taste blood, and everyone waited for the inevitable next step—Bakhtiar's ouster or resignation. Most of us believed that his government did not stand a chance. Bakhtiar was perhaps the last person in the country to understand that the opposition would only listen to the trembling voice of Imam Khomeini. He was now truly alone. Everyone from intellectuals to freedom fighters, communists, and human rights activists now chanted *"Allah O Akbar"* with Khomeini. Too scared to venture out of the Prime Minister's office, Bakhtiar and his cabinet held endless meetings but could only ask a question that had no answer: "What can we do?" In the end, Bakhtiar merely ordered the arrest of more defenseless former government officials. It was an easy show of power that accomplished nothing.

The Shah's own end was near, though few people knew it. Despite the ruler's tremendous ego, he was, in fact, a shy, timid man. The world's most advanced health equipment and best medical specialists had been within his reach, but he had placed himself in the hands of second-rate doctors. It was years since his physician, Dr. Ayadi, had practiced medicine, and his personal Austrian physician, Dr. Flinger, was known as an "international quack."

After the revolution, it was revealed that the Shah suffered from Waldenstorm Disease, a form of cancer. Efforts to keep the illness secret had prevented him from getting correct medical treatment, and his cancer medicines had been disguised as vitamin supplements. Many Iranians believe that if the public had known of the Shah's illness earlier, his associates could have prepared the appointment of a Regency Council and confirmed the sovereignty of the Crown Prince, drawing on the sympathy and compassion of the majority of the population.

The people of Iran respected and loved the Shah as a strong leader, but after his infamous apology speech, they understood that he was already dead. Well-wishers, "ambassadors," and his wife had worn away his resistance, leaving him weak, helpless, and ill. It was just a matter of time.

CHAPTER 24

SULLIVAN'S DEADLY GAME

The American Embassy advised American citizens living in Iran to leave the country and refused to take any responsibility for their safety if they remained. Although Helen was alarmed and suggested that we send the children to stay with her parents in the U.S., she herself had no intention of leaving. But under the circumstances, I explained, her presence in Iran only added to my worries. It would give me more peace of mind knowing she was safe at home, and I was finally able to persuade her, reluctantly, to return to the United States.

It was a gloomy Wednesday when I said goodbye to my family. The future was grim. No one wanted to say it, but we all knew that this might be our last time together. Helen came with Cyrus and Lisa to visit me, looking sad and worried. When I asked where Cathy was, Helen began tearing up. After a moment, she explained that Cathy had refused to come because she said it would be impossible to say goodbye to her father. She was afraid that if she saw me, she wouldn't be able to control her emotions. Since that would only add to my troubles, she stayed home and cried. Cathy had always been the most sensitive member of the family, and Helen's words cut me like a knife. I was on the verge of breaking down, and words of the poet Saadi came to my mind:

Let me cry as clouds in springtime.
Even stones cry out when taken from their kin.

I tried to control myself. I should be a refuge for my family, I thought; any sign of weakness would shatter their hopes for our future. So I tried my best to reassure them of my well being, promising to join them very soon. I don't know if they believed me, but they cheered me with their loving smiles. I told the children that, since they would be far from my reach, they had to be good, study well, and help their mother. I told Helen that she had always been an ideal mother to our children; with a crack in my voice, I said that from now on she would have to be their father too. God would be with her, I added. As we said farewell, she told me she would pray for my freedom each moment of the day. I asked them to give a message to Cathy to be strong and that I would always remember her penetrating eyes. And then they left. All I had was the memory of their tearful faces—Cyrus's confused frown, the anxious care on Helen's face, and Lisa's tears. They have stayed with me forever.

My courageous friend General Mehdi Rahimi sent his car and driver to take Helen and the children to the airport. A patriot, Rahimi was the military commander of Tehran at the time. He sent his wife, Manijeh, to visit me in prison. She said how distressed he was to witness the downfall of the regime and how much it pained him to stand by with his hands tied. His soldiers stood defenseless on the streets, able only to stand witness to the terrorism perpetrated by guerillas and fanatics. He considered our imprisonment a destructive plot by the nation's enemies, but as a soldier he could do nothing except stay true to his solemn oath of loyalty. He would remain loyal to the Shah and the monarchy, she said, and there was nothing they could do to help me. "But," she added, "we have hope that you will find your own way to freedom." There was a note of finality to her words. Then, suddenly, she changed the subject. "How is your health?" she asked me. "If you have any medical problems, you know, the army has excellent doctors who can take care of you." I wasn't sure what to say, so I just nodded my head and thanked her for her concern.

A week later, out of the blue, I was informed that I had been approved for a dental appointment. I wasn't having any dental problems, so I was confused at first. But then I remembered my conversation with Manijeh, and it occurred to me that maybe Rahimi was trying to help me. Perhaps there would be an opportunity for escape. And when I saw the dentist at the base, a colonel, he told me that I had some problems that could become serious and offered to send me to a specialist off base. This seemed unlikely, since I hadn't noticed any symptoms. I was now sure that something was going on, though I didn't know what it was. In the end, however, it all came to nothing. I heard a week later that the colonel had been transferred, and I was never sent to an off-base clinic. Even after the revolution, I was never able to learn if there had been a plan.

Meanwhile, the Shah had departed, leaving a gaping hole in the military's chain of command. He had created the position of joint chief of staff at the behest of the U.S. government, but military commanders still reported only to him. The Shah had never believed in having a second in command, and when he left Iran, the commanders ignored Chief of Staff General Gharabaghi.

The U.S. had hoped to keep Iran's armed forces viable and intact, and the increasingly visible cracks in the army's unity caused great concern. So President Carter requested that Alexander Haig, commander of NATO forces, dispatch his deputy, General Robert E. Huyser, to Iran. What Huyser was supposed to do was less than clear, even to General Haig. Conversations in the White House suggested that he was supposed to help organize a military takeover of the government. Officials at the State Department, however, were saying the opposite.

Confusion plagued Huyser's mission from the very beginning. When he first arrived in Tehran, Sullivan handed him a wire from Secretary of State Vance directing him to ignore all prior instructions. Huyser was ordered not to make contact with the Iranian military, as originally planned, and he was instructed to do nothing until he received further word from Washington, D.C. Since the State Department had one view of the situation and the Department of Defense another, Huyser found himself reporting to the Secretary of Defense, then receiving countermanding orders from State the next day. His mission, according to the Pentagon, was to see that Iran's Armed Forces remained intact under a strong commander; the long-term aim was to keep the present regime together by force, if necessary, even by a coup d'état. The State Department, however, favored accommodation with opponents of the Shah's regime and wanted to keep the military from interfering. When Sullivan told Huyser that it was futile for Bakhtiar to establish a government, Huyser couldn't believe his ears. The President's ambassador was assuming defeat before the game had even begun and was laying the groundwork to turn the government over to Khomeini.

It didn't take Huyser long to realize that Sullivan was following his own agenda. The U.S. Ambassador had decided that the Shah's government was finished. Persuading the monarch to leave the country was part of his larger strategy: to degrade the army to the point where the opposition could take control of the country. Huyser had been tasked, however, with strengthening the Iranian army—recognizing that the mullahs would never be able to control the country if the army was united. Sullivan was a highly experienced politician who was supposed to help Huyser but was actually sabotaging him. Perhaps Huyser had spent too much time in administration instead of the field. What really doomed Huyser's mission, however, was the complexity of politics in Iran due to the disagreement of the U.S. State and Defense departments and the fact that the President was unaware of theie conflicts and could nor make a decision. Huyser was unwilling or unable to adapt to these contradictory conditions.

In his first encounter with Iran's armed forces, Huyser tried to discover who was in command in the army. His inquiries, however, elicited blank stares. The generals insisted that the Shah was still the Commander-in-Chief and that they had never heard of the "Joint Chief of Staff" position. Apparently, no such organizational post actually existed; General Gharabaghi held a title that was created merely to placate U.S. military advisors.

Since Huyser's most urgent priority was keeping the army unified, he decided to form what he called the "committee of six" of Iran's highest generals, who would meet regularly to keep lines of communication open and prevent factional struggle. Having an American organizing the Iranian army was nothing new. Iran's army had been equipped and "advised" by American officers for decades, and many of the highest generals had been educated in the United States. Huyser, however, was spectacularly unsuccessful. He had hoped to mold the generals into a body capable of acting collectively as commander-in-chief, but the generals refused to offer their direct opinions at meetings. When forced into any kind of decision-making, they merely referred all questions back to the Shah. The commanders were willing to attend meetings and go through the motions, but none of them believed in the process that Huyser was trying to put in place. In his book, he claimed that the generals were afraid of one another or feared the Shah. But the fact was that the Shah never delegated authority, and Huyser should have realized it was far too late to reform the army. Such things took time, and with Khomeini practically at the front door, no general was willing to risk his position or his neck.

Huyser also didn't know that General Fardoust was by far the most powerful and important of the Shah's generals, even though he held no official post in the military hierarchy. Fardoust's special connection to the Shah, as the monarch's friend and companion of a lifetime, meant that almost everything went through him in the Shah's absence. Although Huyser didn't include Fardoust in the committee of six, the general kept his eye on the committee's every movement. He was also several steps ahead of Sullivan and made sure that General Gharabaghi, the Chief of Staff, and Moghadam, chief of SAVAK, were Sullivan's main contacts in Iran's military. Both these men owed everything to Fardoust, who was able to manage things from behind the scenes and subvert the Shah.

It was never clear why Fardoust ultimately turned against the regime and supported the revolution. Some believed it was a matter of revenge for a slight, while others traced it to his long connections with the British. But Fardoust always claimed that he was trying to avoid bloodshed, and he may have believed that a smooth change in regime would be Iran's easiest path. In any case, Huyser recognized Fardoust's role much too late; as he said in his book, he didn't learn until he was back in Washington that Fardoust had been leaking the military's meetings to the BBC. Someone at the embassy, with the help of Fardoust's men, had also been leaking everything to the *New York Times*. These regular updates on the army's lack of progress helped reassure the revolutionaries that the military was incapable of opposition.

Meanwhile, Sullivan, through Moghadam and Gharabaghi, was negotiating with Khomeini's top deputies—Beheshti, Yazadi, and Bazargan—in hopes of achieving a political settlement after the Shah's government collapsed. Sullivan hoped to ensure the Iranian government's continuing anti-communist stance and recognition of existing oil agreements. He grew warmer toward Khomeini once the cleric's deputies assured him that Islam was fundamentally opposed to communism. As far as oil was concerned, too, Khomeini's spokesmen were also glad to commit in principle to existing agreements. On the question of the armed forces, Khomeini asserted that many of the high command were corrupt and untrustworthy, and he wanted to have them sacked, tried, and punished. On this point, however, Sullivan stalled.

He passed along the substance of these talks to Secretary Vance. President Carter was startled by these negotiations, called a meeting of his entire foreign policy team, including the Secretary of Defense, the National Security Adviser, the Secretary of the Treasury, and the Director of the CIA. Sullivan's activities, as well as the State Department's handling of the situation, came under heavy criticism. Brzezinski was tapped to inform Sullivan that, on the President's direct orders, all negotiations with Khomeini should stop.

Sullivan, however, was far from Washington. President Carter began sending communications directly to Bakhtiar, completely bypassing Sullivan and the embassy, Sullivan continued acting on his own and directly contradicting the President's orders. In his book, Sullivan wrote that he considered resigning his commission at that point and was angry and deeply insulted that his actions were criticized. But he felt he was in a unique position to do what needed to be done, so he decided to do it. Despite Washington's orders to the contrary, Sullivan carried forward his own agenda and continued to talk directly with Khomeini's group. In this way, he got his revenge on Carter, the Shah, and the Iranian nation, all at once, by playing a crucial role in bringing the two thousand-year monarchy to an end.

The disintegration of the armed forces was Iran's single biggest problem, but the top generals refused to take any action. Huyser tried to raise the possibility of a military coup, but only three of the seven agreed to go along, and the others refused to answer. They all wanted someone else to take responsibility. If the Shah had ordered them into action, they would have obeyed. If Huyser had received authorization from the Shah, they probably would have obeyed him, too. But Huyser was simply not the right man for the job. He lacked the necessary character or resolve to mount a military action in the face of obstacles. The Iranian commanders wanted him to play the role of the Shah for them; they wanted him to command them, but he was unable to do it. Confused by the difference in opinion between the Defense and State Departments, he, like Carter, was indecisive. So Sullivan outmaneuvered him, placing obstacles in his path and poisoning the atmosphere until Huyser was completely checkmated.

Had Huyser been a different man, with Washington's support, he might have been successful, even at that late date. Iran's armed forces had a strong tradition of military discipline. The opposition of a small group within their ranks would have been insignificant if they had direct orders from their leaders, and past experience had shown that strong action from the government always led to support from the country's silent majority.

Ultimately, however, Huyser realized that Gharabaghi and Moghadam, at Sullivan's behest, had reached an understanding with Khomeini's deputies. He knew that his moment had passed, and he sent word to Washington that he wanted to terminate his mission and leave Iran. Dean Brown, the new

Secretary of Defense, angrily ordered Huyser to remain at his post, assuring him that steps were being taken to facilitate his mission. And, almost immediately, it did appear that the situation was changing. The U.S. embassy suddenly began working with Huyser, and Bakhtiar sent him a message of cooperation and tacitly approved the idea of a coup d'état. Huyser wondered why he hadn't dealt with Bakhtiar from the beginning.

By now, however, it was too late. After the G-8 conference, United Press International reported that the heads of the United States, the United Kingdom, and France had all agreed that the era of the Shah was over. Although the U.S. did not specify why, it was clear that America would no longer support the Shah. At the same time, however, President Carter sent a message to Khomeini, who was then in Paris, urging him to stop opposing Bakhtiar's government. In his book, Dr. Yazdi—who later became Khomeini's foreign minister—recalled that someone referred by the French Ministry of Foreign Affairs personally delivered Carter's message to Khomeini. It read:

> The President of America asks the Ayatollah to cease all opposition to Bakhtiar's government. Attacking Bakhtiar is a gamble that can only result in bloodshed, and it is the opinion of the United States that preventing violence will be in the best interests of all concerned. The Ayatollah needs to realize that all violent activity can only worsen the situation, and negotiation can only proceed after a period of calm. President Carter wishes to keep this message confidential, but urges that a direct line of communication be established between him and Khomeini, to the mutual benefit of both Iran and the Ayatollah.

Yazdi recalled that Khomeini laughed at the message, perceiving correctly that Carter had no clear sense of what he was trying to accomplish. "I shall not support Bakhtiar," he said, "and I am not scared of bloodshed. If Carter wants to bring about calm, he should gather up the Shah's possessions for him and deliver the country over to the Muslims." Either Carter was totally unaware of what was happening in Iran or the message was a political bluff. Khomeini had always enjoyed support from the British, and now, with the French on his side, he hardly needed to fear America's warning.

In any case, President Carter's own man in Tehran was busy dismantling the armed forces. While Carter was at the G-8 meeting, Sullivan was, at that very moment, negotiating surrender with Khomeini's group, with the collaboration of generals Gharabaghi, Moghadam, and Fardoust, who later confessed to being a British agent. Bakhtiar was now so powerless and isolated that he didn't even dare to venture out of the Prime Ministry. Khomeini hardly needed to bother about him. Had Carter really thought that any message he could send would persuade the Ayatollah to give up anything? The country was now practically in his hands.

Khomeini announced that he would return to Iran, and all indications were that this would spark a final confrontation between the military and the opposition. Bakhtiar had been promising that the law of the land would be forcibly upheld and that acts of terror and chaos would be crushed by force. General Gharabaghi came out in support of Bakhtiar's initiatives, and Huyser was elated at this indication of resolve. But Bakhtiar's actual response to Khomeini's return was something else altogether. In a politely worded letter, he pleaded with Khomeini to delay his return until the Prime Minister could visit him personally in Paris. Unsurprisingly, Khomeini recognized the emptiness of Bakhtiar's threats, and the letter had no effect. As an Iranian poet writes,

'To show weakness to a tyrant is a folly.
The tears of a kebab just increase the fire.'

Without even referring to the letter, Khomeini informed Bakhtiar that he would receive him only after he submitted his resignation. Bakhtiar canceled his trip to Paris, and Khomeini announced the date he planned to return to Iran. He let it be known that he was coming to overthrow Bakhtiar's government and put the Prime Minister on trial.

Bakhtiar had no choice but to try to prepare for the confrontation. At his instruction, the National Security Council outlined a series of contingency plans. Iran was under national emergency status, so all the airports would be placed under the control of the armed forces. It was decided that Khomeini's airplane should be intercepted, if possible, and redirected to Kish, an Iranian island near Dubai. There, Khomeini would be isolated and unable to stir up trouble. The government also asked the French government to ban the Air France flight carrying Khomeini to Iran. If these actions failed and the result was armed confrontation—a likely outcome—the military was to take direct control of all key government organizations, including the oil industry, customs offices, police departments, and other sensitive installations. Huyser was a key part of these plans, and—in conference with Dean Brown at Defense—worked to prepare for every contingency. The first problem the military would face were gasoline shortages, since the armed forces had not stockpiled enough emergency supplies to keep themselves equipped and ready. So Brown immediately dispatched a fuel tanker to an Iranian port on the Persian Gulf to make sure the military would be well supplied.

When Sullivan got wind of the National Security Council's plan, he immediately met with Prime Minister Bakhtiar and tried to convince him to avoid force. He said he had reliable information suggesting that the armed forces would not support Bakhtiar if he ordered them to oppose Khomeini and would probably disintegrate, with the country's stability. It was America's wish that the Iranian armed forces remain intact, he said; taking action now would compromise that goal.

That same day, Bakhtiar called an emergency meeting of the Security Council. The participants sat in stunned silence as he announced that he had decided to change policy. Rather than quelling the situation by force, he said, the government would now take a passive stance and allow Khomeini to enter Iran peacefully. His rationale? With all the propaganda fundamentalists were spreading, he said, the public was under the impression that Khomeini was a saint returning from heaven. But his actual presence in Iran would give the public a closer look at him, and people would soon realize that he was just another mullah in a turban.

The commanders were suspicious that some kind of compromise was afoot, but a new plan was approved by the committee. Tehran's Mehrabad airport would still be under the strict control of the military, but Khomeini would be allowed to land. A limited number of his supporters, vetted by the government, would be permitted to welcome him. The rest of his supporters would congregate in nearby Shahyad Square, where, after the initial welcoming ceremony, Khomeini would be transported by helicopter and presented to his followers. From there, he would be driven by car to the Behesht-e Zahra cemetery, where he would lead a brief prayer session. After that, he would be flown by helicopter to a residence that the government had prepared for him. If there were any outbursts of violence, the army was authorized to use swift force; otherwise, all troops were to remain passive.

In the meantime, Sullivan ignored both Bakhtiar and the instructions of the Defense Department and continued to negotiate directly with

Khomeini's top leaders, preparing the ground for the surrender of the armed forces. Khomeini considered several hundred of the military's top brass to be untrustworthy. He wanted them tried and convicted, but his deputies ultimately accepted Sullivan's suggestion that these individuals be permitted to leave the country. At all times, Sullivan, Gharabaghi, and Moghadam kept their negotiations with Khomeini completely secret, especially from Bakhtiar and other military commanders. After the fact, Khomeini's promises were not fulfilled: most of the top brass in the Iranian military were either executed or sentenced to long terms in prison.

On February 1, 1979, Khomeini entered Tehran at nine o'clock in the morning. His arrival was broadcast, like the World Cup, unedited and live on all radio and television stations. The entire country was shut down. His motorcade route from the airport to Tehran was swarming with hundreds of thousands of supporters, while people in the provinces gathered around their televisions and radios to follow his historic return.

In prison, we were watching the event, too. As soon as Khomeini's Air France plane entered Iranian airspace, the TV camera focused on the Ayatollah's face. An animated foreign reporter asked him, through Qotbzadeh, who acted as interpreter, "After all these years of exile from your native land, what are your feelings on returning victoriously?" Khomeini, with an emotionless face, grunted, "*Heechi*." Qotbzadeh thought Khomeini had not understood the question, so he repeated it, but Khomeini only said again, in a louder voice that was heard by millions of Iranians "*HEECHI!*" Qotbzadeh had no choice but to turn to the stunned reporter, saying, "He has said he feels nothing."

In prison, as we watched this repulsive scene, Rouhani, former Minister of Agriculture, suddenly shouted out, "What kind of an Iranian is this man, who has no feelings for his country? And yet he claims to be fighting for its 'freedom and prosperity!'" Kianpour, former Minister of Justice, observed that, of course, Khomeini felt nothing for Iran. He was, after all, trying to place Iran once more under the domination of the culture of the Arabs, to complete the task started some fourteen centuries ago. "He doesn't recognize us," Kianpour said. "His country is Najaf and Karbala. His nation is a mass of ignorant thugs with no fixed home. Iran is *heechi* to him."

In the prison, sorrow was on everyone's faces. This spiteful old man in his black turban and robe had arrived, and we knew that even the baldest truth—that Iran was nothing to him—wouldn't break the spell he had cast over the country. And yet, he was also predicting the future: what good could we look forward to in this country? *Heechi.* Nothing. It should have been an eye-opener. It was the first chance the Iranian people had to see what kind of future Khomeini was bringing them. But too few understood the full meaning of that word, and it was too late.

Sullivan's success would reap the whirlwind. The American ambassador in Tehran had engineered a secret agreement with the armed forces and SAVAK, and they surrendered the country to Khomeini and his fundamentalist mullahs. General Huyser was still in Tehran, under orders from President Carter to either save the Shah's government or instigate a coup d'état to preserve order, but Sullivan thwarted them all.

At nine-thirty in the morning, after the flight carrying Khomeini had landed at Mehrabad Airport in Tehran and the Ayatollah had been welcomed by one of his guards, Khomeini took the microphone and, in his Arabic-inflected Farsi, declared that Bakhtiar's government was illegal and that he would soon introduce his own government. After the press conference, Khomeini was transferred by army helicopter to Shahyad Square, where he was received by a massive crowd of supporters. Seated in a land rover, he then led hundreds of buses and cars to the Behesht-e Zahra cemetery, where he gave a speech. He was then transferred to a government helicopter, which was to transport him to the government-sanctioned place of residence. During this flight, however, the pilot was informed that the Imam was not feeling well and demanded to be taken to a hospital. When the pilot landed, Khomeini's men were waiting, by prior arrangement, and whisked him away, out of the government's hands. Bakhtiar's carefully laid plans fell apart when Khomeini tested them.

The world closely followed the developments. The *New York Times* reported that the United States was willing to recognize Khomeini's government. A BBC report announced the names of the members of Bazargan's cabinet. Iranian newspapers followed suit, printing the Revolutionary Council's proclamations on their front pages. Opportunists who had once opposed Khomeini were now singing his praises, and the newspapers were filled with confessions and formal letters of apology from Khomeini's many one-time opponents. The flatterers who had bowed to the Shah were now kissing Khomeini's slippers, afraid for their lives.

After learning through the news that General Gharabaghi would not be attempting a coup d'état, Huyser asked Sullivan to prepare an airplane for him in case he needed to flee the country. Sullivan's reply was blunt: perhaps he had better leave Iran immediately. Huyser was, at this point, nearly frantic with anxiety. He was bombarded with attacks on his performance from newspapers in London, New York, and Moscow, and Farsi newspapers were also taking him to task. Sullivan personally showed Huyser an article that called him a bloodsucking executioner. Finally, Huyser received personal assurances that General Rabii, the Commander of the Air Force, would get him out of Iran safely should the need arise.

In a telephone call to Dean Brown, Huyser asked permission to end his mission in Iran and return home. Brown was surprised. What had happened to the proposed coup d'état? Huyser insisted that the lack of cooperation between the commanders had made it impossible. When Brown asked if it would help if the Shah returned, Huyser insisted that that would also be impossible. He had by then firmly made up his mind to leave Iran, at any cost. Even though all six commanders had told him that a coup d'état would be feasible under the Shah's command—and Brown had offered to arrange for the Shah's personal authorization—Huyser had decided there was nothing to be done. Frustrated, Brown ended the conversation, ordering Huyser to stay where he was and promising that he would hear from him again shortly.

The day after Khomeini landed in Iran, the top U.S. foreign policy officials convened a conference call. President Carter had had his fill of bickering in his cabinet and ordered both sides to work out their differences. Everyone was involved: Cyrus Vance; Dean Brown; Zbigniew Brzezinski; General Jones, head of the Joint Chiefs; Warren Christopher; General Gast, head of the U.S. Army Advisers in Iran; Sullivan; and Huyser.

Sullivan first reported that Khomeini enjoyed the support of the majority of the Iranian people and relayed that, for all intents and purposes, he had already taken full control of the country. The armed forces had lost their ability to act, he said, since ordinary men in uniform would no longer obey their officers, especially if they were ordered to oppose Khomeini. Glad to do everything in his power to put the last nail in the coffin, Sullivan declared that Bakhtiar's government was incapable of standing on its feet, no matter how much support the U.S. provided.

Up until this point, Huyser had maintained that a coup d'état was a viable option. During this conversation, however, he lacked conviction and was even somewhat incoherent. Since Huyser was the point person for the military option, his doubt and uncertainty spoke volumes. Although he claimed that the proposed coup d'état would have succeeded if there had been strong leadership, it was obvious that he was not the leader the situation demanded. After that call, Brown finally recognized that Huyser was incapable of achieving anything in Tehran and gave him permission to return to Washington.

The rest of the discussion was inconclusive. Vance and Christopher had a heated exchange with Brzezinski and Brown, but there was no progress in bringing the sides together. Brzezinski believed that a strong Iran was vital for American interests and that an immediate intervention by Iranian armed forces was clearly necessary. Vance, however, argued that a coup d'état would not be successful, insisted that Bakhtiar was a dead duck, and maintained that America should be negotiating with Khomeini. Although nothing was accomplished, everyone now realized that Huyser's mission had failed.

Before Huyser left Iran, at his farewell meeting with the army commanders, he asked them a vital question: if Bakhtiar's government collapsed, would they be ready to take over the country by coup d'état? His question produced absolute silence. What he didn't understand, even then, was that the commanders were as confused as he was. Would the U.S. support the coup d'état or not? Should the army listen to Sullivan or to Huyser?

In the meantime, assaults on police, assassinations of army officers, and rebellious mutinies in military barracks became daily events. By March 31, 1979, leftist guerrilla groups such as the Mujahedin Khalgh and the Fedayan Khalgh had already overrun and occupied most police stations. The opposition even controlled Tehran's Mehrabad Airport. Khomeini had already set up his supreme revolutionary council, with branches in every neighborhood mosque, each headed by a mullah loyal to the Ayatollah. With machine guns in hand, they stormed defenseless armed forces bases, police stations, and other government departments, with little or no resistance. They massacred thousands. Khomeini was rapidly establishing the cruelest theological dictatorship in the world. It was a template for Muslim fundamentalism.

CHAPTER 25

INTO THE FIRE

In his last days as Prime Minister, Bakhtiar announced that he was going to bring the corrupt detainees in his prisons to justice. We understood immediately that he meant us. We had no desire to be executed by him or Khomeini's regime, but all we could do was wait and see. Was it going to be the frying pan or the fire?

Inside our cells, we watched the dominoes fall. First, the Speaker of the National Assembly announced the dissolution of Parliament. Then, from his command center in Jamaran, Khomeini officially approved the ten ministers who would form Bazargan's cabinet. Bakhtiar's government faded away into silence. His ministers were hiding in one place or another, and we stopped hearing anything from them. The fighting became more and more chaotic. Leftist guerillas fought Islamic radicals in the streets, each trying to occupy Tehran's government buildings, but Bakhtiar's people were no longer visible.

Since our situation was going to be resolved soon, one way or the other, each of us thought about how and when we were likely to die. We sensed that it could be any day, and we were all worried about our families. Those who had not already made arrangements for the safety of their wives and children now tried to do everything they could to protect them. Some of us asked others to give messages to our loved ones, in case we died and others survived. Mansour Rouhani gave me a message for his son, who was living in the United States. I asked him to help my young American wife and our children and to tell them that I loved them very much and was sorry to have to leave them. Some wrote coded messages disclosing where they had their money. Many of us thought about what our last wishes would be. I hoped that, if the worst happened, the authorities would let me see Helen and the children at least one last time and say goodbye.

That was our darkest hour. Some of my fellow prisoners began writing defense briefs for themselves, as if they expected to face a meaningful tribunal. I didn't bother. Especially after Rahimi's aborted attempt to help me escape, I had thought long and hard about my situation. I had come to the conclusion that I would either escape or die in prison. Months earlier I had planned an escape with a friend who was in the police department, but after discussing it with Dr. Sheikh, we decided to cancel the plan because there was only a 50 percent chance of its success. I didn't know what new chapter had opened for Iran, but I understood, now, finally, that if I was to be saved, I had to have to do it myself. So I waited, with my eyes wide open.

On March 11, General Gharabaghi officially announced that the armed forces would henceforth remain neutral and would not "interfere in politics." Everybody knew what that meant. Soldiers soon disappeared from the streets, and in their place came Khomeini's guerillas. The sounds of gunfire bursting from automatic weapons, tearful cries, and bloody chaos were now commonplace as the country fell into the hands of the mullahs. Volleys of wild gunfire sounded the last rites for Bakhtiar's government and two thousand years of the Persian monarchy, and they heralded the rise of the first autocratic theocracy. Khomeini's reign of terror had begun.

In those last days of the government, news from outside was our only lifeline. One prisoner would stand guard in the doorway, straining for the sound of the guard's footsteps, while the rest of us gathered around the portable short-wave radio we had smuggled in, taking turns listening through a single precious pair of headphones. In those interminable days, radio broadcasts, the crackling *Voice of America* reports, and intercepted police and army communiqués were our only focus. But the radio just vomited an endless stream of horror—reports of more police stations and military installations that had been captured by revolutionaries, followed by reports of government and military officials who had been arrested or killed.

So much had changed. When I first arrived here, I was full of hope. Though we were confined to a few windowless rooms, we could sometimes get a glimpse of the complex where we were imprisoned, with its parading soldiers and officers swaggering through drills. It was easy to believe what we had been told, to laugh when SAVAK tried to strip us of the dignity of our positions, and remind ourselves that we were the men who ran the country.

When they brought us army fatigues to wear, only a few of us agreed to put them on, because we were political prisoners. Events since then had shown us how foolish we were to have put any faith in the Shah's honey-coated assurances of a fair trial. We had long ago been marked for death by the revolutionaries, and our captors had made it clear they would hold us here until the end. And so, as the radio broadcast more and more bad news, we knew it was only a matter of time before Jamshidieh, the Army base where we were held, would fall.

When we learned that insurgents had captured General Mehdi Rahimi, Tehran's military commander and head of the national police, we knew our time was coming. If a patriot like Rahimi was in custody and branded an "enemy of the state," surely our turn was next. Soon, Khomeini's new Prime Minister promised to put us on trial and execute us, bragging that the mullahs had already prepared firing squads. But what could we do? No matter who won, we were like the chicken in the Persian proverb—wedding or funeral, the bird ends up in the pot.

Then, one afternoon, the sound of shouting and a general alarm drew all of us to the single window in the hallway, wondering if our time had finally come. I scrambled on top of a radiator to look out. At first, I only glimpsed soldiers milling around in confusion. Where were the officers? I searched for the source of the disturbance, and I found it in a moment. Across the courtyard, at the compound's great iron gates, a hundred or so men wrapped in Palestinian scarves and brandishing guns were shouting and gesturing at the two guards on duty. Behind them, perhaps a few hundred feet back, a larger crowd of men, women, and children were waiting and watching. We were under siege.

The two guards, rifles in hand, stood tense and motionless at their positions; they were the only barrier between us and the mob. Our jailers were now our protectors, it seemed. But not for long. Minutes later, Panjali, the unarmed soldier who took care of our daily needs, appeared at our door. A plain, simple, smiling person who loved everyone, Panjali ran errands for us in prison and took care of us like we were the most important people in the world. Now, he brought dreadful news: "There's been a communiqué from army headquarters!" he shouted. "The army is to stand down!"

I stepped away from the window. As we later pieced the story together, the army had decided not to involve itself in "politics," and "non-involvement" was equivalent to signing our death warrants. For the first time, everyone in prison began realizing that the end of the government had truly come. The strutting peacocks in SAVAK still tried to look confident, as they always did—what else were they to do?—but only minutes later the sound of the gates crashing open clanged through the base, silencing their bravado.

Wild shouting and the sounds of men and women chanting floated up from the courtyard into our building. There was no gunfire yet, but we knew it was just a matter of time. Panjali informed us that the officers in command of the base had already left. Only conscripted soldiers were still at their posts, and we knew they wouldn't last long; without their officers, rank-and-file soldiers had no desire to put up a fight.

The shooting began slowly—first isolated shots, then an occasional burst of automatic weapons—but it grew steadily. By the time the invaders broke down the doors of the army base, I could see from my perch that men in Palestinian scarves were carrying armloads of guns into the courtyard and passing them out to the crowds that had followed them. Soon, shooting began in earnest. We began to feel the impact of the gunfire as sounds of heavy machine guns cut through the air. I couldn't see where the firing was coming from, but the dull roar of those guns drowned out the scattered fusillades that had broken the silence.

I nervously backed away from the window and was glad I did: as soon as I stepped down from the radiator, the window I had been looking through was shattered by gunfire. An instant later, windows on the other side of the hall exploded, and I fell to the ground, covering my head with my hands as glass sprayed across the room from both sides. We were under attack from every direction. I heard no sign of resistance in our section. In moments, all the windows were shattered, and the firing never stopped. The building's brick walls were chipped away by the hail of bullets, and dust filled the air. Terrified, we huddled close together on the floor, as far from the windows as possible. Our ears were telling us what our eyes couldn't see: there was no hope for any soldiers defending the complex. When the sounds of fighting gave way to an even more terrifying silence, we knew that most of them had been killed. We began to smell smoke, and I realized that we were living our last hours.

By then, the SAVAK agents had gone, bolting the doors behind them. There was nothing to do but wait, alone and abandoned. In those tense moments, we almost wished for our captors' return. Then, suddenly, a pale young guard appeared at the door. With a trembling voice, he told us that Panjali had been shot, and he had carried him to the pantry where we took our meals. "Can one of you doctors help?" he asked. Immediately, Dr. Sheikh stood up, and, after waiting for a brief lull in the shooting, I followed him out the door.

In the pantry, we were shocked to see Panjali sprawled on the floor, motionless, blood soaking through his clothing into sticky puddles. Together, we lifted him onto a table and struggled to find his pulse. He was barely alive. Although he couldn't possibly have been conscious, his face was contorted in pain, and his breathing, labored and slow, rattled in his throat. Dr. Sheikh and I looked at each other. Artificial respiration would probably kill him; the color of his skin told us that he had lost too much blood. We tried to staunch the bleeding by stuffing kitchen towels into his wounds and applying pressure. But just like that, it was over. Panjali was gone. Like a piece of meat, the guerillas had butchered him. As Dr. Sheikh closed the boy's eyes, I saw tears in his own.

For a moment, we stood staring down at his young, lifeless body. It is difficult to put into words my feelings at that moment. Panjali had been such a good person; he was a friend, and years as a doctor never inured me to the pain of having someone die in my arms. But even though Panjali had been a patriot who loved the Shah, he had been killed as a traitor. He had been a believer, a faithful Muslim, but he was killed by misguided fanatics in the name of Allah. He had been a soldier, always been proud to wear his country's uniform, but he had never carried or used a gun. Though he had never lived by violence, his fate was to die by it.

We covered Panjali with a tablecloth, and Dr. Sheikh began walking out of the pantry. But I stood where I was. As I looked at the corpse of my friend, I suddenly knew that if I went back, I would share his fate. "Wait!" I shouted, and took Dr. Sheikh by the arm. "It would be suicide to go back now," I said. "If the government has fallen, what would be the sense of locking ourselves back in our cells? The only question is who would kill us first."

Dr. Sheikh shook his head sadly. "If you want to go out there and be killed by those animals, just like Panjali," he said, "I can't stop you. But I'm going to wait with the others for whatever comes next." As he started to walk back, I didn't follow him.

CHAPTER 26

ESCAPE

I leaned against the counter in the prison pantry and tried to compose myself. I hesitated for a moment, but I knew what I had to do; I had imagined this plan many times. From the pantry, it would only be a short trot to the other wing of the building, which housed the Homafars, a group of imprisoned air force technicians who had supported Khomeini from the beginning. If I could blend in with them, I would be safe.

As I rounded the corner into the Homafars' ward, everything was in an uproar. All the doors to the cells had been smashed open, and there were no guards in sight. About a dozen Homafars had clustered at the exit, struggling to push their way out and save their lives. No one seemed to be looking my way, so I joined their group. We were all dressed alike in soldier uniforms, with no rankings, which had been given to us when we entered the Armed Forces prison. I was probably the oldest person in the crowd, but I hoped that in the excitement no one would look closely. Fortunately, there was no electricity, and it was starting to get dark. The horizon was turning orange and black as the setting sun and smoke from the gunfire cast a pall over the entire base.

Looking back, it is difficult to make sense of what happened next. In that maelstrom of roaring machine guns, blood, terror, and the cries of the dead and dying, we all shared a single thought—escaping alive. The main exit door of the building opened into another courtyard, and as we streamed out of the wing, we came upon an armed guard who was crouched by the door, peering outside with his back to us. As we approached him, he suddenly turned and started to raise his gun. The lead Homafars didn't even break stride, seizing the gun and then the guard, pushing him to the floor. But as soon as the first prisoners stepped into the courtyard, there was a crackling of gunfire. At least three Homafars fell to the ground and didn't move. The rest of us ducked back into the building, frozen in shock. What should we do?

In the silence, there was a hurried conference. Someone suggested that since *we* didn't know who was shooting at us—revolutionary guerillas or soldiers—perhaps the shooters didn't know who they were firing at. Another pointed out that, since we were wearing army fatigues, and the first man out the door carried an army rifle, maybe the shooters thought we were defending the barracks. So the Homafars began shouting, "Brother, why are you shooting? We are prisoners! We are supporters of the revolution!"

After a tense moment, someone outside shouted back: "Come out then! One-by-one, with your hands on your head!" There was a pause. Then, shaking with fear, we began to edge out the door, slowly and carefully, as if we would have a chance to duck back to safety. In a moment we might all be dead, I thought, but at least we'll die trying to escape. The thick, acrid smoke from burning tires stung our eyes as we walked out into the open, picking our way past the bloodstained corpses of soldiers and guerillas. I tried hard not to tread on them. I focused on steadying my quivering step and trembling hands and keeping my spinning mind, half expecting a hail of gunfire, from holding me back.

As we marched forward, bullets cut down three Homafars, but the rest of us made it to the main guardroom, a four-sided glass building littered with scattered corpses of soldiers. They hadn't been fighting; they had looks of surprise on their faces, and most hadn't even unholstered their guns. Some weren't carrying weapons. They were simply slaughtered. We then saw about a hundred and fifty men carrying machine guns, their faces hidden behind scarves. They were haphazardly firing around the defenseless base, mopping up or celebrating. These savages, hiding their cruel faces behind a mask of God and religion, reveled in their brutality. The Homafars were cheering these thugs, hugging and kissing some of them on their cheeks, as they moved forward toward the prison gate. I seized the moment, embracing the armed man nearest me and shouting "Long live Imam!" He mumbled a few words in Arabic—probably the only ones he knew, since many revolutionaries merely imitated the mullahs and pretended to speak the Arabic language.

As we passed through the gates of the army base, we saw a group of men, women, and children standing and watching. It was a sad moment in Iranian history. They had come to crush corruption and oppression, and now they were witnessing a slaughter by bloodthirsty thugs. Making my way forward, I tried to blend into this crowd. From the way people eyed me, however, I understood that I was conspicuous. Of course! I was still wearing my prison fatigues over a black t-shirt and jeans. Once I made it to the other side of the crowd, I ducked behind the cover of a parked VW Beetle and tore off my outer garments, the last remnants of my days of humiliation.

Just like that, I was free to go—where? I thought of Dr. Mahani, a surgeon and long-time friend I could trust. His home clinic was just a short distance away. It was so close to the prison that I had once sent him a message, through Helen, that I would seek refuge there first should I ever escape. I hurried along the darkened lane, trying to stay close to the shadows, but I quickly realized that running made me more conspicuous, so I slowed to a businesslike trot.

As I did, my steps unconsciously fell in time with military marches that blared from the radios that shopkeepers kept outside in the streets. I thought of the *Noheh*, the march of young Shia men beating their chests with chains and mourning the martyrdom of Imam Hossein. Who was being martyred today? I thought about the first Arab invasion of Iran, fourteen hundred years ago—one of many times that Iran had been invaded by its neighbors. In the past, foreigners had claimed victory, only to discover that Iran was more easily defeated than conquered. Ever since, Iran had adopted its own brand of Islam, Shia and used it to maintain its independence. But today, Khomeini had transformed radical Shia into a weapon against us and was using it to wage another invasion, transforming our national heritage into grief, tears, and sorrow. I wondered how the next chapter would be written and what beat and whose drum I was marching to.

Along the main thoroughfare, Amirabad Avenue, I knew I ran the risk of being accosted by Pasdars and other gun-toting thugs, but it would take me longer to reach Dr. Mahani's along the back streets. I should have been more cautious. Just as I arrived at a major road junction, a pick-up truck screeched to a halt in the middle of the avenue. Two scarf-clad revolutionaries jumped down, shouting that the Imperial Guard had attacked the national television station and that they were on their way to help. One grabbed me, but after I praised Khomeini profusely, I begged him to release me. I said that I first had to tell my wife and children where I was going and promised to join them and do my patriotic duty. He looked unpersuaded but accepted my word. The men leaped back onto the truck as it drove away. In a moment, they were gone, and I stood in the street with my knees shaking. It was much too close.

Determined not to be caught again, I dashed off the main road and down the first tiny street I came to, but it was a cul-de-sac. When I turned back, I saw that there was some kind of commotion. Spotlights or headlights were shining into side streets and alleys, and I couldn't get back onto the main road without being seen. "What's happening?" I asked a woman near me, trying to suppress my panic. She told me with relish that Hoveyda and other ministers and associates of the Shah had escaped from the Jamshidieh, where they had been incarcerated. The sound and commotion came from guerilla groups that were searching for them—searching for me.

My world went dark, and my mind shut down. I backed away from the crowd, but in my confused state I had no idea where to go. The cul-de-sac seemed to offer the only sanctuary. I surveyed the doorways, desperate for a house I knew or a familiar face. But I saw nothing. A young girl, standing outside her front door, looked at me carefully and pulled her chador tightly about her as I returned her gaze. She had a kind demeanor. Could she help me? I had to do something. I tried to pull myself together, and asked, in a steady voice, for a glass of water. She nodded curtly. Following her inside, I closed the door behind me and carefully took the glass she handed me. After I took a sip, she suddenly said to me, "Your face seems familiar. What is your name?" Not knowing why, I told her the truth. She apologized for not knowing me sooner and shouted up to her mother, "Mama, come down! Dr. Aram is here!"

An elderly lady's voice told her to put on the kettle, and I heard movements upstairs. In a moment, I knew, she would come downstairs. Did I want her to see me? I searched my memory in vain to recall who these people were. Had they really recognized me? Did they know who was standing inside their doorstep? Would they hand me over to the guerillas, fearing what those barbarians might do? Or could I rely on their Persian hospitality and kindness?

As the girl went to prepare tea, I heard a voice calling my name from the street outside: "Assad, do they know you're here? Can you let me in?" I instantly recognized the voice of Iraj Vahidi, a fellow inmate and former Minister of Energy. He must have escaped, too, and seen me enter the house. How long had he been following me? I thought quickly. Was anyone else following me? I had passed unrecognized so far, but I knew that if I was standing next to Iraj, one of the tallest men I knew, I would be more conspicuous. Even if the occupants of this house were willing to help me, I worried that they wouldn't be able to shelter two. So I opened the door—not to let Iraj in, but to let myself out, telling him that I didn't know who lived here. After wishing Iraj the best of luck, I left him standing there.

Outside, the lights, crowds, and commotion had dispersed, and there were no more signs of the guerrillas on the main road, so I hurried toward my destination, past Farah Park. The crowds were slowly dispersing, and only a few knots of people still lingered in conversation here and there. Most were armed, but the way they held their weapons made me guess that they didn't know how to use them and weren't likely to. I scurried along, keeping my head down so I wouldn't be recognized. I suddenly noticed, however, a man walking beside me, wearing an enormous fur hat. It was my friend Mansur Rouhani, and we saw each other at the same time.

"Where are you going?" I whispered, "And for God's sake, take off that hat!" We ducked into a tiny alcove, out of sight, and spoke for a brief moment. He was heading to his mother's home, he said, but he wouldn't be able to stay there for long, since it would be the first place they'd look. He warned me not to go to my own home, and I should have given him the same advice. Days later, I heard that Rouhani had been apprehended at his mother's house and arrested.

When I finally arrived at Dr. Mahani's house, the adjacent street was filled with people, and I started ringing the doorbell like a madman. There was no reply. I kept ringing—what else could I do?—but there was no response. Minutes passed, and I knew I had to get off the street, but where could I go? In despair, I started pounding on the door.

Finally, a lady from the house next door opened a first-floor window and told me the electricity was off. "The bell doesn't work," she said, "but they'll hear you if you knock on the garage door." When I did, Maryam's voice instantly called out, the first welcome sound I had heard in like an eternity. I was so glad to get off the street that I don't remember how I entered the house or whom I saw first. To be greeted by friendly faces and embraced by friends was a gift from God!

When I calmed down, Maryam and Dr. Mahani said they had been waiting for me for hours, ever since they heard that Jamshidieh had been "liberated," as the radio put it. Dr. Mahani had even driven near the complex several times, hoping to find me. Apparently, by fleeing with my face in the shadows, I had successfully hidden from my friend too.

Before I did anything else, I knew that I had to make a telephone call. Since I was sure that the events of the past few days had been broadcast in the American media, I was afraid that Helen and the kids would be frantic with worry. I began telling Maryam that I needed to phone my wife, but then I stopped. All international calls would be watched; if I called Helen, I realized, it could lead my pursuers straight to me.

On the other hand, Maryam wondered, was anyone really bothering with matters like that in the present chaos? I could use the public phone booth across from the house, and if I kept the call short, I would be off the street long before anyone could find me. I quickly agreed. After scouring the house for enough loose change and making sure that the street was clear, I headed for the public phone. Cathy's voice came through at the first attempt, and I could hear her beaming across the distant miles. "Where are you?" she cried. "What's happened? Are you well?" I was so glad to reassure her, at least for the moment. "Rest easy," I said. "I'm out of prison and free, but I can't talk much now." She cried with joy and gave the phone to her mom. Helen was overjoyed hearing my voice and knowing that I was out of jail and alive. She immediately asked me to be careful and not to return to our home. "I love you so very much", she said. I told her that I would try to call her soon, "kiss the kids for me, I love you all."

Returning to Maryam and Mahani, I was wracked with emotion. I was so far away from my family, and it was hard to imagine when I'd see them again. But my friends took care of me. Anticipating my escape, they had prepared a cozy hiding place for me, in the hidden room that all old Iranian houses had to hold valuables and other secrets. They had made me a warm little nest with blankets, food, and everything else they could think of. Together, we sat on the floor of my new home, sipping chilled vodka and snacking on little morsels that Maryam had prepared. It was my first taste of freedom again; even if I was locked away as my enemies searched for me, I felt warm and safe here, in the bosom of friendship.

But eventually, inevitably, we thought of the future. What should I do next? I was out of the frying pan, but flames were crackling at my feet. According to the radio, the revolutionaries had opened the doors of the Shah's prisons but had no idea who they were setting free. They were astonished to learned that the Shah had left so many of his people to his own enemies, like lambs bound for the slaughter. They were quick to recapture many of the prisoners. Within hours, we heard that several, including Dr. Sheikh, had been found wandering along Amirabad Avenue and were now "safely" back in custody. A general search was raging in the streets. I thought bitterly of Iran's former elite, who had fled in ease and comfort—taking their wealth, servants, lovers, and pets—while we were imprisoned as scapegoats, then trapped here, waiting to be found.

I had originally considered it a stroke of luck that Dr. Mahani's house was so close to the barracks. But the more I thought about it, the more it seemed like the most dangerous place in the world for me to hide. It was common knowledge that Dr. Mahani was a friend of mine, and the search parties that had caught Dr. Sheikh might be closing in on me even as I listened to the radio reports. I knew I couldn't hide at the Mahanis' for long. My loyal friends feared for my safety and urged me to stay, but when I insisted that we search for a new hiding place, they agreed to try.

This was easier said than done, however. If I contacted any of my old friends and associates, search parties would sooner or later find me, because so many of my colleagues now supported the opposition. Whom could I trust who couldn't be linked to me? I thought of the many university lecturers, doctors, and others, with different ideologies, who had returned to develop Iran under my guidance. How many would turn me in now without a thought? How many had been swept away by the wave of fanaticism? I didn't want to know and was afraid to find out.

In a telephone call to Dr. Sheikh's wife, Mahvash, I expressed sorrow that my friend had been rearrested and expected her to share my anxiety. But Mahvash laughed at my concern. In the people's court that the mullahs would set up, she declared, her husband would easily prove his innocence. She urged me not to deny the inevitable, either, and to present myself immediately to the revolutionaries at the Alavi School, a religious training center they were using as a temporary court, jail, and execution site. She was convinced that remaining in hiding would only hurt my chances, and we argued for a long time. Finally, she suggested that I discuss the matter with Dr. Shahgoli, who, she said, knew more about what was going on.

The former Minister of Science and Higher Education, Dr. Shahgoli was well known for his resourcefulness. I knew that he had extensive connections behind the scenes and assumed that he was laying plans to save himself from capture by the revolutionaries. But when I telephoned him at home, I found that he, too, was sitting and waiting, as though he didn't have a care in the world. After my experience with Mahvash, I didn't try to convince him to save himself and instead asked him if he'd heard any news.

Dr. Shahgoli knew what had happened to Dr. Sheikh and told me the story. After leaving prison in the confusion, Dr. Sheikh had been arrested by a physician who was a resident at a Ministry of Health hospital and a member of an armed guerrilla group called Fadaee Khalgh. The resident had initially intended to deliver Dr. Sheikh straight back to prison. After much pleading, however, Dr. Sheikh had persuaded him to consult another doctor, Dr. Barazandeh, a department chairman at the hospital and one of the Georgetown physicians whom I had convinced to return to Iran. Dr. Barazandeh took charge of Dr. Sheikh, and, after consulting with a mutual friend, they decided to approach Dr. Ibrahim Yazdi, a revolutionary leader. Yazdi was in charge of bringing prisoners to trial, and his answer was blunt: they must deliver Dr. Sheikh to the Alavi School, where he would be in "safe" hands. My friends believed him, and Dr. Sheikh was taken to the authorities right away.

Dr. Shahgoli advised me to do the same and urged me to speak with Dr. Barazandeh. I was shocked that he seemed so calm—perhaps because he had never tasted the bitterness of prison life—and knew better than to expect justice from those thugs. How, I asked, could he expect me to trust those men? They would kill me first and ask questions later. "Don't you realize they might be coming for you as well?" His tranquility exasperated me.

I had two friends who were close to the top revolutionary leaders, Dr. Barazandeh and Dr. Molavi. To my surprise, Barzandeh told me that he now shared my view of the situation. He was badly frightened, he feared for Dr. Sheikh's safety, and he urged me to avoid recapture. "Everything is in a state of flux," he said. "Since no one yet knows who is really in charge; don't show yourself until you have a better sense of what is happening." I agreed. Once we understood who had real power behind the scenes, we would be in a better position to know what to do. I then called another friend, Dr. Molavi, and found that he had a similar opinion. "No matter who is in charge," he said, "there are deadly elements out there, and they're liable to do anything." Dr. Sheikh's arrest, it seemed, had shaken them all.

As I talked over the situation with Mahani, our minds gradually converged on the same name: Ata Khazani. If anyone could help with this kind of business, it would certainly be Ata. And no one would know that he was connected to me. I had met Ata thirty years ago, when he was still a wood merchant in Bandar Gaz on the Caspian Sea. In that small community, we had been close friends, and as the years passed, our friendship continued. Our families knew each other's homes well, and we had no secrets from each other about our personal lives. Despite all our long years of friendship, however, we had never had the slightest financial dealings, although he took pride in offering help to any friend who needed it.

Dr. Mahani was right: if anyone would know what to do, it would be Ata. He wasn't just a self-made man: he had remade himself over and over again—so many times that it was hard to keep track of where he was and where he'd been. When he was young, Ata had lost his father and quit high school to provide for his family. Their dire need left him with an indomitable will to survive and succeed. So, although he began life as a manual laborer, he had worked his way from being a fisherman to being a commercial middleman, a real estate broker, and finally a sort of civil servant. Ata had a way with people; he was a man of a thousand faces and a jack-of-all-trades, and he had the right kind of ruthless ambition to profit from any turn of fate. After making handsome profits selling real estate and commercial goods, he had seen the revolution as an opportunity and found ways to profit from it. When Khomeini declared that a law degree was no longer necessary to practice law, he cheerfully stepped forward and registered himself as a lawyer. With Ata, it was all about people; he was a likable man, and others never tired of his company, so he fit into any group that he chose to join. Whether he was with *bazaari* (the merchant class), at parties of the upper classes, in religious ceremonies of the mosque-goers, or in meetings with high-rolling traders, he was never ill at ease. Ata had never met a stranger.

As it turned out, making contact with Ata was almost too easy. He appeared at Mahani's front door less than ten minutes after my call. As we sipped vodka together, it seemed like nothing had changed. He had already been searching for me when he heard the news. Having found me, he seemed so positive and relaxed that even I started to believe there was hope. As we drank, he began telling us what he called "real stories" to lighten the mood, and, for a few minutes, he made me forget my anxiety. Then, in a serious tone, he assured me with absolute certainty that he would soon have a new hiding place for me. I must have looked unconvinced, since he affected a kind of mock astonishment, pounding me on my shoulder and demanding in his thick, northern Iranian Gilaki dialect, "Why are you so tense? I will *guarantee* your safety!"

It was sometimes hard to know how seriously I could take Ata's words, but at that moment, his confidence was a lifeline. By his own admission, he had two great weaknesses. He was a compulsive liar, which he freely admitted, and he was always on the lookout for easy money. But it was rare to find people who would really complain that he had cheated them. Every new acquaintance was potential prey, and if there was any profit to be made from them, you could rest assured that he would find it. What some might call extortion Ata claimed was merely a matter of helping people with their problems and receiving a just reward for doing so. Who could say that he was wrong? I was simply glad to have Ata on my side.

We quickly got down to business. After discussing possible hideouts, we agreed that my best option would be to contact Shahrokh, a retired police officer whom we all knew. Shahrokh had retired from active duty years ago, but he was still spry and hale, so Ata set off to sound him out and see if he could help. Just a few hours later he returned, telling me that I would be going to a new hideout early in the morning.

It was late when I finally went to bed, but I couldn't sleep. My mind wouldn't rest: dreams of freedom were interspersed with nightmare visions of arrest and torture. It was nearly sunrise when I finally fell asleep, and it seemed just minutes later that I was awakened by Ata's knock. He brought me a fedora—a style we called a "chapeau hat" and knew from detective movies—and he fussed with it, making me try different ways of wearing it before he was satisfied. I bid goodbye to my faithful hosts and, after getting into Ata's old Mercedes, set off with him to Shahrokh's place of business.

Shahrokh met us at the door with the humble air of a man receiving guests for tea. He was a solid-looking man of about fifty. Like me, he had piercing blue eyes, which is atypical for Iranians but not unusual for those born close to the Russian border. We embraced and, after scanning the nearby streets, he escorted me upstairs to his office to talk. He worked on the second floor of a two-story building, above a vacant ground floor, and there wasn't much to see in his office. In the chaos of the past months, Shahrokh's business had been stagnant, and now it was almost non-existent. This would be a safe place.

Shahrokh showed me the musty storeroom that was to be my home for the foreseeable future, and I felt distinctly like I was going back to jail.

Shelves lined the wall, stacked high with samples of Shahrokh's merchandise, from stationery and office supplies to bags of rice and wheat, canned food, and toys. Pulling aside a section of shelving, he opened up a small, narrow space among the bags of goods, a nest formed out of two blankets and a pillow. In a corner, he set up a table and a chair, with a jug of water and an electric kettle to make tea or coffee. It was like prison, I thought glumly, but here, at least, I knew I had the key.

Three employees worked in the office during the day. Since it would be too risky for them to know about me, I would have to stay quiet and motionless until sundown. If anyone came looking for me, Shahrokh said, I was to pull everything out of sight and stay hidden behind the shelves. Shahrokh would try to give me warning by asking in a loud voice outside the door, "Has Ata had been here today?" After the employees had all left, he would bring me some food and let me know if there was any news. Despite how much he was doing for me and how much of a risk he was taking, he apologized for the circumstances of my visit.

During the day, the sounds of people going about their daily business calmed me. At night, however, I slept uneasily. Scattered gunfire and the sounds of cars tearing through empty streets at breakneck speeds continued from dusk till sunrise. Every sound reminded me that I was a hunted man. In the morning, when I asked Shahrokh the reasons for all the gunfire, he shrugged. Who could tell? Government forces no longer existed, so the chaos that Khomeini unleashed ran wild in the streets. There were many rumors, but it was impossible to say which groups were fighting each other. We only knew for sure that we were under siege.

On the second night, the shooting was louder and closer. At times, it was so near that I thought guns were firing at our building. I dragged myself into my hiding place. Pulling the shelves in behind me was difficult, but after many repetitions, I was able to enter and seal myself up at a moment's notice, even in the dark. There was nothing to do but wait, sleepless and terrified, for the night to end. During the daytime, I tried to sleep; at night, the gunfire made it impossible to close my eyes.

In the evening, Ata would sometimes bring me newspapers, filled with bloody pictures and lists of officials and fellow inmates who had been arrested. I was one of the only people who had not yet been recaptured. He couldn't tell me much about the fighting; most people thought the street skirmishes were between different revolutionary factions, like the Fadaee

Khalgh guerillas and the MKO, but no one knew for sure. Having torn down the Shah's government, these thugs were now slicing the country up like a cake, dividing government buildings and people's homes between them as spoils of war. I read the paper each day and heard all the grim rumors from Ata. I usually regretted it.

One day, Shahrokh brought me a small portable radio that I could listen to quietly at night. No one would be able to hear its tinny broadcasts over the noisy gunfire in the streets, but I wouldn't take any chances and kept the volume so low that even I had to strain to make out the sound. Gradually, I got used to the incessant gunfire and managed to get a few hours sleep at night. But the radio reminded me of the chaos that was all around me. With the endless chanting of Muslim slogans, sermons on Imam Hussein's martyrdom, and the news of arrests and executions, it only added to my depression. But I couldn't turn it off, any more than I could turn of the gunfire. For a week, it was my only reality.

Once, when the radio was playing a military march, an announcer began reading out a list of "eighteen of the most important officials of the Shah's regime" who were now declared to be fugitives at large. My breath caught in my throat when I heard my name. "These men stand accused of committing treacherous crimes against the nation during the Shah's era," the announcer said, "and the Revolutionary Council has condemned them to death. The public will fully cooperate with the authorities in their apprehension. Anyone who makes the mistake of aiding and abetting these criminals in any way will be severely punished." I was surprised to hear Dr. Shahgoli's name, too, on the wanted list.

I was in the dark, gasping for air. It is one thing to know that you are hunted, but it is quite another to learn that your worst fears are true. My photograph would be circulated daily in the newspapers and probably broadcast every day on television. I could feel a rope settling around my neck and saw the apparition of an executioner stepping out of the darkness, his footsteps coming closer and closer. I didn't know if I was awake or caught in a nightmare; at this moment, there didn't seem to be any difference.

The next time Ata visited me, he said that guerrillas had been visiting the homes of my mother, sister, and brothers. My family had been questioned and intimidated, he said, but no one was hurt. I wasn't reassured. How long could this go on? When I saw Shahrokh, I swore to him that I would find a way to leave, so he could be rid of me. But he just smiled. "No one is going to find you here," he said, and he took my shoulder in a brotherly fashion. "I was a policeman for many years, and I am always on my guard. You will stay right here!"

By then, Bazargan's government had been officially appointed and was taking control of the government's ministries and civil services. As Ata told me, however, everyone knew that the real center of power was at Jamaran and the Alavi School. The Revolutionary Council, a group of turbaned mullahs, had taken complete control of the country's affairs, setting up executive branches in mosques under their direct supervision. We could feel the country starting its long slide into theocracy. Most of the time, though, we could only guess what was going on. The revolution was apparently succeeding, but fighting continued, and everything was happening under cover of darkness.

One evening, Ata brought a woman in a black chador to see me. When she lifted her veil, I was startled to see the face of my old secretary, Firoozeh. She was distraught to see me in my condition and tearfully urged me to leave Iran as soon as I could. Then she asked if I remembered a man named Naghdineh. Did I ever! Naghdineh had graduated from a university in the U.S. and had then returned to Iran as an expert in medical equipment standards. He was employed with a good salary and enjoyed a comfortable life style. Apparently, though, that wasn't enough. One day, I learned that he had asked a foreign consultant for a bribe. At the time, the news was unexpected and upsetting. Corruption was endemic, of course, but I had a hard time believing that a newly arrived graduate from a U.S. university could so quickly throw away everything that he had come here to do.

Naghdineh confessed. Since he seemed to regret his action, he was given light punishment. He was allowed to keep his job, although he was demoted. Everyone hoped that, because he was a young man with so much promise, he would reform. But, as Firoozeh informed me, Naghdineh was now sporting the thick black beard that had become fashionable and was active in one of the newly formed radical Islamic groups, loudly proclaiming to anyone who would listen his plans to purge the Ministry of Health of all elements of the former regime. After personally arresting several ministry officials, Firoozeh had heard him speak specifically of me. "The rumors that he has escaped in an American helicopter are false," Naghdineh declared. "I have personally seen him riding in a Mercedes Benz on Vozara Avenue. I was too slow to act, and the coward disappeared before I knew it, but I shall not rest until I have arrested him."

Firoozeh's eyes were misty. "He is very dangerous," she told me. "We are all frightened of what he may do. For God's sake be careful!" Ata and I exchanged a wordless look. Naghdineh had correctly described Ata's car and the street we had driven along. Apparently, he had even mentioned the hat that I had been wearing. After Firoozeh left us, Shahrokh, Ata, and I sat down to discuss my future. If Naghdineh had correctly identified Ata's car and discovered where it had taken me, I was as good as dead. I was not altogether reluctant to leave my hiding place behind the shelves, with gunfire as my lullaby, but what new flames would I tumble into? After some discussion, we decided that Ata would speak to my sister and brothers in hope of finding a distant relative who was trustworthy and courageous enough to hide me.

That night, the sound of gunfire near the office was deafening and unabated. I couldn't sleep at all. As I lay there, the sudden sound of glass breaking somewhere on the second floor sent terror shooting through my heart. Was someone breaking into the building? I seemed to hear footsteps, but behind the shelving, in the dark, I wondered what I could possibly do to save myself. I had no hope of escape. I shut my eyes tight and waited for my fate to reveal itself.

After a while, the noises ceased. Ironically, when this sleepless night finally came to an end, I realized that it was Friday, Iran's day of rest. In the morning, Shahrokh was quick to repair the broken windows, but he didn't know how they had been broken, nor could I think of anything to tell him. My anxiety was contagious. For the first time he, too, seemed visibly worried. But later that day, Ata appeared unannounced and told me to collect my things. We were going off to stay with my Auntie Batoul.

CHAPTER 27

SAFE HOUSE

Auntie Batoul was an energetic and free-spirited woman. Despite the permanent smile on her face, her piercing black eyes told you straightaway that she had no fear. My mother used to joke that Auntie Batoul was a woman and a mother to her children, yet a man and a father as well. She was a fighter. She lost her husband while she was still young, but she worked and raised her five children alone and ensured them first-class educations. She never remarried after her husband's death. As my mother said, Auntie Batoul could be her *own* husband!

When I was a university student in Tehran, she had taken me into her home for a few months and treated me like one of her own children. She had three daughters and two sons. All of her kids were educated in the United States, except her eldest son, who studied architecture in Italy. In recent years, however, I had only had second-hand news about Auntie Batoul. Ata told me that she had moved into a new house a few weeks before the revolution and had contacted my brother, asking about me, when she found out that I hadn't been captured. Ironically, the constant radio announcements about fugitives at large were a source of comfort to my family and friends, since it reassured them that I was still free.

"Nobody knows the address of my new house," Auntie Batoul told my brother. "Assad would be safe here. If you know where he is, for God's sake, tell him to come. I will look after him as I look after my own two eyes."

When my brother told Ata what she had said, they went to visit her together. After a quick study of the house's layout and a few words with Auntie Batoul, Ata agreed that it would be a safe place to hide.

As always, Ata played the secret agent—disguising me in a pair of glasses, a false mustache, and a beret that, I felt sure, only made me look comical. But Ata knew best. To make sure we weren't followed, we switched cars twice along the way, then took a brisk walk to my aunt's door. Scenes in the streets had changed since I had last been out there, before the revolution. All the men now sported beards and looked dirty and disheveled. The women, draped in black chadors, all looked like crows. Piles of garbage and refuse were everywhere. Although most radio programs were still broadcast in Farsi, there were more and more programs in Arabic. I felt like I was in an underdeveloped Middle Eastern city, breathing the polluted air and dust of fanaticism. But after seeing the tearful eyes of my beloved aunt, who took me tightly in her arms, I felt my troubles melt away. She was my guardian angel. "You can rest easy here," Auntie Batoul said. "No one will bother you." Her reassurance was a sedative for my nerves, and I felt better than I had in a long time.

Like Mahani and Maryam, Auntie Batoul had prepared a small room for me. The house was mostly empty; the only other person living there was her son Farzad, who was a senior in high school. The room was comfortable, with a bed, a portable radio, magazines, a chess set, a pack of cards, a variety of snacks, and a few books, including some by Iranian poets Hafez and Sa'adi. I was to leave the room only to visit the bathroom or, on rare occasions, to watch televised news broadcasts. My room was on the second floor, and dark drapes covered its view of the street around the front door. Auntie Batoul would check the identity of visitors, open the door as required, and give me prearranged signals in case of danger. If I had to escape, I could pass through two corridors, jump over a wall and across three flat rooftops, then climb down a short wall into a small alley, called a *koucheh* in Farsi. If I could manage this feat—which was no sure thing—I was then to make my way to Shahrokh's building and use the key he left me to enter my old hiding place. We didn't discuss what we should do if I were captured; it was worth taking the slimmest chances of escape to avoid that.

I stayed at Auntie Batoul's for ten days. On radio and television, the news was always dismal—the harassment of citizens on the streets, assassinations of army officers and politicians, and a continued litany of arrests, humiliation, and torture of anyone targeted by the new regime. The homes of those who had left the country were looted and plundered without hesitation, particularly in the affluent northern part of Tehran. Auntie Batoul told me that expensive oil paintings, furniture, and antiques could be purchased on the streets for almost nothing.

The courts presided over by fanatic mullahs made kangaroo courts seem reasonable by comparison. Seeing the ashen faces of top cabinet members under the Shah—including Rouhani, Azemoon, and Nikpay—on TV, I remembered the hours they had spent preparing their defenses in prison. They had been so certain that a "people's court" would heed their arguments and evidence. After all, weren't they innocent? Instead, the architects of Iran's renaissance were thrown to the wolves, for the sole crime that their names were familiar to those who condemned them. How they had lived never mattered, so they all died together in a hail of gunfire in the name of God and religion.

There is a Persian myth about an ogre named Zahak who had snakes growing out of his shoulders—great serpents that needed the blood of a hundred men, women, and children each day to stay alive. This demon fed on the people of ancient Iran until they drove it away. But unlike this ogre, the mullahs weren't satisfied by spilling the blood of innocents. These monsters also needed to desecrate their bullet-torn corpses by kicking and jumping on them as if for the sheer joy of it. Every day, a new group of hapless victims was paraded before the cameras, their skinny bones and drawn faces under a banner calling them "Enemies of God." The next day, only pictures of their bullet-riddled corpses, treated like punching bags, would be left to remind us they had once existed.

As I waited for deliverance or damnation, the sight of these barbarians brutally beating dull-eyed victims and corpses became unbearable. I could no longer watch. In my room, I cried for hours over memories of my patriotic friends and fellow inmates—many of whom I had seen so recently and who were now gone forever. These noble souls had given their lives to their Shah and their country, so willingly and with so much energy. Now they were being methodically rubbed out at the hands of ignorant, medieval thugs. Their names were besmirched with the foul word "traitor," while the real traitors—shameless hypocrites who marched under slogans like "Defense of Freedom," "Human Rights," "Justice," and "Struggle against Oppression"—trod everything noble into the mud. Where were the supporters of human rights now—the *New York Times*, the BBC, Cyrus Vance, Valery Giscard d'Estaing? Why were they all silent?

One day, Ata brought word that the revolutionary guards, the Pasdars, had ransacked and confiscated my house. For years, I had co-owned and shared a three-story house on Farmanieh Avenue with a friend and colleague. He and his Danish wife and children had lived on the second floor, while we occupied the first. Mir Assad, our servant, lived on the ground floor. In the early stages of the revolution, our friends had left for Denmark. When my wife and children went to the States, only Mir Assad and his family remained to look after the house.

He had told Ata what happened. Just after sundown one day, five armed Pasdars jumped the wall, shouting that anyone who didn't keep down would be shot. After interrogating Mir Assad, they searched the house thoroughly—ostensibly for incriminating documents, but in reality for valuables that they could carry off. They turned the house upside down, overturning furniture, emptying closets, even smashing walls in the bedroom and library in hopes of discovering hidden safes. After failing to find anything worthwhile, Ata told me, they had justified their intrusion by claiming as evidence photographs of me with the Shah, Indian Prime Minister Shastri, and Soviet leader Leonid Brezhnev. They cited my Order of Merit from the Mexican government as a piece of particularly incriminating evidence against me, as well as the Order of Homayoun, which the Shah had given me, and the Order of Knighthood, with a Sash and Ceremonial Sword, bestowed by the Vatican.

At first, the Pasdars had wanted to evict Mir Assad and his family, but when he vigorously protested, they lost interest. They had bigger fish to fry. Not satisfied with what they had found, they took a five-dollar stone statue of a frog that I had given Cathy, apparently believing it was an expensive jewel. Such items were not listed on their report. Their disorderly looting didn't last long, however; the Pasdars returned the next day with a sense of purpose, carefully dividing among themselves all the household goods that could quickly be liquidated. For several days, our house was turned into a place of business and pleasure. During the day, the Pasdars sold our household belongings in the yard. At night, they brought in any unfortunate women they had arrested, enjoying themselves in evenings of debauched comfort. Mir Assad said that he saw one poor woman wearing my wife's clothes. Perhaps they were a "gift."

It was hard to hear this kind of news, to wait and do nothing while things steadily got worse. The Pasdars were looking for me everywhere, and they were daily searching the homes of my mother, sister, and brother. I was extremely careful not to see them or contact my family, since all international telephone calls were censored. In the communication vacuum, revolutionaries spread lies and disinformation. My mother, who lived in the Caspian Sea town of Sari, was informed that I was killed in Washington, D.C. They told her that I had left Iran by helicopter, wearing an American Air Force uniform.

In reality, I was in a safe place, but each day brought a continued bombardment of stories about plundering, executions, injustice, and chaos. I envisioned the day when my turn would come, when I would follow my friends down that one-way road. I would be arrested and tortured. After I had been executed, my murderers would kick my dead corpse with the same brutality with which they had kicked earlier victims. Nothing could wipe these thoughts from my mind.

One day, Prime Minister Bazargan's rhetoric became more strident, and his ministers appeared on television. Bazargan spoke of law and order and promised that summary trials and executions would soon end. It was a hopeful sign, especially when he announced that the use of firing squads would be halted for the time being. But of those men who had been imprisoned with me, General Sadri, Khorram, General Nassiri, and former cabinet members Azmoon, Nikpay, Kianpour, and Rouhani had already been executed.

I learned later that Rouhani, after escaping from prison, had walked to his mother's home near the base, as he told me he would. His sick, aging mother lived in a small, two-story house, where an employee in the Ministry of Agriculture lived downstairs and looked after her instead of paying rent. The telephone line had an extension into his ground-floor apartment so that, in case of emergency, the old woman could get his attention by tapping the handset. When Rouhani reached the house, he used the phone to call a friend, to say he was safe and discuss a safe hiding place. The ungrateful downstairs neighbor listened in and reported him to the local *commiteh*. Within minutes, the Pasdars arrived at the house and arrested Rouhani. He was quickly executed.

Hoveyda was more difficult to dispose of. In the Shah's memoir, *Answer to History,* he wrote that "If a just trial in accordance with all the required legal criteria had been held, Hoveyda and a few of his ministers would most certainly have been able to defend themselves and would have been exonerated. I had suggested to Hoveyda that he go to Belgium as the Iranian Ambassador. But he was so sure of himself that he refused." Hoveyda had been in line for the firing squad, but he gained a temporary reprieve when Bazargan halted the summary trials and executions. After the Shah left the country, Hoveyda was held under house arrest in northern Tehran. When SAVAK disbanded and released Hoveyda, he refused to listen to the pleas of his friends and colleagues to escape from Iran while he still could. Instead, he insisted that he would give himself up to the Islamic Revolution, Iran's new "government."

Mullah Khalkhali, Khomeini's notorious "Hanging Judge," was in no mood to show mercy. He regarded the execution of Hoveyda as a personal mission and, with stone-hearted savagery, stated in an interview that he and Hadi Ghaffari "would torture Hoveyda to death." Hoveyda, however, had many important friends in Europe and the Middle East—including numerous heads of states, prominent writers in France, Belgium, Germany, Lebanon, and Greece, and humanitarian groups around the world—who tried to secure his freedom and save his life. They sent telegrams and letters to Bazargan and Khomeini, urging them to spare Hoveyda the death penalty. Khomeini supposedly threw these letters in the trash, but Bazargan persuaded Khomeini to try Hoveyda in a court of law. There was little chance of justice in Iran, but when Mullah Khalkhali learned of the possibility of a trial, he went to see Khomeini, who told him to ignore Bazargan. That response, Khalkhali recalled, "was enough for me. I went to Hoveyda's prison," he wrote,

and had him brought to me. I ordered that all telephone lines to the prison be disconnected. I was worried that the decision I had made would be leaked. I gave orders that nobody was to leave the prison compound. I said to Hoveyda, "Write your last will and testament." He insisted that he should be given time [a two-week grace period] to write down or recite what was on his mind. I told him no. "You have spoken quite enough already," I said. "You have nothing further to say." The sound of a helicopter began to be heard. I handed Hoveyda over to Hadi Ghaffari to finish him off.

Hoveyda's request for a grace period only accelerated his execution. Hoveyda had wanted to shed light on Iran's contemporary history, but the planners of this revolution did not want their secrets revealed. Ghaffari shot Hoveyda once in the head, and he and Khalkhali stood over him, laughing at his agony. Khalkhali fired the final bullet that ended Hoveyda's life.

At last, when Hoveyda and so many officials from the former regime were being savagely detained and punished, international human rights groups began to take notice. In response to their queries and complaints, Bazargan promised that the rule of law would soon resume. But those in the know realized this concession was just window dressing. In reality, the Revolutionary Council had taken charge of the day-to-day running of the country, issuing its orders through local *commitehs* stationed in each of the mosques. Pasdars enforced the *commiteh's* orders, occupying all the police stations and establishing a network of inspection points and roadblocks on all major intersections in the cities. Members of the former regime and any wealthy individuals who had been named *taghouti* were declared fugitives and enemies of the new state. Khomeini took the word *taghouti* from the Koran. He used it as a derogatory term to describe the former regimes' elite and anyone else that the regime wanted to charge and eliminate.

Before long, the Pasdars learned the ways of deceitfulness and cunning from the mullahs. At first, they merely expressed their frustration and rage by spitefully murdering SAVAK agents on sight. Who is to say that some of their victims didn't deserve what they got? But the goals of the Pasdars quickly changed once they had the full run of the country and began focusing on acquiring wealth for themselves. They even began employing remaining SAVAK agents to help them. There was a brisk business in extortion and bribery. The arrest and murder of citizens reached a terrifying point, and we came to learn that it a person risked his life if he was accused of any crime, for any reason.

Auntie Batoul struggled to help me survive this new reality by finding a foothold in the local mullah's sphere of influence. She somehow arranged a meeting with the Friday prayer leader and put herself forward as a zealous believer who could represent women in the area. Her offer was met with a powerful welcome. It was agreed that, henceforth, she would always be consulted on all local women's affairs, and she began to work her way into the councils of power brokers in the region. This access allowed Auntie Batoul to monitor affairs of the neighborhood and keep her ear to the ground for my safety.

One day, Ata entered her house smiling from ear to ear. "Now they've done it!" he said. "They consider me one of their own. Even the *commitehs* trust me!" We sat down over some tea, and Ata told me what he called "a story well worth sitting down to hear."

The tale had begun much earlier. Apparently, in the last years of the Shah's regime, my old prison friend Rahimi Ali Khorram had acquired a large plot of land through some kind of collusion. Part of the parcel included land that legally belonged to Ata. Khorram started developing this land into a huge amusement park, while Ata and others launched court proceedings to recover the property. Khorram made threats. When Ata ignored them, Khorram called in his SAVAK allies. As a result, Ata had spent twenty days in prison while being tortured by the infamous SAVAK interrogator Sultan Zadeh. His punishment was so severe that he gave up his land. But now that the regime had changed, Ata's prison sentence was a certificate of credibility with the revolutionaries. As always, Ata had transformed a loss into a gain and began exploring a new niche as the legal representative of the "oppressed masses." Hearing of his new status, I was as happy for myself as I was for Ata.

As days passed, my cousin Farzad told me that things seemed to be easing up a bit. Ordinary people were beginning to come out on the streets again, and businesses were starting to revive. Farzad and I spent a lot of time together playing chess. He was frustrated with the Pasdars and resented the fact that he was forced to pray in school. He brought me a set of weights that I could use as part of a fitness routine, and the exercise helped my mental outlook a great deal. I also tried to put my enforced inactivity to good use by reading books that I had never had a chance to read before, including Ferdowsi's *Shahnameh*, I was sure that the government was going to denounce Ferdowsi for his anti-Arab beliefs. He had written in the Farsi language after the Arabs attacked Iran, burned Farsi books, and forced Iranians to read and speak Arabic. If not for Ferdowsi, perhaps Iranians would all be speaking Arabic today.

Gradually, friends of mine who had opposed the Shah's regime and thrown in with the revolutionaries began to despair of reaching their goals. The mullahs had pledged that the clergy and leadership would retire to Qom and engage themselves in promoting Islam once Bazargan's government was established. Their promises had bought them the time they needed, but they were empty. As the Islamic Republic's true face was revealed, the distasteful reality of the revolution my friends had supported became more obvious. Many people in whom I would have feared to confide began sending messages, urging me to stay hidden until some order was reestablished. But they were daydreaming, because any opportunities for order had by now been squandered. Some of them still waited for Bazargan's government to take charge of the situation and for Khomeini and his mullahs to peaceably retire to Qom. But we were witnessing something altogether different. The prophets of ignorance dominated the councils and *commitehs* of the Revolution, and my friends realized that they, too, were coming close to danger.

Unlike so many, I had escaped from the frying pan, but I was teetering at the edge of the flames. While the mullahs were promising heaven on earth and in the future for martyrs, I was in a living hell without any future. I gradually realized that there was no hope for me in Iran, and I began to think seriously about escaping. I never thought that I would have to leave my country. Was it even possible? I had heard many rumors about people who had fled, but no one knew anything for sure. After all, people said that *I* had managed to escape! There were also rumors that Shapour Bakhtiar had made it across the border—with Bazargan's help—by disguising himself as a member of an Air France flight crew, but we knew nothing of the facts. The only news that we could trust were the lists of people who had been captured, tried, and executed by Khomeini's government.

CHAPTER 28

ON THE RUN

In hiding, I often thought about Sadeq Qotbzadeh, my friend from student days in America. Since Khomeini first arrived in Paris, Qotbzadeh had been a prime mover in the revolution. Foreign journalists called him and Dr. Ibrahim Yazdi the Imam's "godsons." Now, as head of the state's radio and television organization, it seemed as though Qotbzadeh could do anything. If I contacted him, I wondered, would he help me, or would he do what Dr. Yazdi had done to Dr. Sheikh?

I hadn't seen Qotbzadeh much since I left Washington, so I didn't really know how he had changed. Once, by chance, two years before the revolution, I had run into him in Paris with a mutual friend of ours, and we had all had coffee together. He was wearing a very smart business suit, and the fine leather briefcase in his hand gave him the air of a successful *homme d'affairs*. When I asked him what he was doing with himself, he replied that his business in Europe, the Middle East, and Africa was keeping him busy. He said that he was content with his life; then he shut his mouth. Naturally, I knew that he was greatly involved in efforts to oust the Shah, so I was cautious when he jokingly said, "I hear you've become somewhat of a VIP. I wonder if you can do something for me."

Did he want me to help him come back to Iran? I had helped our mutual friend Ali Ershadi return. He was now become a professor at Tehran University, with an important government position on the side. Ershadi had not been politically active since he returned, but SAVAK harassed him constantly. Only with Hoveyda's help could he do his job with any peace of mind, and he was eventually appointed to the board of directors of the Refah

Bank. Qotbzadeh, Ershadi, and I had known each other well at Georgetown, but I wasn't sure that I could help Qotbzadeh return to Iran, if that's what he wanted. I had known Ali well enough to be sure that SAVAK's grudge against him was unfounded, but Qotbzadeh was something else altogether. In the years since our lives parted, he had become one of Khomeini's most important lieutenants and involved himself with terrorist groups from the Middle East, Libya, and Palestine. So I changed the subject, and Qotbzadeh smoothly told me that he had only been joking and was far too involved in what he was doing to stop. That was the last time I had seen him. Still, as Ata and I talked it over, it seemed like contacting him might be worth a try. He could probably help me if he chose. But would he want to?

I sent word to Ershadi, who quickly came to meet me at Auntie's house. When I broached the subject of asking Qotbzadeh for help, he said that, while Qotbzadeh was a revolutionary and eccentric in his ideas, there was no doubt that he was a patriotic Iranian and loyal to his friends. Ershadi wondered, however, whether he had the influence he seemed to. After all, he had always been a hard-line nationalist and had opposed the fundamentalist tendencies that were on the rise. We decided that Ershadi would try to contact Qotbzadeh and get a sense for how he would react, without revealing my whereabouts.

After a couple of days, Ali came back with apparently good news. Qotbzadeh had agreed to see him at once and had expressed delight at hearing that I was alive and well. "Where is he staying?" Qotbzadeh asked. "I know he was not corrupt and that he never killed anybody. He will have no problems with us. I will send an official car with guards to bring him safely here to my house, and we will clear his name." When Ershadi asked him how he would do that, Qotbzadeh responded that I would have to go to court and answer questions that the judge would put to me, but I was not to worry.

Ali Ershadi's account of this meeting left me speechless and deep in thought. We had often heard that Khomeini held Qotbzadeh in high esteem. Perhaps my old friend would, indeed, be able to help me. But then I recalled the horror on Dr. Sheikh's face when he had been condemned to death. I also remembered the news photo of the bullet-riddled bodies of Mansur Rouhani and Azmoon, next to the Koranic phrase "God kills evil." A sense of utter revulsion overcame me. Could I really trust anyone who had anything to do with all of that? I remembered Dr. Yazdi, who had been as important as

Qotbzadeh in Khomeini's eyes. He had made similar promises to Dr. Sheikh, and my friend was now awaiting his execution.

Ershadi agreed that, if I threw myself into the lion's den of these courts, Qotbzadeh probably wouldn't have enough influence with Khomeini to save me. I asked Ali, then, to call Qotbzadeh and, after thanking him on my behalf, tell him that all I wanted to do was leave the country. If he could manage to arrange for my escape, he would save my life and I would be eternally in his debt. When Ershadi relayed this request, however, Qotbzadeh said that it would be impossible.

Qotbzadeh had been an adventurous revolutionary, dreaming of a future filled with power. Instead, as we suspected, he was a puppet in Khomeini's bloody hands. He was eventually arrested and condemned to death by his former master. It was said that Qotbzadeh begged Khomeini for forgiveness on his hands and knees. Khomeini then ordered him to stand in front of four thousand prisoners, confess his crimes to them, and ask their forgiveness. If they accepted, Khomeini said, he would pardon his former "godson." But these prisoners were also the sorcerer's puppets, and they shouted in unison, "Qotbzadeh is a traitor! Execute him!" It was done.

Dr. Sheikh was hardly more fortunate. Bazargan promised that officials from the former regime would be treated fairly. He also pledged to Western governments that tribunals would process detainees in accordance with law. In the end, however, Khomeini handpicked his most bloodthirsty mullahs to help him "clean up" every remaining element of the Shah's government, and "hanging judges" like Khalkhali lived up to their names.

The mullah's "trials" proceeded in a standard way. Officials from the former regime were divided into two groups. They were placed in rooms marked "A" and "B" and informed that they would soon be interrogated. After hours of waiting, they were taken to another room and asked a few pointless questions. That was all. After this brief charade of due process, they were cursed and insulted for not confessing their guilt and were usually subjected to physical violence. After their "interrogation" they were taken to the roof in the dead of night, where a firing squad finished them off.

As I learned much later, Dr. Sheikh had originally been held in room "A." When he was given permission to use the bathroom, however, he got confused and accidentally walked back into room "B." This turned out to be a life-saving mistake. Everyone in room "A" was murdered that night by the firing squad, but dawn came before the prisoners in room "B" could get their "moment in court." Normally, this would have meant only a brief reprieve, and he would have been executed with the others after nightfall. But it turned out that the long darkness hadn't come yet for Dr. Sheikh and the rest of his lucky group. International organizations and human rights activists were busy, and their campaign to publicize Khomeini's atrocities were having an impact. While Khalkhali had already executed Hoveyda and General Moghadam, but the pressure was now so hot that the regime placed a temporary halt on executions. It agreed that former officials of the Shah's regime would be tried in a legal court system that was open to international scrutiny. Dr. Sheikh and the others in room "B" escaped certain death, but there was nothing approaching due process in courts that were set up to try them. Members of the public were encouraged to come forward with complaints against the accused, but legal counsel for the defendants was deemed unnecessary. They were also denied access to documents or witnesses for their defense, and the results were predictable. At Dr. Sheikh's hearing, a mullah who served as both prosecutor and judge accused him of defying God and presented as "evidence" allegations that he had misused hospital facilities and computers, purchased unusable vaccines, and performed unnecessary abortions and amputations. Dr. Sheikh was even accused of having illicit relations with women. As I recall, one of the pieces of "evidence" that this mullah introduced concerned a seventy-four-year-old woman on whom Dr. Sheikh was accused of having performed an abortion. But hospital records would have clearly shown that Dr. Sheikh had had nothing to do with the woman; female doctors had removed her cancerous womb in a valid surgery.

Because Dr. Sheikh was an outstanding orthopedic surgeon who was widely respected in Iran's medical community, many doctors tried to step forward to give evidence on his behalf. No one, however, was permitted to testify in his support. One doctor managed to get into the courtroom by pretending to have a complaint; when he tried to give testimony in favor of Dr. Sheikh, however, he was swiftly and violently evicted from the courtroom. In the end, after no real evidence against Dr. Sheikh had been produced, he was sentenced to death.

Dr. Sheikh, however, was lucky again. His grandfather had been a mullah, so his sentence was, in the end, reduced to life in prison, and he survived. His lot, nonetheless, was not an easy one. In prison, Dr. Sheikh was physically abused and subjected to torture. But the mental torture was perhaps worst of all. Guards would routinely bring him and other condemned prisoners to the yard for execution; after shooting a few, they would send the others back to their cells with the promise that their turn would be coming soon. They did everything they could to grind down Dr. Sheikh's will—spitting in his food, forcing him to clean prison toilets, and always standing over his shoulder with whips and curses.

But Dr. Sheikh was a man of great endurance and character. He carried out his duties with such care, and took his punishments with such discipline, that the guards were eventually astonished at his forbearance. They came to respect him a little and became more lenient in his treatment, which helped him survive. Dr. Sheikh also busied himself in prison by giving free twenty-four-hour medical care to other prisoners, as well as to the prison guards and their families. He even made phone calls to his colleagues in hospitals when they needed medical treatment.

Dr. Sheikh's connections ultimately came to the attention of a notorious senior cleric, the Ayatollah Giyani. A hard-liner, Gilani had executed his own son over a political conflict. He had been unable, however, to get an appointment with a British eye specialist for a procedure that would save his mother's eyesight. Dr. Sheikh used his influence and arranged for the appointment. In gratitude, Ayatollah Gilani visited the doctor in prison to thank him personally and was impressed with his popularity among inmates and guards. A few months later, when Dr. Sheikh asked permission to establish a small clinic inside the prison, Gilani agreed. Before long, Dr. Sheikh was a popular medical consultant for revolutionary leaders and their families, and eventually, after five years in prison, he was pardoned and freed. Today, Dr. Sheikh still practices orthopedic surgery in Tehran.

As for me, the hope of freedom was the only thing that kept me going during that long, cold winter in hiding. Gradually, however, the weather began changing. Green leaves were budding on the trees. I could hear birds chirping and market vendors shouting the names of warm-weather fruits. All around me, Iranians were preparing for the first day of spring—*Now Ruz*, the Persian New Year—a time-honored tradition that had been the backbone of our culture for a thousand years. The Islamic Republic had hoped to pass *Now Ruz* in silence, draping our Persian traditions in the same blackness with which they had shrouded the entire country. But now, perhaps for the first time since the uprisings began, the Iranian people were beginning to see the mullahs as they really were. Before Persians became Muslims, we all had been and still were Iranians, and our pride in our cultural traditions ran deeper than the mullahs realized. So that year, *Now Ruz* was celebrated, with particular fervor, as an act of protest. People stood up, however quietly, and let it be known that nomadic traditions from the outside would never replace a custom like *Now Ruz*, which is celebrated everywhere the Persian language is spoken.

Auntie Batoul laid out a traditional *Now Ruz* table with the *Haft-Seen*—water, live fish, a mirror, and foods that all start with the Farsi letter "s." After she placed a picture of Helen and our children on the table, we prayed together to the almighty that I would soon join them. Another part of the *Now Ruz* tradition is to celebrate the arrival of each New Year by visiting with family and friends. My mother had superstitiously believed that the first visitor to come into the home on *Now Ruz* would have good luck that year, and she had almost always chosen me for that privilege. Alas! I could now hardly consider myself lucky or the bearer of good fortune. Indeed, if I put my foot into anyone's house, I would be risking the life of my host.

Auntie Batoul had decided that she would not visit anybody that year, and she had kept her new address secret to forestall visitors who might inadvertently discover my presence. Some of her deceased husband's relatives, however, managed to find her new telephone number and informed her that they would all come to visit her on the following Tuesday. There was nothing that she could do to stop them without raising suspicions, so we decided that I would remain quietly in my room during their visit.

It was a little past eleven in the morning when a mixed group of a dozen or so men, women, and children arrived at Auntie's house. They were happy and boisterous, and I could hear them greeting, hugging, and kissing each other and wishing everyone a happy new year. For almost an hour, they drank tea with traditional *Now Ruz* sweets, speaking of news and catching up on old business. Iranians say that people from Mazandaran speak louder than their countrymen. As I listened silently to the visitors gossiping and laughing noisily, it seemed to be true.

Eventually, because it was a new house, the visitors demanded the grand tour, and Auntie was unable to refuse. I listened silently as the group moved slowly from room to room, laughing and chatting. When they arrived at the door to my room, my heart was in my mouth, but I shouldn't have worried; with great poise, Auntie declared that the room was storing her daughter's belonging, and that her daughter, Farzaneh, had taken the key with her. Before anyone thought to ask when Farzaneh had left, Auntie swept the group back downstairs.

After the tour, everyone ate lunch, and, even from above, I could tell that Auntie Batoul was trying to bring the visit to a close. One of the women suddenly asked my aunt if she had ever heard what happened to Dr. Aram. Auntie had anticipated such questions, so she answered quickly, "I don't know and I've heard nothing. Some people," she added sadly, "say that he has already been killed. But Assad's mother prays night and day for his safety. We all hope that he has found some way to save his life."

At that point, a man who had been quiet until then said that he had heard from reliable sources that the Americans had helped me escape on a U.S. helicopter. "They said that Dr. Aram was wearing an American naval uniform," he added. Another man chimed in, claiming that I had been seen in Washington D.C. They all marveled at my good fortune—if only it were true. "Put your mind at ease," the first man said soothingly, "You can be sure he is safe." Hearing my deepest wish related as plain fact was a strange experience. I had to feel my arms and legs to be sure I was still there and not merely an apparition. Auntie Batoul simply said, as calmly and sadly as she had before, "I hope it is true."

The day after *Now Ruz*, Ata walked into my room with a determined look on his face, and we began talking seriously about how I was going to leave the country. "If you don't take the plunge soon," he said, "something will happen when you least expect it. We can't wait forever. Now that the grass is growing again, we cannot let it grow beneath our feet." There was no doubt in my mind that if they captured me, they would torture me to find out the secrets I knew or the money I had. Since I had neither, I would either die under torture or be half-dead when they finally executed me.

While I was in hiding, Ata had been collecting information, investigating possible routes of escape, and weighing risks. Air travel was under tremendous scrutiny, so he had eliminated that as a possibility. Smugglers, on the other hand, were doing a brisk business. In tumultuous times, Iran's borders with Turkey, Pakistan, and Iraq were more difficult for the government to secure and more profitable for those willing to take risks. The smugglers were in full bloom that spring. But dealing with those types would not be easy, Ata cautioned. If they knew how important their client was, they would demand exorbitant fees. Since duplicity was their stock in trade, there was no guarantee that they wouldn't turn me in so they could collect money from all parties. Some smugglers could be trusted, but many were incompetent or abandoned their charges along the way.

During the day, when I had nothing to do, I would make a small opening in the curtains and peer down on the street. I would watch people go by— civil servants, guerillas, Pasdars, street vendors, children, and mullahs—men in loose-fitting clothing and women hiding their beauty and flaws under black chadors. After *Now Ruz*, I seemed to see fewer gun-toting thugs and more mullahs wearing turbans—or at least that's what I wanted to see. I'd study their faces, clothing, and actions, trying to divine their experience and what was on their minds. By watching the streets, I would also, I thought, know if someone was coming to arrest me. And then, one warm spring day, a man who had been standing on a street-corner for hours attracted my attention. He was watching cars as they passed, taking note of the people inside. Sometimes, when a car stopped, he would approach and speak to the driver before returning to his post. Occasionally he would speak to a passerby. I turned the situation over in my head. What could he be doing here? Was it a coincidence? Something didn't seem right. I became more and more apprehensive and started noticing that he occasionally fixed his eyes on our house. I couldn't take my eyes off him. As I rehearsed the emergency escape plan in my mind, I had to wipe sweat from my palms. When Auntie Batoul returned home that afternoon, I excitedly told her about the man, and she grew agitated. She put on her chador and sternly commanded me to stay put until she could find out more. But when she returned, the sound of laughter greeted my ears. The man was nothing but a laborer waiting for someone to hire him for the day. I realized, at that moment, that it was becoming difficult to keep a level head in my position, and I understood why Ata believed something had to be done. Imagine if I lost my head and tried to flee?

One day, Ata visited and told me an interesting story. He had gone to a memorial service for a mutual friend, Dr. Fereidoun Ibrahimi. A well-known dentist in the city of Rasht, Ibrahimi's father had been a major landowner in the provinces of Azerbaijan and Kurdistan. At the service, Ata and Ibrahimi's wife talked with a man from Kurdistan who was complaining about the lack of rain and its effect on agriculture. Mrs. Ibrahimi observed that when farmers complain about poor harvests, they often want to persuade the landowner to accept less than their fair share of the profit. But the farmer explained that nobody was interested in farming any more, because the best business was trafficking in human beings. "Before," he said, "it was most lucrative to smuggle things like cigarettes, whiskey, or arms, but today, there is no question—it's smuggling people."

Hearing those words, Ata started questioning the man closely. It turned out that his village was situated along the Iranian-Turkish border. Ata then invited the Kurdistani for lunch the next day, and the man openly admitted that he knew of an army general and a rich landowner who had been smuggled across the border to Turkey. He himself was not directly involved, he explained, but he knew the people who had been. Ata suggested that perhaps they could make some kind of arrangement. The man professed ignorance of details and prices, but he promised to try to set up a meeting.

For Ata, the light of hope was finally twinkling at the end of a very long, dark tunnel. He thought that this method of escape would be feasible. Given his experience, he knew what he was talking about. It would be expensive, he warned me, and there were no certainties. Smugglers were not people we could trust, but I would have to trust them with my life. Still, the thought of escape worked magic on my mind. I wasn't worried about the money; I had many friends who could loan me whatever I needed. Auntie Batoul had brought me a message from my mother just a few days earlier, urging me not to worry about her and to do whatever I needed to do to see my family. "She said to tell you she has thick skin," Auntie Batoul told me. "Watch out for yourself. She will pray for you, and God will be your protector."

Three days later, Ata returned from a meeting with the smugglers with good news. "Pack your bags," he told me. "We've come to an agreement. The route is as safe as it can be, and the price is right—$50,000. If we can get you to Tabriz, they will take you the rest of the way, across the border to Turkey."

Getting to Tabriz, however, would not be easy. The mullahs had forbidden people to leave the country, and all the borders were closed. International flights no longer existed, and even private airplanes, except under very special circumstances, were not allowed to fly. Traveling inside Iran was also heavily restricted. Cars, buses, and even trains were subject to frequent inspections, and the few domestic flights still operating were under extreme surveillance by the new government. In cities, there were inspection check points at major intersections, where Pasdars questioned and searched people in taxis and private cars, as well as pedestrians. They had the names and photographs of people the Revolutionary Council wanted to arrest. Since television had broadcasted my picture and newspapers had published it, I would have an extremely difficult time trying to avoid capture.

Since so few people were traveling these days, we decided that a car would draw too much attention. The bus seemed like the best option; with so many people on board, I might be able to slip under the radar more easily. Buses left Tehran for Tabriz on a daily basis, morning, noon, and night. After giving it some thought, we decided that the night bus was probably the best choice; there would be fewer inspection stops, and the inspectors would probably be tired and pay less attention to their duties.

Getting to the bus stop, however, might be a problem. Private cars were stopped and searched regularly, and the Pasdars would be sure to recognize me. Taxis were stopped less frequently, but one never knew which drivers could be trusted. Simply walking to the bus stop might have been a possibility, but Ata shook his head. The distance was too great, and after dark, I would be far too exposed to curious eyes.

As we discussed the alternatives, the siren of a passing ambulance gave me an idea. Before the revolution, I had worked to set up Iran's first emergency medical service, and, ironically, all the fighting in the streets had proved the usefulness of this network of ambulances and health technicians. As the revolution had dragged on, emergency responders were some of the only government officials respected by all sides, because they worked bravely and tirelessly to save both soldiers and revolutionaries. Back when it had been my personal project, I had been in contact with the emergency services twenty-four hours a day and had developed a close working relationship with many technicians and ambulance teams. Perhaps an ambulance could take me to the bus terminal.

I dispatched my former secretary to feel out Reza Omidvar, one of the head technicians, and see if he would be willing to meet me. Auntie Batoul was incredulous. "How can you trust this man?" she asked. "These days, *everyone* is a Khomeini supporter!"

I believed Reza wouldn't betray me, but she was right; these days, who could be sure of anyone? But we couldn't wait for a safer option to come along. Ata had convinced me that something had to be done. The longer we waited, the more likely we would be surprised by a turn of events we couldn't control. As it turned out, however, our fears were unfounded. Reza was delighted to help. He warned me, though, that ambulances weren't exempt from inspections. Sometimes even critically injured patients were stopped on their way to the hospital, their life blood draining away while they were scrutinized for political subversion. But Reza had an idea—I could pose as the ambulance technician, and he could pretend to be the patient.

After discussing the idea with Ata, we agreed it was sound, and Reza set out to obtain an ambulance technician's ID card for me. With all the media publicity, photos, and descriptions being circulated, Ata suggested that I disguise my appearance. Since my blue eyes were so identifiable, Ata obtained a set of brown contact lenses from a friend at the Tehran Clinic. And since beards had come into fashion, we agreed that I should stop shaving and become stylish. A beard would help me blend into the crowd, Ata pointed out, and hide any signs of fear on my face if I were questioned.

With wild, unkempt hair, baggy trousers, and an unwashed jacket, I would no longer be Dr. Assad Aram, Deputy Minister. For the bus ride to Tabriz, I would also need a new identification card, so Firoozeh acquired a blank Ministry of Health card. Together we fashioned it into a passable imitation of an ID badge for a pharmacy technician named "Hussein Nikbakht." Reza affixed a new photograph of me to the identification card, along with the official seal of the Ministry of Health. He also made sure that I was issued a formal letter from the Health Ministry, assigning me to Tabriz for a week. Then, as a finishing touch, we filled a plastic shopping bag with a small Quran, a box of sweets, some bread and cheese, and a small book of Khomeini's writings on top.

Ata would meet me at the Tabriz bus terminal with my passport and all the necessary cash, since it would be too dangerous for me to be caught carrying them. In the meantime, we decided that I needed someone to watch over me, trailing me like a shadow without anyone knowing that we were together. If something unforeseen happened, he would be able to assist and—in an emergency—help me escape capture, since that would mean my death. Hamid, a young relative of Auntie Batoul, fit the bill. An athletic young man from Azerbaijan, he had an easygoing manner that would help smooth over any difficulties. Hamid himself purchased our tickets on a Mihan Tour bus. He would sit in the second row, and I would sit two rows behind him.

Ata flew to Tabriz on the day of my departure. My brother came to see me before I left, and it was one of the most joyless farewells that I have ever known. We knew that we might never see each other again. Even if I managed to escape, it would be hard to imagine that I would ever return to Iran. I hugged him tightly and asked him to hug our mother for me. Who could tell if I would ever see her again, either? Then the ambulance arrived. Reza and I exchanged clothing, and Auntie Batoul, with tears in her eyes, passed a Quran over me in ritual blessing and tossed a pitcher of water on the trail behind me for luck and protection. And so I left.

Inside the ambulance, Reza lay down, pretending to be a patient. Another technician drove, and I sat beside him in front. Since most ambulances had two emergency technicians, it would have looked suspicious to have only one EMT in the ambulance with the patient. Reza was able to find another trustable emergency technician at the last minute. Firoozeh, my former secretary, sat next to the patient, wearing a black chador. Without encountering any problems or being stopped, we arrived at the bus terminal and parked close to the station. I changed out of my uniform, said goodbye to the emergency technicians, and walked toward the bus. My secretary carefully looked over the passengers to make sure that there was no one there who might recognize me. After she signaled that all was well, I stepped onto the bus as the last passenger. As I walked to my seat, I saw Hamid sitting quietly in the second row. Even though we made no contact, his presence calmed me. The passengers gave the traditional blessing in unison, and the bus set off. I watched as Firoozeh waved goodbye, and as she faded into the darkness, I thought about how loyal and kind she had been to me.

Once the bus was well underway, I surreptitiously looked over my fellow passengers. They were a scruffy lot, but I fit right in with my ragged clothing. It was already getting dark when the bus turned onto Eisenhower Boulevard. I heard Hamid proclaim, "Let us render another *salavat* to Mohammad!" Whenever the name of Mohammad is mentioned, everyone shouts "Peace be to him," and I tried to join in without changing expression. When we reached Shahyad Square, a Pasdar checkpoint, however, my stomach suddenly seized up. As the bus came to a halt, the passengers called out in unison *"Allah o Akbar,"* but this time I remained silent.

The driver descended and handed a piece of paper to the Pasdars. I tried to look like I was yawning while I wiped cold sweat from my cheek. After being confined for so long, the thought of hiding in the open, under lights, filled me with anxiety; then, when two Pasdars boarded the bus, fear shot through the center of my being. I forced myself to remain expressionless and focus on the seat in front of me, trying to look bored and sleepy. But surely, I thought, they would recognize me! They had my picture; they would know who I was—how could they not? As the Pasdars moved forward toward me, they looked over each passenger, slowly, one at a time. When they asked a few sharp questions of the passenger in front of me, I tried not to fidget. Then, suddenly, they passed by me without a word, moving down the bus to passengers behind me. I was in a daze; had they really not seen me? A moment later, the inspectors got off the bus and waved us on.

Was that it? Would all the inspections be so easy? As we departed Shahyad Square, I had to contain an urge to burst out laughing. In Farsi, *shahyad* means "in memory of the Shah," so Khomeini had renamed the square "*Azadi*," or "Freedom." For once, his claptrap was appropriate. I was free! I didn't want to look back, and as the bus rolled on, I stared out at the dark road ahead of us. In the outskirts, night seemed to snuff out the city lights like a blanket over a candle. By the time we reached the countryside, the road was all but deserted, with only occasional Pasdars in pickup trucks breaking the silence.

Other passengers were starting to drift off to sleep, but I was too excited to close my eyes. As we rolled on and the minutes turned into hours, however, my elation turned into anxiety again. I wasn't out of the woods yet; it was still five hundred miles to Tabriz, and I had little notion of what I'd find there. Then the bus's radio sound system started broadcasting a parade of sermons, reports of brutalities—called "triumphs,"—and ominous proclamations from the central authority, reminding me that I was still far from safe. I was a hunted man. When we reached Karaj, however, about forty miles from Tehran, I wondered if I was only frightening myself. The Pasdars simply asked the bus driver a few questions from the road and waved us on. Most of the other passengers were still asleep, and the sight of the checkpoint receding in the distance made me giddy.

The next checkpoint, however, was different and thorough. We pulled into an enormous open square and parked behind a long line of buses. I heard Hamid joking with other passengers, but I couldn't mimic his carefree demeanor. When our turn came, two young men boarded the bus, wearing different uniforms but carrying identical weapons. They looked like they were only twenty years old, but their unkempt hair, long beards, and angry expressions made me nervous. In the first row, they shouted at a youth who had replied too quietly to their questions. "Louder!" they demanded, "Have you lost your voice?" To a woman whose chador had inadvertently slipped under her foot, they screamed "Woman! What kind of *hejab* [the Islamic term for women's "covering"] do you call this?" The two steadily worked their way forward, checking the names of passengers against a list they carried, tearing through some passengers' bags—picked at random, I suppose—while ignoring others, shouting at some and, for no apparent reason, passing others by. When one of the Pasdars demanded my name and occupation, I told him my alias with surprising calmness. He wanted to know if anyone was accompanying me. I shook me head, and he walked on. For all his harsh speech, he had barely looked at me. We drove away.

Two hundred miles later, we stopped at the entrance to the city of Ghazvin. Again, there were a great number of buses waiting for inspection, so I knew the Pasdars were being thorough. A crowd milled listlessly around the buses, and I heard someone remark that he had been waiting for more than two hours. Some passengers were eating from their bags, but the thought of food revolted me. As others closed their eyes and began to snore, I envied them. Would I ever be able to sleep that soundly and fearlessly again?

The driver got off the bus, and, after an hour or so, Hamid stepped off, too, to find out what was going on. In a few minutes, he returned and whispered to me that the authorities were searching for fugitives, checking everyone and everything with the greatest scrutiny. My worst fears had come true and paralyzed my mind. Had I made mistakes? Was there anything more I could have done? I could think of nothing. I looked around in the darkness to see if there was any way to escape from the bus, but that was a stupid thought. There was no chance of getting away; I was as penned in as I had been in prison.

After another hour of waiting, two bearded men carrying firearms boarded our bus. They looked similar to the last two Pasdars, with the same sulky expressions. It was obvious that they had received the same kind of training, since they shouted at any passengers who asked questions or provoked them. They demanded documents from some passengers, forced others to open their bags and luggage, and ordered two passengers off the bus for further questioning, with a kick for emphasis. The Pasdars questioned Hamid aggressively, accepted his answers and moved on. My heart started to throb, because I was next. The youth doing the questioning placed his automatic rifle across his chest and fixed me with an angry glare. His hair was unkempt, his long beard was untrimmed, and his expression was tough and brutelike. He reminded me of a Neanderthal from the dawn of history. He stared at me during a long pause, and then we exchanged words in quick succession:

"What are you?"

"A pharmacy technician."

"Where are you going?"

"Tabriz."

"Who are you with?"

"I'm alone."

"Get up!"

I stood, trying not to look frightened. He looked me over contemptuously, then shoved me in the chest, shouting, "Sit down!" I did, and just as I was thinking that it was all over for me, he moved on.

In relief, I dropped my guard for a moment and exhaled loudly. The Pasdar reacted instantly. "What is your name?!" he shouted at me. As I tried to reply, he demanded my reasons for visiting Tabriz, how long I would be there, and who I knew in the city. As I tried to answer, my story began swimming in my mind. He pulled a wad of papers out of his jacket, unfolding them as he kept shouting at me. I glimpsed pictures of men who'd been my cellmates in prison—Nahavandi, Majidi, and Homayoun. I felt like a black cloud was descending around my head, and my legs were trembling. Then the Pasdar reached my picture, a badly Xeroxed copy of an old photo. In the picture, I was smiling; as he hesitated over it, I thought my chest would explode. I was caught. I stared at his Uzi. Could I snatch his weapon and throw him to the ground? What about the other Pasdars? Could Hamid help me escape? What if I got outside the bus? What then?

Staring at me intently, he again asked how many days I would be staying in Tabriz. "One week," I said. He nodded and walked on to the next passenger. As I sank back in the seat, I grabbed my head in my hands. If he had waited longer, or looked more carefully, I might have acted! I had nearly brought death on myself. My head was swimming. I closed my eyes and tried to calm myself down, but my heart was pounding too hard. It wasn't until we pulled away and the bus resumed its journey that I could breathe normally.

By the time we entered Zanjan province, on the border with Azerbaijan, it was nearly daylight. No one came out to inspect the bus—perhaps the Pasdars were too sleepy to interrogate us—so the driver took his papers to be stamped at the inspection post. When he returned, we set off again. A little further on, we pulled up at a roadside restaurant, where the driver announced a twenty-minute stop for breakfast. Fresh bread, cheese, fried eggs, and hot tea drew the passengers off the bus. Though I didn't have much of an appetite, I stepped outside for some fresh air. It was spring, but still bitterly cold.

I wasn't wearing warm clothing, so after a few minutes, I went back inside and drank a cup of hot tea to warm myself. Here, in this elevated region, the plateau had not yet surrendered its cold winter chill, and the wind gusting from the mountains cut me to the bone.

As I drank my tea, Hamid spoke to me, under his breath. "So far, so good," he said. "God willing, we will arrive safely."

"*Inshallah!*" I replied.

After Zanjan, we began to enter the Azerbaijani areas of northwestern Iran—a part of the country where people spoke mostly Azeri and had their own very distinct culture. The entire region had once been a part of Iran, but Russia had seized a large part of it, annexing it into what would become the Soviet Union and later the nation of Azerbaijan. Tabriz, my destination, was the third-largest city in Iran, but it was also a place where you could go far without hearing a word of Farsi.

When the bus reached the road sign for Bostanabad, two Pasdars on the side of the highway waved us to a stop. One Pasdar stood by the road, smoking a cigarette and looking through the windows. The other stepped on board and cast a cursory look over the seated passengers. "Where are you coming from?" he asked.

"From Tehran," the driver answered.

"Where have you been inspected?"

"Everywhere!" the driver said, smiling.

The Pasdar, who looked tired and sleepy, was hardly listening. He stroked his beard and looked over the passengers again, then took a piece of paper out of his pocket. He glanced at it for a minute. "Is there anyone here named 'Hussein'?" he asked in a flat voice. Two passengers raised their hands and, after a moment's hesitation, so did I. We "Husseins" were ordered off the bus, and we obediently stepped out into the chill of the morning.

The Pasdars conferred for a moment, and the one smoking the cigarette kicked the ground. To no one in particular, he announced that we would have to accompany him to Bostanabad for a more thorough inspection. When the driver asked how long they would have to wait for our return, the Pasdars conferred again. "You can leave," he said, finally deciding. "*These* people must stay with us."

The other two Husseins looked irritated, and I fought to contain my panic as I realized the real danger I now faced. I turned to the driver and tried to sound more annoyed than frightened. "Please!" I implored. "We have been inspected many times already. If you leave us here, how will we get to Tabriz? What have we given you money for our ticket for? Why can't they carry out their inspections here?"

Haidaroghli, the Azerbaijani driver, was a pleasantly disarming man, and he spoke without fear to one of the Pasdars. "Ah, my friend, this is a small matter," he said. "These people have been inspected and questioned so many times they're lucky they still even *remember* their names. They're just ordinary workers and traders. I'll vouch for them." At the same time, Hamid stepped off the bus. "Sir!" he said, in his thick Azerbaijani, "These men are supporters of the Islamic Republic. Why are you causing them this inconvenience?"

The Pasdars were as annoyed to deal with us three Husseins as we were to be dealt with, and they clearly had no interest in arguing about it. They exchanged a few words, and, after looking over our miserable clothes and ragged appearance again, they asked, "Have your documents been examined?" Before we could say a word, Hamid loudly shouted, "Yes!"

The Pasdars relented and let us back on the bus. As it set off, the passengers gave a loud blessing. And as the Pasdars faded in the distance behind us, Hamid cried out joyfully, "Long live Khomeini!" Indeed. As the bus rolled on, the sun rose from behind the mountains, and its warming rays bathed the green pastures of the Bostanabad country. The inspections were beginning to feel routine. These Pasdars seemed as disinclined to catch me as I was to be caught. I had fond memories of skiing here on Bostanabad's snow-covered mountains in winter and picking fruit from its orchards in summer. But my memory of the spring morning when two tired Pasdars decided whether I would live or die is the one I carry closest to my heart.

At the inspection point outside Tabriz, the Pasdars were no more zealous in their duty than the previous guards. After a quick scan of the passengers, they accompanied the driver to the inspection office. A moment later, Haidaroghli returned to the bus with his papers stamped, and we entered the city.

CHAPTER 29

THE SMUGGLERS

Tabriz! I had spent two years here as a newly commissioned army lieutenant, leaving behind the poverty of student life for the first time. I had my first successful medical practice here, and in my memory, Tabriz was a city of friendship and good fortune. I hoped it would be again.

When the bus arrived at the terminal, there were no Pasdars in sight, and I saw no one I recognized—and more importantly, who would recognize me. I collected my goods, like the other passengers, and got off the bus, bidding a silent goodbye to Hamid, who would return to Tehran. The atmosphere was quiet and calm; nothing was suspicious. I wish I could just have gone about my business, but until Ata arrived, I had no business to attend to, so I stood on the curb and waited. After about thirty minutes, Ata walked up. He greeted me casually, and when he took my arm, we looked like two friends out enjoying a nice spring day. We had to be careful not to stand out, he warned, but the chances of anyone recognizing us were slim.

We found a tea shop that Ata was looking for and went inside. He and I sat by the window and drank cups of tea, keeping an eye on the street without looking suspicious. A middleman would meet us here and take us to the rendezvous point. Ata had made the contact and all the arrangements. An orange Peugeot soon pulled up outside the tea shop, and Ata stood, saying, "This is our ride!" We got into the car, and as we drove through town, it was easy to forget how much had happened in the country over the past year. In this place, so different and far from Tehran, nothing seemed changed. With the exception of a few armed Pasdars idly wandering the streets, there was no sign that there had been a revolution. There were no street inspection points on the route we took, and no one stopped us. There were no beards or *hejabs*, and we didn't hear recorded revolutionary marches blaring from every storefront.

We arrived at a motel. The driver instructed us to tell the manager that we were friends of Hajj Ali and would spend the night. At seven o'clock the next morning, someone would arrive to take me on the next step of my journey. Hearing the name Hajj Ali, the hotel manager nodded, gently pushed the guest registry book aside, and took us to a room without a word.

We settled in. There was one bed, but no table or chair. Ata and I sat on the floor, and I told him everything that had happened so far. Always practical, Ata decided that, before anything else, we should think about our stomachs. He left the motel and returned with fresh bread, cheese, tomatoes, cucumbers, and halvah. I realized that he had been right, as usual. Once our bellies were filled, I felt much better and reflected that, however close I had come to being caught, I was closer to freedom. We spent the entire night talking about the trip I was about to take. I tried to imagine what could go wrong, but Ata focused on what would go right. He gave me my passport, which he had carefully bundled away, along with three thousand dollars that I would need for the journey. My aunt had sewn a cloth pouch into my trouser waistband to hide my money. I would also carry some gold coins—the currency of choice for bribes—and a hundred American dollars in my pocket, with some Iranian rials thrown in for unexpected expenses before we got to the border. Ata gave me a diplomatic passport, with my true name and identity, so carrying it was a risk: anywhere inside revolutionary Iran, it would mean my death if it were found. Once abroad, however, I would need the document to get political asylum. Since every step took me closer to freedom, I appropriately hid the passport in the sole of my shoe.

We were too excited to sleep and talked of many things, from the hardships of the mountainous journey ahead of me to the smugglers into whose hands I would be delivered. I had heard stories about this part of the country and the hard-hearted, pitiless lot who plied their trade back and forth across the border. I would be at their mercy. Ata struggled to dispel my fears, telling me how peaceful the area was and assuring me that all the smugglers he had ever dealt with were remarkably brave and trustworthy. It was cold—the room had only a small kerosene heater—but we talked for hours, warming ourselves with good cheer. Just as the sun was beginning to rise in shades of pink and orange, we fell asleep.

Somehow, we managed to wake up and were sitting outside by seven, and the car that was to pick me up arrived only about an hour late. The two people who were in the car got out. After some talk, Ata handed them an envelope, containing half of the agreed-upon sum of money. The rest would be delivered upon my safe escape. After casually checking the envelope, the smuggler coldly gestured for me to get in the car.

Standing beside it, I hesitated for a moment, because Ata's face took on an expression I had never seen. He suddenly looked tired, and he looked worried. I realized, for the first time, how much stress my escape had been causing him. I hugged Ata tightly, kissed him, and assured him that I would be safe. "Call me from Turkey," he said "God willing," I replied, getting into the car.

As we pulled away, I studied the features of the two men who held my destiny in their hands. The driver was a strong, stocky man with a chubby face and a bushy mustache. The man in the passenger seat looked about fifty, with thinning hair and a mustache covering his upper lip. His thin, bony face had a sulky expression. We drove in silence for a while, but a few minutes outside Tabriz, they began talking together in a low voice. After a moment, I realized they were speaking the Azeri language. I had learned Azeri when I lived in Tabriz, but it was a long time ago, and their dialect was thick, so it was difficult for me to follow their conversation.

I sat in ignorance for many kilometers, wondering where we were going, how long it would take, and when we were going to cross the Iranian border. They didn't seem interested in telling me. Who were these men? They didn't speak to me at all, even to ask my name. Ata had told me that if anyone asked, I was only to say that I was a traveler crossing the border to buy weapons. But it was clear that I was in no danger of that kind of interrogation. Even when I tried to introduce myself, they completely ignored me; I suppose I was just cargo to them, and one doesn't converse with cargo. As they chain-smoked, I overheard that we were heading for Marand, seventy miles from Tabriz, where we would take delivery of something. I only understood that it involved a great deal of money.

In Marand, we stopped in a grassy square filled with plants and flowers. They both got out of the car, and the driver took a bundle wrapped in cloth from under the front seat and placed it carefully in the trunk. I was sure it was an automatic weapon of some sort. The driver told me to stay put—the first words he had spoken to me—and they walked toward a small, nearby bazaar.

As I waited, I noticed that people were going about their lives with none of the religious claptrap that was unavoidable in Tehran. There were no public broadcasts of the Quran in Arabic here, and the fashion was behind the times. There wasn't a chador in sight. Occasionally, I saw armed men without uniforms—either members of local *commitehs* or self-appointed vigilantes—but that was rare.

Just then, a young man wearing a sort of half-uniform, carrying a rifle on his shoulder, passed the car. A moment later he doubled back and passed me again, taking a good look inside before walking away. I didn't know how much longer I would have to wait, so I worried a little bit. What if an official inspected the car and discovered the Uzi in the trunk? What could I say? I tried not to get agitated, and when the young man with the rifle returned, I struggled to remain calm. But when our eyes finally met, he simply smiled and gave me a friendly, reassuring wave. Then he walked on.

After an hour's anxious wait, my smugglers returned, carrying a large parcel. After putting the cloth-wrapped Uzi back under the front seat, they carefully placed the new parcel in the trunk. The driver also produced a handgun and slid it under his seat. In the backseat, next to me, they piled cartons of Marlboro cigarettes, and we set off. They seemed to be irritated at something. After a series of choice adjectives, I figured out that they were cursing the owner of the restaurant where they just had lunch. They didn't ask if I was hungry, and I didn't care. Food was the last thing on my mind.

As we set off, their conversation suddenly became very interesting. I was becoming more attuned to their way of speaking, and I soon made out that they were old convicts who had been released when the revolutionaries emptied the Shah's prisons. They seemed to have many enemies and often referred to a prison guard named Ghadamali. Perhaps he had mistreated them in prison; I gathered that they had a complicated plan for finding him and taking revenge, poor man. There was also a particular Pasdar who had been creating problems for their business lately. They debated the best ways to eliminate him and remarked that his disappearance could serve as a warning to other Pasdars. I shivered listening to them, but at least I was on the wrong side of the law *with* them.

I didn't learn what they had originally been imprisoned for, but it was clear that, on their release, these men had taken to the smuggling trade with verve and gusto. I learned a great deal, actually, as they argued over the pros and cons of different cargoes—cigarettes, alcohol, petrol, carpets, drugs, and weapons. They seemed to have moved anything there was a profit in selling, and hearing the ins and outs of the trade made the miles pass quickly. But they agreed that human beings were the best cargo of all.

The road signs and mountain scenery told me we are heading towards Mahabad, in Iran's Kurdistan region. As we drove through verdant valleys, the radio began broadcasting only Kurdish music. We passed local men working in the fields, and it was pleasant to see women wearing colorful clothing instead of black chadors. How long, I wondered, would the Kurdish people hold onto their customs under the oppression of Khomeini's laws?

When we stopped again, I was beginning to feel hunger pangs. I realized that the smugglers were hungry, too, when the man in the passenger seat got out and walked toward a roadside restaurant. He returned shortly and sat in the car. After a few minutes, a man carrying a covered tray approached us. Even from the car, the smell of grilled meat set my stomach growling. Without even a glance in my direction, the two smugglers ate heartily, savoring thick, juicy kebabs and rice to catch the grease. The aroma in the cramped space made me salivate, but they ignored me. From the way they were drinking from a soda bottle, I realized the waiter had served them something alcoholic. I tried to contain myself, but soon I could no longer control my hunger. Suddenly, in Azeri, I burst out: "I'm starving to death! Could you please order me something to eat? I will pay for it myself."

Whether it was the booze or my Azeri accent, my outburst brought a sudden grin to the driver's face. "You speak Azeri!" he cried out. "Why didn't you say you were hungry?" Like winter into spring, the atmosphere changed. He heaped a portion of meat onto a piece of bread, and I seized it gladly. "Do you drink booze?" he asked, and I responded, laughing, "Why not?"

When I was through with the second portion of kebab, the light was back in my eyes, and over vodka, we started talking like old confederates. I told them I was a gun dealer named Hussein Aga, on my way to Turkey; if they doubted my story, they had no interest in knowing the truth. Their names were Morad and Ali Aga. With no hesitation, they told me how they had spent ten and twelve years in prison, respectively, for smuggling narcotics.

They had no interest in politics or religion, but since a religious revolution had freed them from the Shah's prison, they gave their prayers and thanks to the only God they respected: the almighty dollar.

We were busy in conversation when a blue pick-up truck passed us, and Morad pointed it out. "That's the one," he said, and we accelerated to catch up with it. After attracting the driver's attention, we come to a halt by the roadside. Following a moment's conference between my smugglers and the truck's occupants, I was hustled out of the car and into the van. I never saw Ali and Morad again.

I was now tightly squeezed between two new companions in the front seat of the vehicle. The driver, who called himself Saeed, was blue-eyed and clean-shaven and wore tailored jeans. On my other side was a man with a serious, sour-looking face. Saeed introduced him as Arsalan, adding that he was a Turkish citizen.

Saeed was a different breed than the rest of the smuggling fraternity. He spoke constantly and laughed a lot, but through all his joviality, he saw the fear in my expression and reassured me. "Don't worry," he said, gripping my shoulder, "By this time tomorrow, we'll be in Turkey."

After an hour of driving on asphalt, we turned onto a rough dirt road and had to slow down. After another 10 kilometers, we turned onto yet another road, hardly more than a dirt trail, and the car moved at a crawl. Although it was difficult to make out the trail, the driver never faltered.

We saw no dwellings as we made our way through the hills,. When we reached a summit, however, several small houses came into view. There was no road—we simply drove the car straight up the hill—and as we approached the dwellings, I saw two women washing dishes in a nearby stream. When they saw us, they invited us into their homes. We parked the car, and they escorted us into a large, plushly carpeted room. In one corner, there was an enormous pile of cotton mattresses and bedding, indicating that this house hosted many guests.

Saeed was interested in learning the whereabouts of a certain Hajj Agha. One of the women said he had been called away and left instructions for us to remain here until he returned, and she urged us to accept her hospitality. We gladly agreed; it had been a long journey and our throats were parched. Haji's wife, a heavy-set woman in her early forties, prepared the tea and chatted in Azeri. Her hands were covered with henna of a local color, and her hair was also colored with the reddish tint.

We were drinking our second cup of black tea, brewed over a charcoal fire, when we heard approaching hoof beats. From the window, we saw four figures on horseback, and from Saeed's satisfaction, I could tell that one of them must be Hajj Agha. The riders dismounted from their saddles, and Hajj Agha warmly greeted Saeed and Arsalan, hugging and kissing them both, then vigorously shook my hand. He was a tall, slender man, tanned and dressed in a wrinkled black suit that had once been of very high quality but was now covered with tobacco dust. We sat down on the carpeted floor together, and Hajj Agha's wife brought us tea and a long Vafoor opium pipe. After drinking tea with us and inhaling with great satisfaction, he announced how much better he felt and politely asked after my business. I replied with pleasantries. "God be praised," we all said. Everything was fine.

After a few more minutes of polite talk, Saeed and Arsalan proceeded to explain their difficulties. All the chaos in the government, shortages of foodstuffs, and problems at the border were making life challenging for them. The crux of the issue seemed to be Saeed's share of the profit. As the discussion grew heated, it was clear that neither he nor Arsalan felt that their responsibilities were being adequately compensated. The three continued their discussion in another room, and I started to get nervous, but they returned with amiable expressions, having apparently come to an agreement. We all had a fourth cup of tea together, and Arsalan took a parting puff on the opium pipe before we bid farewell to Hajj Agha and set off.

By now the sun had gone down, and clouds overhead made the twilight darker. As we drove, we saw no signs of life around us; only the pick-up truck's headlights gave us a glimpse of what was hidden in the inky dark. Saeed found his way through the wilderness—I don't know how—and after changing directions several times at prearranged landmarks, we finally arrived at an asphalt road. There was no traffic, so we sped along, heading toward a distant twinkling of lights ahead in the distance.

Suddenly, out of the darkness, a shoplike building appeared, and we slowed to a halt. Two Pasdars carrying grimy weapons came up to the car, and Arsalan stepped out to negotiate with them. He handed a paper to one of the Pasdars, and they continued talking. Suddenly, Saeed leaped from the car and snatched the paper out of the Pasdar's hands, saying harshly that he should be ashamed of his actions. "These two are my guests!" he shouted in an aggrieved tone, and he walked back to the car hurling expletives. As we drove away, Saeed was suddenly all smiles again and explained what had happened. One of the Pasdars was his first cousin and the other a close friend. Before the revolution these men had been street thugs, fugitives from the police. But with the revolution, the hunted had become hunters.

We passed through another small village, then followed a dirt road until we entered an even tinier village. There was barely room for our van to pass between the peasants' dwellings of mud brick. The fronts of the buildings were used as pens to corral cows, sheep, and goats, and everywhere were piles of dried cow manure that villagers used as aromatic heating fuel. Stopping the car in front of one of these dwellings, Saeed announced that we had arrived at his father's house.

Inside, the three of us entered a dirt-floor kitchen made of mud brick, with a blue- painted wooden window hanging on a wall. We took off our shoes in the entryway and passed into a room with a kelim-covered floor, where a chubby middle-aged woman and a pair of young girls, age ten or twelve, sat on the floor. The woman was pouring tea into teacups, while an old man sat on a small carpet, studiously smoking opium, and ignored our presence. This was Saeed's father, a man who was supposedly sixty years old but looked much older. After a moment, he acknowledged our presence with a nod. The woman brought us tea, and I sat down on the floor to drink it. Saeed gulped his standing up, telling me that, since we would not be able to leave until later that night, he and Arsalan were going to run some errands. For three days, I had only slept a little, in fits and starts. Saeed urged me to relax and rest until they returned.

The old man finished smoking and, discovering that he had a captive audience, decided to pass the time by telling me his life story. He had been a renowned smuggler in his day, he said, the foremost practitioner of his profession. Nobody could stand up to him, and his enemies had a habit of falling off cliffs or being sent to prison for various offenses. But he had also been a very generous man, he added, who fed and took care of many families.

He was still an expert marksman, he boasted, and with that happy thought, he sent one of his daughters to fetch his rifle. In a moment she returned with a Czechoslovakian Brno, a rifle that had been popular in Iran during Reza Shah's rule. The Shah didn't like to use Russian or British goods, so Iran imported as much as possible from Czechoslovakia and Germany. It was a sparkling clean, well-lubricated weapon, and it looked like it received regular use. He dropped a bullet into the chamber, pushed the bolt home, and raised the gun as if aiming at an imaginary target across the room.

Suddenly he swiveled the barrel of the rifle and brought it level with my chest. I froze. What had I gotten myself into? Did this man simply like to terrify people, or was he going to extort money from me? Was he a government informer?

Suddenly the man laughed and dropped the rifle to the floor. "Did I frighten you?" he asked. I was quick to assure him that he had.

"You needn't have worried," he said with a toothless grin. "I swore off killing years ago."

I was not fully calmed by his words, and his little joke seemed to make him more talkative. His stories were hardly reassuring; chuckling at every detail, he told me that he had been sent to life in prison for double homicide. Nevertheless, I was slowly relaxing. After serving eight years, he said, the revolution had been his salvation, because he was freed when all the prisons were opened up. In a grave tone, he stated that prison was not a good place to be. He never wanted to go back. I agreed silently.

When he asked me what line of work I was in, I spoke without thinking. I told him that I was a doctor and that my wife and children were in America without any support. Since the government would not let me leave Iran, I continued, I was prepared to do anything to get out and join them. His expression changed as I spoke; he nodded kindly, but said nothing. The woman brought us more tea, and after loading his pipe with fresh opium, he took two long drags before speaking, solemnly and with great gravity. "I, too, suffered greatly when I was in prison," he said. "I, too, was separated from my wife and children. I know what you are going through."

We didn't talk about my situation any longer. He rolled up his pants leg to show me a painful old injury he got in prison, though it was hard to tell where the pain was coming from. "When I wrote to Hoveyda," the old man told me, "he ordered for me to be looked after. May his soul rest in peace. Now, you say you are a doctor, are you not?"

I was quick to take the hint. Though his treatment was not in my area of expertise, I assured him that I had two friends who were doctors in this region. I promised to write them and ask them to treat him for free. The villages in this area lacked well-equipped clinics, but I told him that if he went to Tabriz or Rezaie, doctors with access to the right kinds of laboratory and radiology facilities would be able to help him. He had heard they had good medications in America, and at his suggestion, I promised to send him medicine from the United States. When I got there, however, I couldn't get a mailing address to send the medicine to him.

All the while, the man's wife had been sitting and listening to us. When there was a lull in the conversation, she began asking questions. I told them both about my family and the years I had spent in this area. By the time Saeed and Arsalan returned, the atmosphere was warm and friendly. I was almost sorry to leave.

Saeed hugged his father goodbye, and we set off. Bouncing gently along dirt roads in the dark, the pick-up truck slowly retraced its path to the main asphalt road. Just as we got onto the main road and were beginning to make good time, however, Saeed told us that we were being followed, perhaps by Pasdars. We couldn't risk finding out. Hitting the accelerator hard, he sent us flying through the night at a frightening pace, jolting across bumps and sliding through curves in the road. As we descended into a low valley, Saeed hauled the truck off the road and cut the headlights. We began driving slowly through the darkness along a rugged trail of stones and shrubs. If any-one had been following us, we had surely left them far behind; the question now, however, was whether or not Saeed had any idea where we were. After a while, he started nodding and pointing to indicate where we had come from. We had gone a fair bit out of the way, he said, but we had lost the Pasdars, if they were trailing us.

After a short drive, Saeed pulled up under a tree and signaled for us to get out. Placing the keys and a short scrawled note in the glove compart-ment—leaving it, he explained, for friends who were coming from Turkey—we began walking. As we hiked through trees and scrub, Saeed announced that it would be about fifteen minutes until we arrived at the foot of the mountain. "Be careful," he warned. "Make sure you don't lose us, because there's nothing we can do for you if we're separated."

By the time we started, a thick cloud had fallen, obscuring the skies and making the night even darker than. It was perfect smuggling weather, I supposed. A light snow was falling, and I was wearing only a locally made anorak; the frigid mountain air cut through it, chilling me to the bone. But nothing was going to stand in my way—I had come this far and would not be stopped by Pasdars, cold weather, darkness, or any obstacle. I knew I was only a few short steps away from my escape, from the end of this long agony. Thinking of freedom, I put my head down and forced myself forward through the cold.

I was lost in these thoughts when a clipped voice called out in Azeri, "Where are you going?" I stopped short, and the shadow of a tall man, carrying a rifle in his hands, loomed in front of me. I didn't see my companions anywhere. "I am going to Turkey," I responded.

"You must have a permit," he growled. I started to mumble, holding my hands out, but he interrupted me, demanding "Passport, identity card, something."

All I could do was shake my head. "You are a brave man," he said, shaking his head. "How have you gotten this far? Are you alone or do you have companions?"

"I have companions," I said, and shouted out into the darkness, "Saeed, where are you?"

A short moment later, Saeed's voice called out in reply, and he appeared out of the darkness. To my relief, he began speaking quickly with the armed stranger. They seemed to know each other well, but I had difficulty following their conversation. Finally, the stranger turned and addressed me, "These two can pass, but not you. Who are you, anyway?"

Saeed barked out, "Listen you! The gendarmerie is disbanded. You are in charge of nothing. Go home." Only then did I realize that the stranger was wearing a gendarme's uniform, from the Shah's rural police force. My fear disappeared. But the stranger still grimly insisted, "I and my rifle are the law. Damn the gendarmerie!"

The two continued to argue. After a minute, Saeed counted out one hundred toman (about $15), and I realized that the entire incident was a prelude to negotiating a bribe. After paying the man, we departed unscathed and continued our climb. Saeed was grinning at my anxious expression. "Put away your frown, my friend!" he said, "Until we reach Turkey, there isn't anyone else to meet, and we've already paid off the Turkish guards." With this reassurance, I had no difficulty climbing to the mountain's top. From there, we descended into a riverbed that my guides assured me marked the boundary between Iranian and Turkish soil. Sharp flint stones bit into my feet and legs as we scrambled down the path. I lost my footing numerous times, but excitement numbed my pain.

At the bottom of the mountain, we started to see some lights across the river, probably from a village or hamlet on the Turkish side of the border. The sky, too, was starting to lighten. Morning couldn't be too far off. The river was about fifteen yards across, but the thought that only water separated me from freedom gave me strength to plunge into the cold stream without hesitation, oblivious to everything but my freedom. The water was cold, but in that icy plunge I felt my blood boiling within me. Without fear or doubt, perhaps for the first time, I knew that I was going to make it.

On the other side of the river, I collapsed in a sodden heap in a grassy field. Lying on my back, I stared up at the black clouds overhead. In my imagination, I saw misery and torture in the shrouded faces of innocents. But the sun was rising and dark clouds receding as morning broke. A voice pulled me back to reality. It was Saeed standing above me. "Are you having fun?" he shouted. "Get up—let's get going!" Suddenly he paused. "Why are your clothes wet?"

I told him I had waded across the river, and Saeed shook his head. "You fool!" he said, almost laughing, and pointed to a bridge that crossed the river. "Why didn't you stay dry?" The bridge was only a short distance away, but in my haste I hadn't noticed it at all.

As we trudged through muddy fields in the lightening dark, I shivered but felt no pain. Arsalan now led us. When a uniformed Turkish guard greeted him politely, I realized he was the headman of the village. Arsalan handed him a twenty-dollar bill, and the man pointed us toward the settlement by the light of his flashlight. The sound of dogs barking greeted us as we entered the village.

Arsalan's house was constructed exactly like the houses in Saeed's village. In a small entry room, we took off our shoes before proceeding into a larger room, its floors covered by delicate kelims. A wood-burning stove stood in the center, and in a corner a mattress was piled high with bedding. My body was limp with exhaustion. One of Arsalan's wives brought us tea, and as we sipped and relaxed by the warmth of the stove, Saeed suddenly asked me what I would do now. I shrugged; only a few short kilometers separated me from the border, but the life of misery, torture, and death I had left behind was not easy to shake off. What *was* I going to do now?

It was almost dawn, but our host prepared a small dinner— some lavash bread and two bowls of vegetable soup—and laid it out on the floor for us. I didn't care for the soup, but between hunger and the desire not to insult my hosts, I had no trouble eating it. After giving us more hot tea, Arsalan's wives prepared the room so we could sleep. His wives slept in the next room, Arsalan slept on the large bed in the main room, and Saeed and I slept on the floor. I didn't sleep very well; my clothes were damp, the floor was hard, and my mind was reeling. But for the first time in a long time, nightmares didn't torment me.

As I lay there, my mind was spinning. I had been saved—some would say because of my innocence. But where were the guardian angels of all those brave Iranians Khomeini's thugs had used for target practice? While the guiltiest criminals lived in comfort and happiness, I had barely escaped with my life. All of my values, the belief that good triumphs over evil—were they anything but daydreams and wishful thinking?

Deep in thought, I heard Saeed whisper to me. "Can't you sleep either?"

"No," I answered quietly. "I have too much on my mind." After a pause, I asked, "Why can't you sleep? Is it money?"

Saeed grunted. "Money can be found anywhere," he said. He was silent for a few minutes. Then, as he began speaking again, I realized his thoughts were parallel with mine. Saeed was a smuggler, he said, but only because the life had been forced on him. He didn't complain. But the chaos and break-down of law and order in Iran bothered him greatly. There was no account-ability, no responsibility. No one knew who was in charge or whether they should be. What was lawful one day was a crime the next. While his own business was thriving, he feared for his country.

Saeed's words moved me, but I didn't know what to say. What words could comfort him? So I humbly thanked him for helping me, taking care of me in good faith, and bringing me across the border. Saeed shrugged off my gratitude. "It wasn't a difficult job," he replied, looking at me with piercing eyes. "You seemed frightened, though," he said. "I don't think you've ever made this crossing before. You were an important person, weren't you? You almost look familiar."

I shook my head. "No, I was a doctor," I answered. "My wife and chil-dren are in America, and the authorities wouldn't let me leave the country." I changed the subject. "How long have you been a smuggler?"

"Not until recently," he said. "When I was drafted into the national ser-vice, they sent me to Tehran. When it was completed, I joined the police department and served as a constable in Shemiran."

I broke in. "Maybe that's where you saw me? I used to live in Farmanieh."

"No, I don't think so," he answered. "I used to work in the Ministry of Agriculture, but then I was transferred to the Ministry of Health."

"The Ministry of Health?" I asked. "Which section were you in? What did you do?"

"I was a guard at the ministry's main gate—checking credentials, escorting VIPs to their cars, that sort of thing. I was there when Professor Puyan was the Minister and during Dr. Sheikh's term." He repeated Dr. Sheikh's name several times. Then he looked again at me and said quietly, "I remember now. You're Dr. Aram aren't you? I used to escort you to your car."

I wasn't sure what to expect, but he repeated my name several times, and then he got up and kissed me on both cheeks. What a coincidence! I couldn't say that I remembered him, but it was good to be reminded of the old days. Saeed continued with his story. After the revolution, he had decided that Tehran wasn't safe, so he left to stay with his father in the country. He had lived at home for a while, waiting to see what would happen, but he couldn't remain idle forever. So, with his family's encouragement, he began a career in smuggling. He had been very successful. He knew people who could help him, he easily made the right kind of friends, he was brave enough to take the risks he needed to take, and he was smart enough to know when to play it safe.

I don't remember when I fell asleep. But by seven o'clock, there was so much noise in the house that I had no choice but to get up. At least two dozen people were using the washing area in the front yard, and I tried to clean my tired face as well as I could. On seeing me, Saeed laughed and greeted me, repeating a famous Persian proverb, perhaps a smuggler's favorite: "Mountains cannot reach mountains, but people can reach people." Mountains stay where they are, but people are always on the move.

Moments later, we were having breakfast when four men entered the house and started a discussion with Arsalan. I couldn't make out what they were saying, because the dialect was different from the Azeri I knew. But their voices were raised and lowered in a way that had to be anger or sorrow.

After the men left, Saeed told me not to worry; it was an ordinary village dispute over stolen cattle. It involved rivalries over smuggling territory with another village. Saeed implied that someone had died or been killed over the matter, but he seemed unconcerned. Then he turned to my problems. He handed my passport to Arsalan, with forty dollars folded in the middle, and sent him off to the border station, several miles away, to get a Turkish entry-stamp. "With that stamp," Saeed declared, waving my passport in the air, "You will be certified to have entered Turkey legally, and you will be able to travel anywhere you choose." He paused. "And since we are still so near the border," he added, "I will see you the rest of the way to Erzurum myself."

I didn't know what to say; I wanted to offer him more money, but I was sure he would refuse it. So I simply clasped his hand, and I think he understood. Presently, however, Arsalan returned, looking dejected and angry. Tossing my passport onto the table, he reported that the border guard had recognized the passport and had refused to stamp it. Since it had belonged to an important official in the Shah's regime, the guard had refused to have anything to do with it. As soon as Saeed saw my worried expression, he angrily shouted, "Ai! You are useless! Had you not thought of this before? Come! We'll see this man together."

They strode off while I waited idly in the garden, strolling about anxiously. My thoughts were on my predicament, but my eyes turned toward the chickens, dogs, and cats who were all peacefully coexisting. Ducks were swimming in a muddy pond, with snow-covered peaks and green, grassy slopes in the background. As the sun warmed the earth, I felt like I was waking from a long, terrible dream. Somehow, the problem of the passport seemed to fade into the background. I had come this far. Surely, nothing would stop me now.

I was right to feel optimistic. After two hours, Saeed returned and with an air of triumph and placed the passport in my hands, with its all-important entry stamp. Smiling, he explained the situation. "You see, my friend, here in Turkey, when an official mentions 'the obstacles of regulations,' it has a special meaning. They want money. If they talk about 'legal impediments,' this means, also, that they want more money. And finally," he continued, "when they mention that it is *absolutely impossible* and *completely illegal*, this means they want a very large sum of money!" Saeed laughed. "Your high position, you see, has cost us an extra hundred dollars." He laughed again and didn't seem to be put out.

Erzurum was the closest city with an airport, and I had to get there. Arsalan's village, however, had no road connections. All local transportation was by horse, mule, or donkey, or occasionally by an intrepid bicyclist. So Arsalan found two donkeys for Saeed and me to ride to a larger village, where a cousin of Arsalan's had an old Nissan that we could borrow. Saeed and I piled into this ancient car, with two other passengers, and headed for Erzurum.

After an hour's drive, we arrived at a small market town. It had a row of shops where brisk sales were being transacted by crowds of shoppers. Saeed pointed out some old American cars parked on the side of the road. After he investigated, it turned out that one of them, a 1959 Chevrolet, was going to Erzurum as soon as passengers had filled up its eight seats. This meant that Saeed did not have to accompany me any further, so I paid five dollars to the driver for a seat.

As we said our good-byes, I offered to pay Saeed more for all that he had done, but he gracefully declined. "Maybe I'll come to America one day. You will be able to help me much more there," he said, smiling. I told him that I would welcome that opportunity. As we parted company in that small town, I felt that I would miss his friendship, but I was no longer afraid to move ahead without his protection.

My fellow passengers, two women and five men, were all local farmers who were going to Erzurum to trade produce for household supplies. The whole road had once been covered in asphalt, but it was difficult to see where the tarmac had been. The frequent potholes and bouncing of the car's aging, battered suspension woke up any passenger who tried to try to fall asleep. So the journey went.

When we pulled into Erzurum, late in the evening, I asked the driver to drop me off at a motel. When he did, the manager met me at the door, rubbing his eyes. "Are you Iranian?" he said. "You certainly look like you've come from that land of blood and fire." I answered that I was and had, and he nodded sympathetically, leading me to a small, cozy room. I desperately wanted a hot bath, but my most urgent thought was to find a telephone to call the United States. Neither was available in my room. I used its small sink to wash my face and hands and sat down on the bed to rest. In a moment, I was dozing, without even taking my shoes off. After a few minutes, however, I woke up, walked out into the hallway, and discovered a bath at the end of the corridor. Its hygiene left much to be desired, but the water was hot. I couldn't remember the last time that I had taken a hot bath without fear and anxiety.

The next morning, I arose at seven. After I had breakfast in the motel's tearoom, I asked the hostess for the address of a travel agency. She said there was one within walking distance. I also asked about a phone, and she told me that there was one in the hallway. I was anxious to call Ata and inform him of my safe arrival, so the smugglers could receive the rest of their money. I also wanted to call and speak to dear Auntie Batoul. Most of all, I wanted to tell Helen and our children in America that I was alive and well. But as I approached the hallway telephone, I overheard a loud voice speaking in Persian. An Iranian was on the phone speaking to someone in Iran. Even in Turkey, he marveled, people were overjoyed by Khomeini's victory over the Shah, and he said, with great joy, that he would soon travel back to Iran to join in the glorious revolution. His words made me shiver, and I decided to forgo the telephone for the moment.

I went straight to the travel agent. Potential flight destinations included Paris and London. I had good friends in both cities who could help me financially and with travel documents. In prison, however, after hours of analysis and discussion, I became convinced that the British were supporting Khomeini. So I booked a one-way ticket to Paris.

After six months of tortuous confinement and forty-five days of life-threatening escape and pursuit, it took less than ten minutes to get my Air France ticket to Paris. Since the plane wouldn't leave Erzurum until seven the next morning, I had the whole day to kill. But instead of returning to the motel—I didn't want to risk running into the Iranian—I asked at the travel agent about local places of interest. I stayed busy doing a little shopping, elated by the sensation of walking free and going wherever I pleased. I bought some things I needed—a shirt, pajamas, underwear, a toothbrush, and some shaving equipment—as well as some souvenirs for Helen and the kids and a carry-on bag for the plane. Then I just strolled around, looking at people, and every step I took felt surreal.

I heard the warm, romantic voice of a Turkish singer and followed it into a traditional Turkish teahouse. Inside, local men were drinking tea and playing backgammon, and the sound of dice rattling on the board reminded me of better days. People were simply passing the time of day. Teahouses in Iran had once had the same happy atmosphere, but I knew that, today, a teahouse there was like a cemetery. Instead of laughter and dice, there were only sermons and Arabic recitations of the Quran.

As I walked the city's streets and lanes, I eventually climbed into its higher-class quarters, a hilly area where clean, cool breezes came out of the mountains and the shops were more spread out and of better quality. I walked and walked—glad to be a stranger in this town, an unknown traveler, and, most of all, to be wandering free. As I strolled, my appetite came on with a vengeance, and I followed the delightful aroma of Turkish "chenjeh" kebab into a clean, well-lit restaurant, where I had a delicious dinner. Then, after resting at the hotel, I took a hot bath and changed into clean clothes, luxuriating in the sheer, sublime joy of freedom.

The next morning, I woke well before dawn and paid my bill at the desk. A few minutes later, I flagged down an ancient taxi and set off for the airport. The radio's soft, happy music matched my mood. The driver guessed somehow that I was from Iran, and he asked me many questions about the chaos at home.

"You Iranians always enjoyed a high standard of living," he told me. "Why on earth would you rebel against such good fortune?" He wanted to know what was wrong with my country, and I wanted to answer him but didn't know the answer. I was still in shock.

"Iranians used to visit us here," he said. "They were all educated, well dressed, and well-to-do. How do they tolerate what these reactionary mullahs have in store for them?" I was silent. "Your country," he said, "will go back many years, and you will lose so much."

When he asked why I hadn't stayed in my country to help, I swore, God willing, that I hoped to go back some day. I then remained silent until we arrived at the airport that would take me away from my homeland, perhaps forever. I boarded the first plane to Ankara without delays. I was happy to be getting farther away from my beloved country, but the happiness I felt was bittersweet.

In Ankara, I got my ticket for Paris and lined up at passport control. Would the authorities accept the invalid diplomatic passport of a fallen regime? Would I need to bribe somebody? If so, who would I bribe? Without Ata or Saeed at my side, I realized that I was a novice in this underground world. But when I nervously surrendered my papers, the officer simply stamped the exit permit and handed it back. In a moment, I was on the plane that would bring me to my family.

Gazing at the white clouds above Ankara's blue skies, my mind drifted back to a day in prison when we had seen an airplane flying far above us, through our small window. I had said to Mansour Rouhani, wistfully, that I would have given anything to be on that flight; I didn't care where it was flying to, as long as it was away. Now here I was, holding a glass of whiskey, sitting in comfort on a plane to Paris. I swallowed hard as I drank to those patriotic Iranians whose only reward for loyalty and dedication had been the firing squad.

When the plane's PA system announced that we were approaching the Charles de Gaulle Airport, I was delirious with excitement. Before me was the famous land of freedom and liberty. I would no longer have to fear for my life. There would be no sympathizers gloating in the country's misery. I didn't have to worry about being caught or spied on. I was free from SAVAK and out of the reach of the mullahs.

At the immigration desk, a police officer inspected my passport. He said nothing, but I saw in his eyes that he'd guessed what I had been through in Iran. With a wink, he stamped my passport and welcomed me to Paris. My luggage was only the carry-on bag I had bought in Erzurum, so I quickly hailed a taxi to the Concord Lafayette Hotel, an old favorite when I had been in Paris before. It was always busy and welcoming.

It was Sunday in the United States. I knew that Helen and the kids would be at church until ten, so I would have to wait at least two hours before I called them. I passed the time shopping for a suit in the hotel lobby, then returned to my room to take a bath and soak off the dirt of my trip and thousands of residual fears and anxieties. As I lay there in the tub, the months of panic melted away; my only thoughts now were of the time stretching before me until it was ten in the morning in Minnesota, and I could hear the voices of my wife and children.

CHAPTER 30

HOMECOMING

"Hello, Cathy dear, is that you?" I said.

In a muffled voice, she said, "Daddy! Daddy, can you speak?"

"Of course I can!" I laughed, "I can even shout! I am free! I am calling from Paris!"

Helen, Cyrus, and Lisa each picked up a telephone in different rooms and were all trying to somehow show me their happiness at hearing my voice. I tried to speak a few words directly to each of them.

When I spoke with Helen, she said that they had just returned from church, where our family's priest of many years, knowing our predicament, had prayed specifically for my freedom. That very Sunday during mass, the organist had played "Edelweiss," though with different words. We knew the song well; in *The Sound of Music*, it was the last song that the Von Trapp family sang before escaping from the Germans. At the sound of it, Helen told me that tears starting flowed down her cheeks. How long, she had prayed, will we have to wait? I promised I would be with them in a few short days' time, and the sound of their joy and laughter rang in my ears as I set down the phone.

My next call was to Ata in Tehran, and I could hear the great relief in his voice to learn I was safe. He had not heard anything about me for the past three days and had been deeply worried. I reassured him that all was well and that I would never forget everything he did for me. He told me that he had arranged for Dr. Shahgoli to escape the same way I had.

I was excited to rejoin my family, but I had some concerns about getting to the States. I had a visa, but my passport, which had gotten me this far, was invalid, and I was worried that I might have difficulties with U.S. customs. When I spoke with Helen, I had asked her to contact the State Department and, if necessary, speak directly to Undersecretary of State Warren Christopher to avoid problems.

In the meantime, I borrowed some money for my journey to the U.S. from my good friend Abbas, who had also managed to escape Khomeini's hell and was staying in Paris. He had been a successful architect and was wealthy enough that Khomeini's hyenas had made him a target, confiscating his house and property in the country. He had been living in the south of France, but he was now in Paris, waiting with his wife and children for American visas. We met at a restaurant and agreed to fly out together. We would be ideal companions; either of us would be able to contact friends and family if there were any problems entering the United States.

As we strolled down the free streets of Paris, I remembered the pleasant days I had spent here with Helen and six-month-old Lisa. I visited the same places I had seen with them, but I now looked on the city with different eyes. Back then, I had been on my way back to Iran, having finished my studies, and my new career and family life lay ahead in the future. Since then, I had always made my work and career the most important thing, but now that world was in ashes. Helen, on the other hand, had always been a mountain of strength for me whenever I faced problems or difficulties. Hiding her own anxieties and pain, she always had a smile for me, and I suddenly longed for nothing more than to lean on her love and strength again. What could be more important than being a good father and husband? I suddenly found myself wanting nothing more in the whole world than to be that.

After boarding a Pan American flight to New York with Abbas and his family, I wrote a few postcards. One was to Naghdineh, the corrupt young employee I had been forced to demote, who had made it his mission to send me to prison. On the back of a picture of the Eiffel tower, I wrote in Persian, "My dear Naghdineh, I have arrived safely in Paris. I don't know how I could ever repay your kindness in helping me. I write this as a small token of my esteem for all your help and kindness. Someday, I hope to be able to return the favor. Your friend, Assad Aram."

I don't know if that postcard had any consequences. My secretary later told me that Naghdineh had spent a few weeks in prison, and word spread that he was suspected of helping a fugitive. Maybe the postcard had alerted the authorities—not that Khomeini's henchmen needed a reason to throw a man in jail. Who knew that better than me? If my postcard gave Naghdineh even a thousandth of the anguish and pain he caused me, I would never feel badly about my "note of thanks."

The flight passed in a flash, and before I knew it, we were at the U.S. immigration desks. After Abbas had gone through, it was my turn. I took a deep breath and handed over my diplomatic passport. The immigration officer read it silently for a moment, his mouth moving almost impercep-tibly, then asked in a loud voice, "His Imperial Majesty the Shah-an-Shah, eh? What ever happened to the Islamic Republic?" I started to answer, but he laughed, and I realized that he had been joking. With a grin, he said, "Welcome to the United States!" and stamped my passport.

Hours later, I was on the short flight from New York to Minneapolis. The closer we got to landing, the faster my heart beat. I was coming home, and home, I now realized, was not Tehran, the United States, or any physical place. It was in my heart.

And then, when I entered the airport's arrival hall, my journey came to an end. Helen and the children ran joyfully toward me. Each tried to draw my attention. Cyrus wanted to know how I had escaped. Cathy plain-tively asked if they had mistreated me. Lisa proudly proclaimed that here in America, there was nothing to be afraid of. And Helen, sweet Helen, wiped tears from her eyes, declaring that the danger was over and we would be to-gether now, forever.

I can never forget those moments. It was like spring after winter, like returning to life after execution! I was alive again, and all that I wanted now, I had.

A passerby, witnessing our joyful reunion, remarked "What a homecom-ing!" Helen looked at him and said, "If you only knew."

"The Cover"

The cover is painted by Zaman Zamani, a famous Iranian artist, known for his water colors and oil paintings. It depicts a street in the city of Yazd, Iran. A painted sign hangs from a noose with the word " azadi ", which means freedom.

Made in the USA
Charleston, SC
15 December 2013